"In this brilliantly structured ⟨
the Chinese Communist Party
tives of ten individuals. Their ⟨
to heated political rhetoric on China that can obscure the
human cost of geopolitical conflicts."

Joanna Chiu, *Toronto Star*

"This collection does something brilliant but increasingly
rare in the present day – to treat the Chinese Communist
movement not as an abstract to be glorified or condemned,
but as a series of human moments: complex, sometimes
contradictory, and always fascinating. Whether it's a
Moscow-returned activist in wartime China or the actions
of a Mao-inspired fanatic in Peru, the extraordinary journey
of this world-changing movement comes to life in this
volume."

**Rana Mitter, author of *China's Good War: How World
War II is Shaping a New Nationalism***

"The rich and complicated stories in these 'ten moments'
call into question the overly simplistic portrayals of the
Chinese Communist Party that dominate our understanding. The erudite but eminently readable tales in this book
make cutting-edge scholarship in PRC history and politics
accessible to a broad audience."

**Aminda Smith, author of *Thought Reform and
China's Dangerous Classes: Reeducation,
Resistance, and the People***

"Edited with care and creativity by a trio of accomplished
historians, this well-paced anthology uses life stories to place
the Chinese Communist Party's first century in existence into
a fascinating new perspective. An impressive volume."

**Jeffrey Wasserstrom, author of *Vigil:
Hong Kong on the Brink***

The Chinese Communist Party

Ten engaging personal histories introduce readers to what it was like to live in and with the most powerful political machine ever created: the Chinese Communist Party. Detailing the life of ten people who led or engaged with the Chinese Communist Party, one each for one of its ten decades of existence, these essays reflect on the Party's relentless pursuit of power and extraordinary adaptability through the transformative decades since 1921. Demonstrating that the history of the Chinese Communist Party is not one story but many, readers learn about paths not taken, the role of chance, ideas and persons silenced, hopes both lost and fulfilled. This vivid mosaic of lives and voices draws together one hundred years of modern Chinese history – and illuminates possible paths for China's future.

Timothy Cheek is Director of the Institute of Asian Research and Louis Cha Chair Professor of Chinese Research at the University of British Columbia.

Klaus Mühlhahn is Professor of Modern Chinese Studies and President of Zeppelin University in Friedrichshafen.

Hans van de Ven is Professor of Modern Chinese History at the University of Cambridge.

The Chinese Communist Party
A Century in Ten Lives

Edited by
Timothy Cheek
Klaus Mühlhahn
Hans van de Ven

CAMBRIDGE
UNIVERSITY PRESS

CAMBRIDGE
UNIVERSITY PRESS

University Printing House, Cambridge CB2 8BS, United Kingdom

One Liberty Plaza, 20th Floor, New York, NY 10006, USA

477 Williamstown Road, Port Melbourne, VIC 3207, Australia

314–321, 3rd Floor, Plot 3, Splendor Forum, Jasola District Centre,
New Delhi – 110025, India

103 Penang Road, #05-06/07, Visioncrest Commercial, Singapore 238467

Cambridge University Press is part of the University of Cambridge.

It furthers the University's mission by disseminating knowledge in the pursuit of
education, learning, and research at the highest international levels of excellence.

www.cambridge.org
Information on this title: www.cambridge.org/9781108842778
DOI: 10.1017/9781108904186

© Cambridge University Press 2021

First published 2021
Reprinted 2021

Printed in the United Kingdom by TJ Books Limited, Padstow Cornwall

A catalogue record for this publication is available from the British Library.

ISBN 978-1-108-84277-8 Hardback
ISBN 978-1-108-82261-9 Paperback

CONTENTS

ILLUSTRATIONS

ABOUT THE CONTRIBUTORS

Philip Bowring is a journalist and historian who was business editor, deputy editor, and editor of the Asian news magazine *Far Eastern Economic Review* for seventeen years between 1973 and 1992.

Timothy Cheek is Louis Cha Chair of Chinese Research at the Institute of Asian Research, School of Public Policy and Global Affairs and Department of History, University of British Columbia.

Jeremy Goldkorn is a South African-American editor who lives in Nashville, Tennessee. He is the editor in chief of SupChina and cohosts the Sinica Podcast with Kaiser Kuo.

Julia Lovell is Professor of Modern Chinese History and Literature at Birkeck, University of London.

Klaus Mühlhahn is Professor of Modern Chinese Studies and President of Zeppelin University in Friedrichshafen.

Elizabeth J. Perry is Henry Rosovsky Professor of Government at Harvard University and Director of the Harvard-Yenching Institute.

Tony Saich is the Director of the Ash Center for Democratic Governance and Innovation and Daewoo Professor of International Affairs at the Harvard Kennedy School.

Hans van de Ven is Professor of Modern Chinese History at Cambridge University.

Xu Jilin is Professor of History at East China Normal University in Shanghai.

Guobin Yang is the Grace Lee Boggs Professor of Communication and Sociology at the Annenberg School for Communication and Department of Sociology at the University of Pennsylvania.

Zhang Jishun is Professor of History at East China Normal University in Shanghai and Adjunct Professor of History at Fudan University.

ACKNOWLEDGMENTS

How to tell the story, or stories, of the Chinese Communist Party (CCP) and the broader history of twentieth-century China of which it has been an integral part? What does that history tell us about the Party and China today? Over the past two years a group of scholars inside and outside China have come together to address these questions. Tim and Klaus brought together a dozen colleagues to review the scholarly field and to rethink our narratives at a workshop in Berlin in August 2018. We considered the flowering of serious academic scholarship on "the revolution" inside China over the past two decades and the availability of so many materials to consult. It was overwhelming.

This little book came out of these meetings as a way to speak to a broader audience. The looming centenary of the CCP gave us focus and a short deadline (for academics). Hans invoked the model of the BBC's *History of the World in 100 Objects*. Instead of offering a comprehensive narrative history, we chose to focus on the experience of those who worked with, led, or had to live with the Party. Our goal has been to give a human face, necessarily partial, to the variety of experiences across a century of revolution and rule. We invited colleagues, with an eye to fine writers, who could meet the short deadline and reflect some different voices. In particular we are grateful to our two PRC-based colleagues, Zhang Jishun and Xu Jilin, who agreed to contribute. All of the contributors "exceeded the Plan" and drafted vivid stories grounded in their considerable research, in a remarkably short time.

It has been a pleasure as editors to work together. Our contributors, old friends and new, made this book a reality. We are grateful to the reviewers for useful comments and suggestions. Lucy Rhymer at Cambridge supported the project through the peer-review process with her usual cheer and acumen, and graced the project with her own careful reading of the manuscript. John Gaunt once again provided excellent copyediting. Nick Stember, finishing his PhD at Cambridge, provided research and organizational help on the images and permissions above and beyond the call of duty. Nancy Hearst once again has saved us and the reader from myriad typos and slips. In all, this has been a collective effort and, we hope, a pleasure to read.

TIMELINE OF THE CHINESE COMMUNIST PARTY

1911	Republican Revolution: fall of the Qing Dynasty.
1919	May Fourth Movement in Beijing opposes the Treaty of Versailles.
1921	Official founding of the Chinese Communist Party (CCP) in Shanghai.
1923	The Communists and Nationalists co-operate in the first United Front.
1927	The First United Front ends in a bloody purge; Communists driven underground and to the countryside; Nationalists rule China from Nanjing.
1934–1935	Communists driven out of their rural base in southeast China and embark on the Long March.
1936–1947	Communists make their new capital at Yan'an, in the northwest province of Shaanxi.
1937	Japan invades central China, beginning World War II in Asia; the Communists join in a united front with Chiang Kai-shek's Nationalists.
1945	August. Japan surrenders, ending World War II.
1946–1949	Civil war in China between Nationalists and Communists.
1949	Establishment of the People's Republic of China (PRC); Nationalists retreat to Taiwan.
1956–1958	Hundred Flowers campaign followed by Anti-Rightist Campaign.
1958–1960	The Great Leap Forward; leads to famine, 1959–1961.
1960	Soviet Union withdraws all experts from China; border skirmishes, 1969.
1964	China explodes its atom bomb.

1966–1969	The Cultural Revolution; first ended 1969, but policies continue until 1977.
1971	PRC takes the China position in the United Nations (replacing the Nationalists on Taiwan).
1976	January: Premier Zhou Enlai dies; September: Mao Zedong dies; October: purge of radical leadership as "Gang of Four," rise of Hua Guofeng as Mao's successor.
1978	3rd Plenum of 11th Central Committee in December confirms Deng Xiaoping and endorses reform.
1980s	China rejoins IMF and World Bank; allows joint ventures; sets up special economic zones; decollectivizes farmland; Hu Yaobang becomes General Secretary and Zhao Ziyang becomes Premier; leadership division over direction of reforms; Hu Yaobang resigns and top intellectuals purged, January 1987.
1989	Student protests in Tiananmen, April–May, and military repression on June 4. Jiang Zemin replaces reformist leader Zhao Ziyang. Berlin Wall falls.
1990s	Popular patriotic education drive; reforms resume 1992 with Deng Xiaoping's "Southern Tour." Double-digit GDP growth most of the decade.
2001	China joins the World Trade Organization (WTO).
2008	Unrest in Tibet; Beijing Olympics; global financial meltdown.
2012	Xi Jinping becomes new Party General Secretary at the 18th National Congress.
2018	Repressive measures under Xi expand: detention camps for Uyghurs in Xinjiang; independent intellectual outlets shut down; more lawyers arrested.
2021	July, one-hundredth anniversary of the founding of the CCP.

MAP OF CHINA TODAY

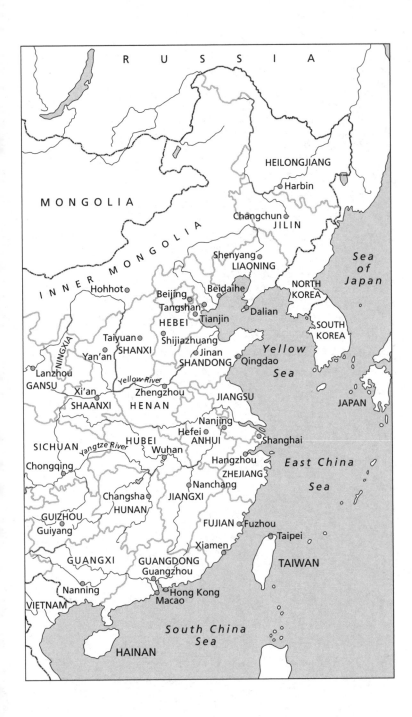

INTRODUCTION
Telling the Story of the Chinese Communist Party

In July 2021 the Chinese Communist Party celebrates its centenary. The world will be offered a series of stories about China and the Chinese Communist Party, most notably by the Party itself. They will combine elements of a coming-of-age narrative with a biblical tale of sin, struggle, sacrifice, and redemption. The Party will tell us about its beginnings as a young, idealistic revolutionary party prone to ideological errors and heroic acts in the fight against the Japanese during the Second World War and the evil Nationalists led by Chiang Kai-shek in the subsequent civil war. In very muted tones, if at all, it will say something about the sins of the 1958–1961 famine of the Great Leap Forward and the torments of the Cultural Revolution decade, 1966–1976. It will then glorify the achievements of the post-1978 reform period, culminating in the wonders of the New Era under Xi Jinping. This narrative is meant to assure China's people that the country is well on the way to realizing the Chinese Dream.

Xi Jinping, Party General Secretary and President of the People's Republic of China, first articulated his Chinese Dream vision during a visit to Beijing's Museum of the Chinese Revolution in November 2012. The Chinese Dream, he explained in 2014, was the fulfilment of "four comprehensives." These were a strong China economically, socially, scientifically, and militarily; a highly civilized China with a culture built on rich historical traditions as well as Western science and modernity; a socially harmonious China; and a beautiful China with low levels of pollution. Xi set two milestones. In 2021 China was to achieve moderate prosperity, defined as per capita GDP reaching US$10,000. By 2049, the country was to have become a fully developed, rich, and powerful country. Being largely an accounting challenge, the first goal will be achieved regardless of what happens, including the damage wreaked by the COVID-19 pandemic. The second is a smart move: it dampens expectations for the present but nonetheless promises a steadily accumulating better future. "Why question the rule of the Chinese Communist Party," goes the message of the two milestones, "when the alternative is chaos, weakness, and backwardness?"

The Chinese media will be full of stories to burnish this image of the Party in 2021. But the stories in international media will form a counterpoint. They will focus on the cost of China's revolution, the mistakes and tragedies of Party rule, and the dangers apparent in China's current party-state. They will dwell on the price at which the Party achieved its victories on the battlefield, including the starvation of 300,000 people by a year-long siege at Shenyang in Manchuria in 1948 during their civil war. This served as a warning to others as the People's Liberation Army began its march to national victory. It worked: subsequently cities preferred surrender to death. Much will be made of the Great Leap famine and the horrors of the Cultural Revolution. After decades of cautious hope in Western halls of power around China's entry into the WTO in 2001, expectations that China might become "more like us" have been dashed. At least some of the intensity of criticism of China today can be traced to the sense of betrayal by those who nourished such illusions – and made their careers from sustaining them.

In recent years things have become even worse. Since Xi Jinping came to power in 2012, China has seemed to behave in increasingly nefarious ways. Domestically, it has shifted from one-party to one-man rule and become a surveillance state using high-tech to monitor the public and lock up innocent people. Abroad, it spies, exploits, abducts, defrauds, pollutes, weakens, bribes, and strong-arms. Chinese "sharp power" is seen everywhere, from the South China Sea to Huawei cellphone systems in your neighborhood. Even more will be said about the concentration camps for Muslims in Xinjiang, the campaign to unmake Tibet by moving in tens of thousands of Han Chinese, the rebellion in Hong Kong, and Taiwan's continued defiance of Beijing. Bolstered by this narrative some will argue for the need to continue the trade war, decouple supply chains, and gird for a new cold war. This is the Chinese mirror reflecting our hopes, fears, and anxieties.

Both stories have some truth to them, but both serve contemporary power constellations and economic interests. Both obscure the complex history of the Chinese Communist Party. The Chinese Dream narrative serves the current government in China which is "led" by the Party. The China Mirror/Foil narrative serves as a metaphor for our hopes and fears, but also specific national political and economic interests in North America, the UK, and Europe. Neither is all that interested in what the history of this century, from the 1920s to the 2020s, was really like for those involved in and living under its rule. This story is more complicated, refusing simplistic categorizations, easy heroes and villains, and blurring ideological storylines.

This book does not offer an alternative grand narrative, a third way of looking at a century of the Chinese Communist Party that mediates between the two positions. Instead, we present a mosaic, made up of ten scenes, ten micro-histories, from the century of the Party, as lived by particular individuals at particular moments. This is not a comprehensive history, but rather a series of snapshots to reflect how different the Party was in different decades and how different the Party could be for different Chinese people over the century. Our goal is to make the life of the Party more vivid, more understandable, and more varied than the grand master narratives on offer. We see successes and failures, hopes and regrets, and most poignantly the contingency of history – what happened was not inevitable but came about sometimes despite the efforts of loyal Party members or ambitious Party leaders. This history is not predetermined, but neither is it random. We see people making sensible choices, taking chances, and responding to unanticipated events. It is a living history that leaves traces of multiple storylines – some have come to dominate the public story, some have been submerged but reappear in different decades, some were plausible but have been crushed. Our goal is to leave the reader with a more intense, more nuanced, more human sense of a century of Chinese Revolution and state socialism under the Chinese Communist Party, and with sufficient information to assess grand narratives, whether of the Party as Savior or the Party as Demon.

Of course, interest in the Chinese Communist Party is inseparable from the increasing power on the world stage of the People's
Republic of China, a Leninist state run by the Party. Xi Jinping may
be the President of China, but everyone knows that what matters is
that he is the General Secretary of the Party. It is the anxieties that
China's rise – its economic clout; its increasing assertiveness in
multinational fora; and its military power on land, on sea, in the
air, and in space – raises in Western capitals that drives much of the
media narrative. As historians, we are committed to the idea that
PRC state ambitions and Western national anxieties should not
utterly cloud our understanding of the history of the Party in
China. When the Party was founded in 1921, China was weak and
divided. When it came to national power in 1949, China was a war-
torn, impoverished nation. When Mao died in 1976, China had
emerged from Cold War isolation to take its seat in the UN and join
the United States in boxing in the Soviet Union. By 2001 when China
joined the WTO, most Western leaders counted on Beijing's "peaceful rise" as an economic power and a "responsible stakeholder" in
international affairs and expected that China was on its way to
becoming "a normal nation"; that is, one congenial to Western
interests and the international market system. Yet we find that in
2021 China has embraced capitalist economics but not liberal democracy, and to the amazement of many, it has prospered.
Authoritarian China is not weak. It is able to project financial power
through its Belt and Road Initiative and military power through a
blue-water navy and advanced armaments, including cyber-warfare
capacity.

This is important. The CCP has produced one of the
greatest economic miracles of all time. It has contradicted by deed
and achievement one of the most fundamental assumptions that
Western social scientists, economists, diplomats, and statesmen held
dear for decades. The belief was that a Communist one-party system
not only robbed its people, but it was above all economically far
inferior to the Western liberal system. That confidence is gone. So is
the idea that underpinned the USA's containment strategy of the
USSR, formulated in American diplomat George Kennan's
1946 Long Telegram. It held that the Soviet Union was expansionist
but essentially weak, so all that needed to be done was to contain it
where it threatened key security interests and wait for its

disintegration. Despite its many failings and shortcomings, the CCP is the most powerful political party in the world, with armed forces to match. US wargames suggest that the USA will not win a war with China in Asia. These are unprecedented challenges – the biggest that Western liberal systems have ever faced.

Nonetheless, and all the claims of the Party to the contrary, it does not control history. Other factors will be in play. China's economic miracle was based on a uniquely favorable demographic situation. It had a large working-age population that was well educated and that had few children or retired people to look after. Now China is rapidly aging. Cleaning up the pollution that China's economic takeoff produced will impose a heavy burden on future generations. It faces a uniquely difficult set of border issues that throughout history have imposed huge costs on China's rulers and not infrequently brought them to their knees. The USA will not leave China's challenge unanswered. There is also the truth that the Chinese Communist Party was designed as a tool for revolution, not as a tool for stable rule. The efforts begun by Deng Xiaoping to make it such have not borne fruit. It is not, or at least not yet, politically stable.

This book does not seek to provide an answer to these challenges. But this book does suggest that the Chinese Communist Party is not one thing, wedded to a single dogma and a set way of doing things. Xi Jinping represents a centralizing, dictatorial, nationalist, even militarist tradition. But our ten stories show that there were important alternatives. Two stand out. The first is a liberal Communist tradition. Its proponents believed that China needed change and that the Party was necessary to achieve it. But they also were committed to intellectual and moral autonomy, the right to criticize the Party, and the decentralization of power. Another was a cosmopolitan one. Its adherents drew from and supported international solidarities, from which the Party originated and from which it drew much strength and critical aid. To them, this was a dream for all people, not just a Chinese Dream. These traditions have been silenced for now. But they did exist. They are a source of inspiration and a font of alternatives for those who want change in China now. Lively Marxism societies on Chinese campuses today make the point. They have articulated stinging critiques of the post-1978 reforms.

The history of the Party in the last hundred years reveals above all one thing: an astonishing degree of determination and a relentless ability to recover from crisis. If there is a lesson to be learned then it is this: a China ruled by the CCP cannot be easily defeated, nor can or should it be isolated. It has been and can be a productive partner and even a leader in global affairs. When the Party leadership embraces its own liberal and cosmopolitan traditions, it behooves us to support it and work together as allies in the war on climate change, economic injustice, and pandemics. But the Party is also too ruthless to trust. When the Party chooses to be a rival pursuing its own narrow interests, which alas it has been doing under Xi Jinping, we should criticize its abuses of its own citizens and resist it internally when it tries to export its authoritarian ways. Yet the Party is dangerous to provoke. A prudent policy by the liberal democracies should treat the Party as the irreducible fact of political life that it is and pursue their policies informed by the whole of the Party's history. This requires us to do everything possible to keep China from becoming an implacable enemy. Managed rivalry is one thing, but intemperate, foolish leadership will end in war. Wise engagement requires knowing China and its dominant Party better. We need a deep historical approach.

The last three decades of engagement have produced an important difference between now and the Cold War. The Soviet Communist Party appeared strong, but was not able to manage its own internal contradictions or match the economic productivity of what was then called the West. The Chinese Communist Party has lasted thirty years longer and is an economic powerhouse. Containment is not an option. There was little contact between the Soviet Union and the West. Now China is connected, an integral part of the world. There is in place a rich, broad, and multifaceted tapestry of contacts between academics, business, journalists, students, families, diplomats, scientists, bankers, and manufacturers linking both sides. At a time when Beijing and Washington prefer to think of the world in terms of a bipolar, zero-sum, Darwinian struggle of the fittest, these diverse linkages will sustain co-operation in many areas. International relations are not made in capitals alone. This book is but one small product of this difference. It is a difference worth preserving.

Chapter 1 – 1920s

The 1911 Revolution in China overthrew the Qing Dynasty and ended two millennia of imperial history. Gone was the Emperor, the son of Heaven; gone were the Grand Council, the Grand Secretariat, the provincial governors, and the county magistrates; and gone were the Confucian classics on which elites had sharpened their minds. When the revolutionary Sun Yat-sen (1866–1925), today still the "Father of the Country" on both sides of the Taiwan Straits, inaugurated the Republic, some were against it and many had doubts. Others, convinced that a republic was more progressive than a monarchy, were enthusiastic. China had stolen a march on Japan, the country that had inflicted a morale-busting defeat on China in 1895 in the First Sino-Japanese War.

The fate of the new republic was uncertain from the beginning. Its first president, Yuan Shikai, even tried to restore monarchical rule with himself as the new emperor. But the First World War of 1914–1918, the October Revolution in Russia of 1917, and the 1919 Paris Peace Conference were fatal shocks. The "Great War," as it was then called, disillusioned many educated Chinese by showing the brutality of the so-called civilized nations of Europe that had set up treaty ports in China. The October Revolution in Russia showed that there were other paths toward the future than European liberal models, one involving mass mobilization, the violent seizure of power, and jumping over several stages of history straight into a Communist future. Finally, the decision of the great powers in the Treaty of Versailles to give former German concession areas in China's Shandong Province to Japan rather than restore them to China incited mass protest. The republic, not a decade old, never recovered.

The Chinese Communist Party was founded in 1921 against the background of these events and in the context of a worldwide revolutionary upswing against imperialism outside Europe and capitalism within it. In China, teachers and students, educated in a rapidly growing number of modern-style primary and secondary schools, as well as universities, read pamphlets and books penned by a wide range of progressives from around the world – democrats, anarchists, Communists. Nothing illustrates the international *background of the origins of the Chinese Communist Party as well as the fact that the Party's first constitution was a translation of the constitution of the Communist Party of America. A variety of groups dedicated to joining the worldwide tide soon emerged in Beijing, Shanghai, Guangzhou, and elsewhere. The Chinese Communist Party came into being when one revolutionary Dutchman, Henricus Sneevliet, traveled from Indonesia to Shanghai via Moscow and met up with Chinese Communists in Shanghai.*

THE 1920s

1 A Dutchman's Fantasy: Henricus Sneevliet's United Front for the Chinese Communist Party

TONY SAICH

What on earth does a Dutchman, Henricus Sneevliet (alias Maring), have to do with the rise of the Chinese Communist Party (CCP)? Sneevliet was not an easy man to deal with. He was arrogant and certain in his beliefs, he spoke no Chinese, and he knew little about China. He nonetheless stamped his vision on young Communist activists in China in the early 1920s. Why were they willing to bend initially to his vision for China's future? Sneevliet's certainty derived from his prior experiences in the Dutch labor movement and the anticolonial struggle in the Dutch East Indies. His experience of making revolution, rather than reading about it, was impressive to a group primarily comprising young students. He was one of the mechanisms by which international communism entered China.

Sneevliet was dispatched from Moscow, the home of the Communist resistance to the traditional capitalist and imperial powers and the seat of the Communist International (Comintern), which was the main vehicle for promoting a radical alternative. The Comintern drew revolutionaries from around the world to the flame of revolution in Moscow and, in its early years, was open to all comers – assisting nationalists in Turkey and revolutionaries in Southeast Asia. Sneevliet's revolutionary pedigree caught Lenin's eye and he was duly appointed the representative to the Far East. Thus Sneevliet arrived with the authority of the revolutionary hero of the day and of the home of the international Communist movement. This authority Sneevliet wielded to knock heads together in China.

The China that Sneevliet entered in 1921 was in flux. The dynastic system of governance, which had persisted for thousands of years, had collapsed in 1911, leaving behind a political and intellectual vacuum. While there was a government in Beijing, which other nations recognized, real power lay with a motley crew of warlords, whose rule only reached as far as their military strength stretched. For young activists, it was a frustrating but exhilarating time as they explored different thought systems that might restore order and pride to the nation – anarchism, republicanism, militarism, and more. The 1917 Russian Revolution offered a path to redemption from the humiliation experienced at the hands of the Western powers and to rebuild an economy devastated by internal revolt and foreign incursions. The victorious Bolsheviks had no hesitation in exporting their revolution beyond their borders and China was viewed as a key country in the struggle between the old world and the bold and new.

Sneevliet proposed and had compelled acceptance of two key concepts that became crucial legacies for the CCP. First, the need for a disciplined, Leninist party was essential to guide activity. Second, for Sneevliet, the Party could not promote revolution in isolation and it was essential to ally with the broader nationalist movement that was stirring in China. Following the fall of the Qing Dynasty, Sun Yat-sen, the father of the nationalist movement, had set about building a force to unify China. With strong support from Chinese overseas, Sun formed the Nationalist Party (Kuomintang, KMT). This was the party that Sneevliet would pressure the Communists to join. He proposed that the alliance would take the form of the Communists joining the Nationalist movement as individuals in what was termed a "united front." While Sneevliet got acceptance of these two concepts, despite his best efforts the comrades in Moscow and China never fully accepted his concept of the united front. Having planted the seeds of the Party, Sneevliet, like so many other foreigners, left China disillusioned, wondering why it could not be more "like us."[1]

A Resistant CCP

Sneevliet arrived in the bustling, cosmopolitan city of Shanghai just in time for the CCP's foundational First Congress

(July 20–August 5, 1921). Shanghai was home to a nascent labor movement and its international ambience meant that not only people but also ideas flowed freely. Moreover, the foreign concessions meant that activists could meet and conspire out of the reach of the Chinese authorities. Thus it was on a quiet side street in the French Concession that thirteen Chinese, a Dutchman and a Russian (Vladimir Nikolsky) gathered together to plot the future.

The participants met clandestinely in the home of one of the participants, huddled around a table, debating vigorously the future of China. The Chinese participants, including future CCP leader Mao Zedong, were disillusioned with their political inheritance and were drawn from an assortment of radical study groups that had evolved across the country, some independently and some with Soviet promptings. The precarious nature of the venture was revealed when an intruder, certainly a police agent, entered the house muttering excuses for interrupting. The meeting was swiftly abandoned and the Chinese participants reconvened on an isolated boat on South Lake in nearby Zhejiang Province. The presence of two foreigners would have heightened suspicions, and so Nikolsky and Sneevliet remained behind in Shanghai to await their return.

Impetus for the founding of a Chinese Communist Party had come from another Russian, Grigori Voitinsky, who had been sent by the Foreign Section of the Vladivostok Branch of the Far Eastern Bureau of the Russian Bolshevik Party under the guise of being a journalist. His remit was to assess the revolutionary potential in the East. However, after his departure, the nascent Communist grouping fell into disarray with squabbling about what kind of organization best suited China's situation. Following his return from China, Voitinsky remained an influential voice in Comintern China policy. He served in the Soviet government of Irkutsk but he is best known as the founder of Soviet sinology.

Different perspectives played out at the Congress, which was a lively, relatively unstructured affair that exposed further divisions over questions of who should be a member, how to engage in the labor movement, and whether Communists should join the National Parliament, which had been established in Beijing as the nominal government. The minority view reflected the bookish, small-study-group origins of the Communist cells. Proponents eschewed labor activism as a priority. In fact, as far as they were concerned, the workers had little understanding of Marxism and so members should take time to undertake education and carry out propaganda. Perhaps, they argued, Bolshevism was not even the most appropriate form of socialism for the Party to adopt and it would be beneficial to study other approaches, such as German social democracy, and then decide what best suited China's needs. Certainly, some type of organization was necessary but not necessarily a Bolshevik-style tightly organized working-class party destined to usher in the dictatorship of the proletariat. Given their predilections, they saw no problem with collaboration with Sun Yat-sen's Nationalists in the South.

The majority adamantly rejected such views. The Congress was chaired by Zhang Guotao, a student from Beijing, who became active in the labor movement, a bitter opponent of Sneevliet's views, and later a major rival to Mao Zedong for the leadership of the CCP. Zhang represented the view that the number one priority was the immediate establishment of the dictatorship of the proletariat: a tough task given that there were only fifty-three members in the Party. Collaboration with "bourgeois nationalists" was ruled out and it was decreed that intellectuals were not welcome in the Party – ironic given the background of those present.

Sneevliet was not impressed by the quality of the debates and although he must have presented an imposing figure to the young activists, not all were happy with his overbearing manner. Sneevliet agreed that work in the labor movement was a priority, but he did not think that the time was ripe for the establishment of a Communist Party. Prior to the Congress, he wrote back to his masters that not too much money should be spent in China and that perhaps in a year or more a "truly well-organized party" might be formed.[2] This negative perception never went away. In July 1922, he told the Comintern that a "propaganda group would have been much better."[3] Right up until he left China in 1923, he retained the preference for propaganda, education work, and activism in the emerging labor movement. These activities, he believed, were more important than establishing a political party. Sneevliet complained that the continual infighting undermined unity, and in June 1923 he made the withering comment that "the fact that it [the Party] was born much too early (in 1920) or better said fabricated, still weighs on the party." Not only was the birth premature but also it was "supported too strongly by foreign means."[4] Far from delighting in the lively debates, he saw the Party's independent spirit as a sign of naivety. China, he felt, was not ready for a Communist Party.

An Important Trip South

Sneevliet's view was certainly clouded by the unwillingness of many Chinese comrades to accept his ideas on how to work with the Nationalists. The leadership of the nascent Chinese Communist Party approved of Sneevliet's view of the importance of the labor movement but they rejected completely his idea of working together with the Nationalists to create a united front. The documents passed by the First Congress reflected this isolationist stance. Capitalists were to be overthrown by the "revolutionary army of the proletariat" and classes abolished under the dictatorship of the proletariat. Other parties were to be confronted with "independence, aggression, and exclusion."

This approach stood in stark contrast with Sneevliet's charge. He came to China armed with his experience in the Dutch East Indies, where, before he was expelled, he had worked in the nationalist opposition to the Dutch colonial administration, and he participated in the discussions that had taken place at the Comintern's Second Congress of 1920. Here, Lenin and Indian delegate M. N. Roy had debated the correct strategy for revolution in the colonial and semi-colonial countries. As a delegate from Indonesia, Sneevliet served as secretary to the commission that was charged with reviewing policies to address the national and colonial question. Despite differences between Lenin and Roy, movements in these countries were deemed "national revolutionary" rather than "bourgeois democratic" to distinguish between a "revolutionary" bourgeois movement that would not prevent the Communists from "training and organizing the peasantry in a revolutionary way" and the "reformist" bourgeoisie that would oppose such actions.

This was why Sneevliet believed it possible to work with bourgeois nationalists. His challenge was that not only did the CCP Congress reject such an approach but also he needed to find a compliant bourgeoisie to work with in China. The trip to south China was revelatory. There he saw revolutionary potential among those gathered around Sun Yat-sen's KMT. Unlike in the north, where he viewed the Party's illegal operations as ineffectual, here Sneevliet witnessed a strong labor movement with a possible ally for the national-revolutionary movement. To a large extent, he defined the KMT to fit his framework for collaboration and then set out to convince the comrades in China and in Moscow that working together was the best way forward. Initially, he was successful but gradually opposition emerged in both places, and by the time he left China even he had clashed with Sun Yat-sen about Sun's obsession with a military solution to China's problems.

Slipping out of Shanghai on December 10, 1921, Sneevliet traveled via Hankou (Wuhan) and Changsha before meeting with Sun Yat-sen at his headquarters in Guilin in southwest China, where he was preparing for a military push north. On arrival, Sneevliet met with Sun immediately and they engaged in lengthy discussions over nine days of meetings. Sun informed Sneevliet about the situation in China and Sneevliet filled Sun in on developments in Russia and its New Economic Policy, which Sun viewed as similar to his own approach. Last but not least, they discussed the reorganization of the KMT, the establishment of a military academy, and possible CCP–KMT collaboration.

Sneevliet was not impressed with Sun's leadership style. For a party that proposed democracy, Sneevliet viewed Sun as more inclined toward a dictatorial style with a militaristic bent. Sneevliet wanted the KMT to be reorganized along Leninist lines. He thought of the KMT as a broad tent that could attract students, workers, and peasants. If propaganda work was strengthened, this would ensure that Sun would not have to rely on the support of a few generals to survive. Sneevliet was baffled by Sun's understanding of Marxism and his belief in traditional Chinese thought. Sun was puzzled why so many young people were attracted to Marxism as "all the basic ideas of Marxism are to be found in the Chinese classics."[5] For Sun, Marxism proposed nothing new as it had "all been said two thousand years ago by the Chinese classics."[6]

Events broke the impasse. Any doubts Sneevliet may have harbored about Sun and the KMT as the right partners were overcome by a large-scale seamen's strike that gripped the south during the winter of 1921–1922. The strike impressed Sneevliet: it was "undoubtedly the most important event in the history of the young Chinese labor movement."[7] The strike brought victory in March

1922, when the authorities caved, agreeing to wage increases of between 15 and 30 percent. Sneevliet thought that the leadership of the strike lay with the KMT but in fact the two key leaders were members of neither the KMT nor the CCP. There were, however, strong KMT links with the Seaman's Union, with Sun Yat-sen having written the calligraphy for the official signboard. Whatever Sneevliet made of the KMT activism, it contrasted markedly with the inactivity of the local Communists, who did not even organize a support movement.[8] While the actions of the seamen were impressive, Sneevliet exaggerated the KMT's role in the strike, in part because he arrived in Guangzhou during the peak of the activity and because all his informants were KMT members. This encouraged him to see great possibilities for long-term co-operation, a view not shared by the CCP leader, Chen Duxiu, in Shanghai.

Reporting Out: Resistance in Shanghai, Acceptance in Moscow

Preparing to leave China, Sneevliet seemed reasonably sat-isfied with what he had seen. Guangzhou was the best place to implement his tactic of CCP–KMT collaboration, with a vibrant labor movement, a political party that had leaders sympathetic to the workers and to the new soviet state in Russia, and a place where Communist propaganda could be openly disseminated. Now, it remained to convince those in Shanghai and Moscow of his tactic. He encountered opposition from both, opposition that grew over time, but he nonetheless prevailed. The KMT was also resistant, but money talked and in 1923 Sun Yat-sen was swayed by the inducement of 2 million gold rubles from Russia to fill KMT coffers.

The first hint of resistance came on Sneevliet's return to Shanghai. In April 1922, he met with CCP leaders and those KMT members who were in the city. For Sneevliet, the way forward was clear. The CCP needed to give up its isolationist stance and work with the KMT to expand contacts with the workers and soldiers in the south, two of the four groups he identified as making up the KMT membership. Sneevliet thought that he had received KMT guarantees that Communist propaganda would be permitted in the areas under their control. He was aware of the need to maintain the CCP's independence as an organization but this was not enough to convince his colleagues. Chen Duxiu wrote to Voitinsky, who was back in Moscow, noting that the various local groups had met to discuss co-operation and all had passed a "resolution of complete disapproval."[9] Chen pointed out that the basic policies of the two parties were different and that KMT collaboration with the Americans and warlords such as Zhang Zuolin and Duan Qirui (militarist leaders of the putative government in Beijing) was unacceptable. The only real base for the KMT was in Guangdong, whereas elsewhere it was viewed as a "political party scrambling for power and profit." Even in Guangdong, working with Sun Yat-sen would alienate the powerful warlord, Chen Jiongming, thus undermining their work. As a result, Chen asked Voitinsky to pass on their views if the Comintern discussed Sneevliet's proposal. The rejection of the proposal by their Chinese colleagues did not immediately influence Comintern thinking, perhaps because, by June, Chen Duxiu's views had mellowed somewhat. While still ruling out the feasibility of a united front with the KMT, he did hope that Sun Yat-sen and the KMT might "temporarily follow the same road as us."[10] For Chen, Sneevliet was simply too optimistic about the KMT's potential.

If the terrain seemed difficult to navigate in China, it was even trickier in Moscow. Over time, opposition from some Chinese comrades influenced the view of key players in the Comintern: Karl Radek, the clever, cynical East European revolutionary; Georgy Safarov, a Soviet sinologist who also helped execute the Romanovs; and Voitinsky. Further, Sneevliet found himself caught between the different priorities of the Comintern and of Narkomindel (the People's Commissariat for Foreign Affairs) – the internationalist and nationalist organizations of Lenin's revolution. In China, he could pull rank and assert organizational discipline to force compliance. Moscow was a much tougher arena as he could not appeal to a higher understanding of Leninism to get his way, nor could he appeal to organizational discipline.

Yet these differences were not apparent when Sneevliet arrived in Moscow to deliver his July 1922 report. In his analysis, the absence of a modern working class, an undifferentiated peasantry, and an ineffective Communist Party organization made him "very pessimistic about the movement in China and its possibilities."[11] The CCP had no independent power base. This confirmed the necessity of working with the KMT.

Despite reservations about Sun Yat-sen's leadership style, Sneevliet devised the novel idea that the KMT was not a bourgeois party based on a single class but rather an amalgam of four groups. First were the leading intelligentsia, many of whom were attracted to socialism. Second were the emigrants living in other colonial countries, and they were the "motive force in the Chinese nationalist movement." They were more important for the revolution than Chinese capitalists who were tied too closely to the foreign powers.[12] They provided Sun with crucial financial support and expected China's reunification with an end to warlord rule and foreign exploitation. Third were the soldiers of the Southern Government. Finally there were the workers. This flexible structure would allow the CCP to operate within the party, and the role of the CCP was to keep the alliance together and push the movement to the left.[13]

This analysis proved convincing to Comintern leaders. Sneevliet took back with him the Comintern's "August Instruction," for which he had provided the draft.[14] In addition, he took with him an instruction for the CCP to move its headquarters to Guangzhou and work closely with Sneevliet. This would permit covert work in Shanghai to be replaced by open work in Guangzhou. This decision was promulgated despite the knowledge that Sun Yat-sen had been driven out of the city, suggesting that Sun was not seen as indispensable to collaboration with the Nationalists. Indeed, some in China, including most of the comrades in Guangzhou, were more supportive of Sun's foe, the local warlord, Chen Jiongming.

The "August Instruction" was a firm endorsement of Sneevliet's tactic. The KMT was declared a revolutionary organization and two tasks were outlined for the CCP: to educate "ideologically independent elements" to form the nucleus of the future CCP and to organize groups of followers within the KMT and the trade unions. Before any split might occur between the petty bourgeoisie and the proletariat, the CCP was to support the progressive elements of the KMT. A propaganda organization was to be established to carry out work independently. For labor, the main task was to establish trade unions. This was to be the united front.

Forging Compliance: The CCP Joins the KMT

Returning to China, Sneevliet had two tasks. The first was to get the CCP to accept his tactic, while the second was to work with the Soviet representative, Adolph Joffe, the diplomat who had headed the Soviet delegation that negotiated a peace treaty with Germany during the First World War. Moscow entrusted him with negotiating a deal with Sun Yat-sen. The CCP's perspective on co-operation with other groups was slowly shifting as well, and by May 1922 Chen Duxiu effectively acknowledged the need for a united front. The KMT was more influential among the workers than was the CCP and Chen called on the CCP, the anarchists, the KMT, and others to pull together in a united front for labor work. The CCP would still play the major role in the revolution. Chen nonetheless remained pessimistic about the KMT as he felt that, under Sun's leadership, there was little hope of reforming the party. Chen Duxiu was moving toward a "bloc without," working alongside the KMT but remaining separate organizations.

Sneevliet, however, pushed the CCP to accept a "bloc within," with its members joining the KMT as individuals. To enforce his tactic, Sneevliet convened a meeting of the Central Executive Committee in Hangzhou from August 28 to August 30, 1922. He carried the two Comintern documents for support as well as an indication from Sun Yat-sen that the KMT would be willing to work with the Communists. Once again, events pushed Sneevliet's agenda along. Sun's expulsion from Guangzhou and his retreat to Shanghai had left him in a weak position, rendering him more willing to accept a closer relationship with Soviet Russia. Sneevliet repeated his view that the KMT was a "strong, democratic, national-revolutionary political party," composed of different social strata. Chen Duxiu and Zhang Guotao in particular resisted his desire for integration, and they gave in only after Sneevliet invoked Comintern discipline.[15] Chen's acquiescence was conditional and he would only support the tactic if Sun Yat-sen revoked the ruling that required new members to pledge personal allegiance and to place their finger-prints on the party oath. For his part, Sneevliet was adamant that he did not invoke discipline to get his way. He reported that there were no serious objections, with comrades from Beijing and Changsha adopting the proposal immediately and with only the comrades from

Guangzhou opposing.[16] Whatever the level of dissent, this meeting took the historic decision for individuals to join the KMT while retaining their CCP membership. The CCP as an organization was to remain to criticize and push the KMT in a more radical direction.

Doubts in Moscow: Is a Mass Party Possible in China?

Sneevliet's second trip to China seemed to have gone well but if he thought his work was done, his problems were just beginning. Key members of the CCP, such as Zhang Guotao, continued their opposition and found sympathetic ears in Moscow. While Zhang continued to resist, Chen Duxiu fell in line, accepting that the first task was to complete the national revolution and only then could the economy and the proletariat be developed under CCP leadership. Further, even after Joffe and Sun Yat-sen had finalized the January 26, 1923, historic Joint Statement with Russia, outlining the relationship between Soviet Russia and Sun's movement, and allowing Sun to receive Soviet financial support, Sneevliet found that working with Sun could be an extremely frustrating business.

Just as the pieces seemed to be falling into place, concern in Moscow increased about Sneevliet's excessively close relationship with the KMT, and views diverged over whether the priority was to build a mass political party or develop the united front. Returning to Moscow in late December 1922, Sneevliet was surprised to discover that he needed to defend the tactic of co-operation. Three main topics were discussed. The first concerned the question whether Sun Yat-sen was the "correct" nationalist to support and whether another militarist might be better. Second, there were concerns that Sneevliet had ignored Comintern work for that of Russian foreign affairs, spending too much time with Joffe. This reflected emerging tensions between pursuing the Russian national interest and maintaining the ethos of an international revolutionary movement. For the two men, in a country such as China, pure Comintern work was impossible and there had to be conditional support for promoting national liberation. Russian policy had to be "nation friendly and anti-imperialistic."[17] Third, the sessions of the Executive Committee of the Communist International (ECCI) were dominated by discussion of the tactic of co-operation with the KMT, the role of the labor movement, and whether a "mass party" could be developed. All of these challenged Sneevliet's model of a united front in China.

Despite the earlier acceptance of his views by the Comintern leadership, Sneevliet sensed a growing consensus that a Communist mass party could be developed in the foreseeable future. As Chinese comrades developed their own lines of communication with Moscow, dissenting views found their way to Comintern leaders, providing them with ammunition to critique Sneevliet. After his visit, Sneevliet wrote scornfully about the idea that just 250 Communists could create a mass party capable of "independent policy activity." Such a path could only lead the CCP into becoming a "meaningless sect." Sneevliet blamed Voitinsky for promoting the view that a mass party was a necessity and he was surprised that there was a cult developing around the northern warlord, Wu Peifu. This created the "delusion" that a policy independent of the Nationalists could be developed.[18] Addressing the Comintern's key policy-making body, the ECCI, Sneevliet stated that anyone who thought that "our own" mass Communist Party could be established in China had no sense of reality. Policy could not be based on "general tactics and view-points" but on realities on the ground.

Sneevliet stressed that there was no alternative to his approach. His critics, ECCI members Voitinsky and Richard Schüller, the fiery Austrian who was a leader of the Communist Youth International, felt not only that the CCP should have its own organization, but also that this should be the focus of work. They refused to accept that the CCP operate as a "mere" branch of the KMT, but rather it should be the central organization. Summarizing the debates, the ECCI chairman, the Russian Nikolai Bukharin, pronounced that no one opposed the CCP remaining in the KMT but he feared that KMT weakness might cause it to seek an alliance with the "bourgeois states." Thus the final version of the "Resolution" adopted (January 12, 1923) called for nudging the KMT toward "Soviet Russia in the struggle against European, American and Japanese imperialism." However, the "Resolution" did tilt toward Voitinsky's view of the development of a workers' political party, containing the phrase, "The specific and important tasks of the CP of China are to enlighten and organize the laboring masses, and to create labor trade unions in order to lay the *foundation* for a strong mass Communist Party."[19]

How to interpret this added phrase became the source of serious disagreement. Bukharin recognized the weakness of the proletariat and thus agreed that a united front was essential, but the lack of an independent proletarian movement meant that the CCP's "special task" was to create one. Each could interpret it in their own way. In a document that angered Sneevliet, Radek argued that for the Communists to become a real force, they needed to organize the "working masses," create strong trade unions, and build a "strong Communist Mass Party."[20] This was music to the ears of Sneevliet's opponents in China. Even the catastrophic defeat of the railway workers' strike in February 1923 did not stop Voitinsky, who felt that further strike action was possible in northern China.[21] Finally, they held that the proposed move south made the CCP too dependent on the KMT, sucking it into the factional divisions within the KMT. As far as Voitinsky was concerned, the KMT had failed to become a national political party, continuing to act as a "warlord faction." If the CCP was to continue working with Sun Yat-sen, Sun needed to be wary of temporary alliances with other warlords and instead should promote building the political party.

Clearly, an alternative path was being explored by influential Comintern members. So, once again, mixed messages were sent to China. In May 1923 their views were pulled together in a directive to the CCP leaders, but fortunately for Sneevliet it did not arrive before the Third Party Congress (convened June 12–20, 1923). However, Zhang Guotao had been in Moscow and must have sensed the shifting atmosphere and he certainly raised objections at the Congress. Radek and Voitinsky drafted the directive to guide Sneevliet at the Third Party Congress.[22] The draft stressed that the CCP's main task was to increase its strength through organizing the workers and establishing and restoring unions to provide a broader base for revolutionary activity that would permit the establishment of the "mass Communist Party." The movement's core task was to push forward the anti-imperialist struggle and the fight against their "running dogs." The KMT was expected to show unconditional support for the labor movement in both the north and the south. Working with Sun Yat-sen was not rejected but his alliances with pro-Anglo-American and Japanese warlords needed to be restrained for fear that it would discredit the CCP and the labor movement in the eyes of the people. An anti-Japanese boycott would provide a good start combined with an anti-imperialist movement to oppose the British and the Americans. Bukharin's revisions to their directive struck a more moderate tone and placed great emphasis on the role of the peasantry with the formation of a worker–peasant alliance to ensure that the leadership of the peasant movement was in the hands of the "party of the working class."[23]

Third Party Congress: Battle Won, but Not the War

Voitinsky's criticism notwithstanding, on returning to China, Sneevliet went to Guangzhou, where he maintained frequent contact with Sun Yat-sen. On March 8, 1923, the Soviet Politburo approved 2 million gold rubles to support Sun and his movement, with the expectation that KMT reorganization would proceed accompanied by extensive ideological and political work. Soviet aid was to be kept strictly secret, with the Russians merely expressing sympathy for the KMT's aspiration for national liberation. Despite Sun's agreement, Sneevliet's experience was slow and frustrating and he began to doubt Sun's sincerity, believing that his military preoccupation was delaying party reorganization. Sneevliet began to think the money spent on Sun was being squandered on the "worthless campaign in the south," with some senior KMT leaders wishing for Sun's defeat as this would benefit the movement as a whole.[24] Money could be better spent on propaganda work in Shanghai.

Sneevliet's last significant act in China was to maintain support for the form of collaboration with the KMT. As noted, the fact that neither Radek's and Voitinsky's draft nor Bukharin's revised directive reached the Third Party Congress in time helped Sneevliet. Despite this, it was still a stormy meeting. The crushing of the February railway workers' strike and the subsequent repression had a sobering impact on the Party and Chen Duxiu's faith in the power of the working class was severely curtailed.

Things started badly, with Sneevliet angry that Zhang Guotao had been spreading rumors that he would soon be recalled to Moscow as the Comintern was unhappy with his work. He was also dissatisfied with Zhang's classification of a "right" on China policy (Sneevliet and Joffe) and a "left" (Radek and Safarov), with

Bukharin holding the center ground, leading him to write, "we should not forget that the Chinese are very immature in experience and most of them lack knowledge."[25]

Once debate of the Comintern's "January Resolution" began, matters did not improve. The "Resolution" noted that the KMT was the only serious revolutionary group in China and thus the "young CCP" needed to co-ordinate actions with it. With a weak labor movement, the central task was the national revolution, necessitating that CCP members remain within the KMT. So far so good for Sneevliet, but now came the complication that Zhang Guotao and others seized on. This work had to be conducted without the CCP losing its identity, meaning that it had to preserve its own organization. It was important for the CCP to create "professional unions" that could "prepare the basis for a strong mass Communist Party." The CCP had to walk the delicate tightrope of carrying this task out independently while not antagonizing the national-revolutionary movement. The CCP could not become entirely tangled up in the KMT.

On this basis, Chen Duxiu drafted a set of theses for approval,[26] supported, of course, by Sneevliet, and the influential leaders Li Dazhao and Qu Qiubai. Zhang Guotao accused Sneevliet's approach of being tantamount to liquidating the CCP, while Sneevliet replied that Zhang suffered from "leftist" tendencies and "illusions" about the speed of development of a mass workers' party. Zhang Guotao's critique raised three questions. First, did the KMT represent the national movement? Second, was there the possibility of reorganizing the KMT? Third, could the revolutionary movement only be developed through this form of co-operation with the KMT? For Zhang, it was clear that the CCP's interests would be submerged if all members joined the KMT. Of course, they had to work closely, but they were two quite distinct parties and the KMT did not represent the entirety of the nationalist movement. Zhang was especially opposed to CCP leaders and those in the labor movement joining the KMT. He took the demand of the "Resolution" that the CCP should preserve its independent organization as sanctioning this. For Zhang, the KMT was only to be supported where it enjoyed good relations with the masses, but not in the north where there was no KMT organization. He found strong support for the view that the CCP should conduct the labor movement independently, with the exception of in Guangzhou and Hunan, where there was no other choice.[27] The CCP's task was to organize the workers and raise their consciousness.

After others had weighed in to support Zhang, Sneevliet spoke to the Congress.[28] Neither he nor Chen Duxiu had any intention of dissolving the CCP and he was not guilty of worshiping the KMT. Sneevliet was deeply concerned that the debate had veered away from a straightforward discussion of practical implementation of the "January Resolution." There was no license to debate whether individuals should join the KMT or whether an "independent labor party" should be established. He was particularly critical of the view that it was not necessary to help the KMT set up branches in the north. Sneevliet backed up his view with an appeal to organizational discipline, pointing out that the ECCI "supposes that even in the CP of China there is something like discipline and it cannot make its resolutions in such a way that some or other ingenious inventor manufactures arguments to make passive resistance and sabotage on the decisions of the IKKI [ECCI] possible." For Sneevliet, Chen Duxiu's theses were the only correct interpretation of how co-operation with the KMT should be conducted. His counterarguments finished, Sneevliet called for a vote. It was a narrow victory, twenty-one to sixteen, indicating that the issue was far from resolved.

Chen's theses were drafted into the CCP "Resolution on the National Movement and the Question of the KMT," which clearly reflected Sneevliet's tactic. There was no need to create a "bigger, more revolutionary party" given that the KMT existed and could serve as a powerful, centralized headquarters for the democratic nationalist movement. It was not possible to create a great mass party at the present time as the workers' movement was incapable of becoming a sufficiently powerful, independent social force. The CCP would work within the KMT to draw in class-conscious elements from the workers' organizations, expanding Communist influence, and thus laying the foundation for the CCP among the masses. It was incumbent on the CCP to stop the KMT from concentrating only on military activities, while ignoring propaganda work. The KMT was to be guided toward Soviet Russia and away from the imperialist powers. Last but not least, the CCP was to help extend KMT organization throughout all of China.

While Sneevliet won the vote, it did not mean that he had won the debate. Opposition continued and, in the following months, there was little forward momentum. Indeed, as soon as the Congress finished, the Party moved its headquarters to Shanghai, baffling Sneevliet, who lamented that he could not understand why the Party "prefers Shanghai's illegality over Guangzhou's legality."[29]

In October 1923, Sneevliet left China expecting to return to Moscow to review his work and get his new assignment. Many key figures in the CCP were happy to see him leave. Within the Comintern, Sneevliet's perceived pro-Sun Yat-sen position was unpopular with the likes of Radek, Safarov and Voitinsky, while his criticism that they were dreaming of the imminent creation of a mass Communist Party did not go down well. Sneevliet's later disillusionment with Sun and his suggestion that the Russians were wasting money supporting him must have confused those in Moscow. It was never likely that his assignment would be extended.

On his way back to Moscow from Shanghai, Sneevliet ran into his replacement, Mikhail Borodin, in Irkutsk in Soviet Central Asia. Borodin was on his way to Guangzhou to implement Sneevliet's tactic, the reorganization of the KMT, and to manage co-operation among Sun Yat-sen, the CCP, and Soviet Russia. It must have been an excruciating encounter, making it patently obvious that Sneevliet's time in China had come to an end. The chance meeting was a clear symbolic moment in the changing nature of Russian engagement in the Chinese Revolution. The moment marked a passing of the baton from the internationalist vision of a global proletarian revolution to one more closely aligned with Russian national interests. What more obvious sign could there be than the exit of the Dutch, globetrotting revolutionary and the entrance of a Russian member of the Bolshevik Party?

The United Front: An Enduring Legacy

The initial legacy of Sneevliet's tactic became entangled in the struggle between Stalin and Trotsky over dominance within the Bolshevik Party. Trotsky and his supporters accused Stalin of sticking with a tactic beyond its usefulness that doomed the CCP to failure. While the conflicting views about the united front persisted, the tactic was successful initially and enabled the CCP to expand membership that would have been inconceivable if left to its own devices. CCP membership expanded significantly and the Party was able to establish strong connections with the unions and among the peasantry. Yet that success caused concern to those on the KMT right under Chiang Kai-shek, who had emerged as the leader after the death of Sun Yat-sen (March 1925). Chiang was far more wary about CCP intentions than Sun had been. Rather than the CCP casting aside the "bourgeois" elements of the KMT and taking leadership of the revolution, Chiang Kai-shek's troops slaughtered the Communists in Shanghai in April 1927.

Over the longer term, the tactic of a united front has been employed in China on a number of occasions to promote the CCP's interests. Despite the massive defeat, the concept of a united front has survived down to the present day and is the most enduring legacy from this period. With the CCP facing extinction in the mid-1930s, it promoted again the united front with the KMT but this time in the form of a "bloc without." The CCP used the alliance both to protect itself against the greater power of the KMT forces and to boost its prestige by opposing the Japanese invaders, who had launched their aggressive attacks in 1937. On taking power in 1949, the CCP used the idea of the united front to encourage the participation of a broad coalition, including private entrepreneurs, public intellectuals, and those who had joined the other eight political parties that existed then in China. The approach was soon abandoned with the private sector dismantled, critical intellectuals silenced, and the other political parties shunted aside. Once economic reforms began in earnest after 1978, the united front was resurrected to attract to the CCP those crucial for helping the Party meet its development goals but who were unwilling to join the Party: technicians, engineers, and intellectuals. Later, the broad coalition was extended to include private entrepreneurs, and eventually some even joined the CCP. Externally, the approach is coordinated by the party's United Front Work Department to connect with the Chinese diaspora and through related organizations such as the Chinese People's Association for Friendship with Foreign Countries to build platforms of support globally for CCP interests and policies.

As for Sneevliet, he continued to work among the small far left in the Netherlands. He founded the Revolutionary Socialist Party

and was elected its representative to parliament. During the Second
World War, he dissolved the party and set up a resistance group to
oppose the German occupation. In April 1942, he was captured and
executed. A street and metro station in Amsterdam carry his name.

BIBLIOGRAPHICAL NOTE

Unless otherwise noted, all the references are to be found in Tony Saich, *The
Origins of the First United Front in China: The Role of Sneevliet (alias
Maring)* (Leiden: E. J. Brill, 1991), 2 vols.

Chapter 2 – 1930s

The 1920s saw a remarkable growth of the newly formed Communist Party. It grew through student study societies and labor agitation in the railways, at mines like that at Anyuan in central China, and in the 1925 May 30th Movement's mass protests against imperialism in Shanghai and other cities. Throughout the middle years of the decade, the United Front between the Nationalists under Sun Yat-sen and his successors and the Communists aided this growth. However, Chiang Kai-shek, the military leader who took control of the Nationalists in 1927, put an end to the United Front in a bloody purge of the Communists in April 1927.

In the decade since that violent falling out, the CCP fought against the odds. With the labor movement decimated and Party organizations broken or driven underground in the cities, a rump decamped to the countryside. One of the local leaders, Mao Zedong, teamed up with another regional Party militarist, Zhu De, to establish a rural base away from the Nationalist authorities in a remote and poor part of central China. After a few years of failed uprisings, this team established the Jiangxi Soviet base in the mountainous border regions of southeast China. The Communists finally learned rural revolution here, replete with harsh "encirclement campaigns" by the Nationalists bent on exterminating the Communists, violent land reform, and murderous internal purges in which the Communists killed thousands of their own on grounds of ideological differences. The central Party apparatus, the inheritors of Sneevliet's and Borodin's Bolshevik training, limped along in Shanghai but finally decamped to the Jiangxi Soviet. By 1934, the Communists were forced to abandon their Soviet base and flee. The disorderly, disastrous, and extended retreat saw the Communists lose 90 percent of their forces.

What was left of the Communist forces finally regrouped in cold, dusty, and unwelcoming northwest China, settling in Yan'an by 1936. The retreat was immediately glorified as a biblical exodus, the Long March. The year of wandering across southern and western China had achieved one thing: a leadership change. Beginning at the rump meeting of Party survivors in Zunyi, Guangxi Province, in 1935, a regional leader, Mao Zedong, took military lead of the rout *and was able to lead the remnant successfully to its new refuge. Mao was on the rise, but he was neither the undisputed leader nor destined to succeed. He and the Party faced daunting challenges – military and political opponents inside the Party, a powerful enemy in the form of Chiang Kai-shek's Nationalist Army, and a record of unsuccessful revolutionary administration in which overly harsh land reform policies and an inquisitional approach to internal dissent had nearly destroyed the Party. Mao would handle his military competitor in the Party, Zhang Guotao, relatively quickly, but his political competitor was more serious, because he was sent to Yan'an from Moscow. Enter Wang Ming.*

THE 1930s

2 Wang Ming's Wuhan Moment: The Brief Flowering of Popular-Front Communism

HANS VAN DE VEN

The Kremlin, November 11, 1937, a cold autumn day. Georgi Dimitrov, the head of the Communist International, or the Comintern, and Wang Ming, the leader of its Chinese delegation, walked into Stalin's office to discuss events in China. They were worried.

Four months before their meeting, on July 7, 1937, Chinese and Japanese units had clashed near Peking. Local commanders were willing to accept a local settlement, as they had done before, but Chiang Kai-shek, China's leader, was not. After Japan had occupied Manchuria in 1931, it had gradually pushed farther south into China, forcing local arrangements that excluded Chiang Kai-shek's Nationalists from ever more territory. Chiang believed that the moment to stand up to Japan was now. Broad fighting broke out. The strong central army divisions he ordered north, though, failed to stiffen local spines. On August 13, he gambled, throwing elite forces against Japanese units in Little Tokyo, the Japanese-dominated part of the Shanghai International Settlement. They nearly succeeded in driving them into the Huangpu River, but Japanese re-enforcements arrived just in time. The Battle of Shanghai became a meat grinder, pitting at its height 700,000 Chinese defenders against 250,000 Japanese attackers. When the Japanese landed forces to the south of Shanghai on November 5, Nationalist forces faced encirclement. Exhausted, panicked, and demoralized, they fled helter-skelter from the doomed city. Japanese units set off in hot pursuit and soon threatened Nanjing, China's capital at the time, hoping that its capture would force China's capitulation.

Stalin, Dimitrov, and Wang had other concerns. There was Hitler. He had come to power in Germany in March 1933. In the years since, he rebuilt the German Army, stoked the economy and, in violation of the Treay of Versailles, reincorporated the Saarland in 1935 and remilitarized the Rhineland region in 1936. In 1936 he concluded the Anti-Comintern Pact with Japan and Italy. Dimitrov had played a bit part in these events. Just a few weeks after Hitler had become chancellor, the Reichstag was set on fire, an act for which Dutch Communist Marinus van der Lubbe was executed. The Nazis accused three others, including Dimitrov, of involvement. At their trial in Leipzig, Dimitrov defended himself, taking on Hermann Goering, the Nazis' number two, provoking the quip that "there is only one brave man in Germany, and he is a Bulgarian."[1] Dimitrov was acquitted but expelled to the Soviet Union. Now famous, he became the head of the Comintern.

Spain was a worry too. On July 17, 1936, a number of generals, including Franco, backed by wealthy landowners, royalists and conservative Catholic clergy, mounted a coup against the Republican government, based on an alliance of liberals, workers' parties, Catalan and Galician nationalist parties, and anarchists. By the end of 1937, the fighting still hung in the balance, but Franco's forces controlled the western half of Spain. About 100 Chinese volunteers, some from China, others from Europe and the USA, served in the international brigades supporting the Republican side. They had sworn, "we voluntarily come here to fight for the freedom of Spain and the world. We are prepared to spill our last drop of blood."[2] Many would do so.

Nor was the Soviet Union itself in good shape. Fearing the hostility unleashed by forced collectivization, the movement of millions of farmers into cities, and the desire of some Soviet republics to split from Moscow, in 1936 Stalin had begun a massive purge. At the end of 1937, it remained in full swing. Stalin's regime faced trouble at home.

The prospects for international communism, in short, looked grim. In the face of the rise of fascism in Europe, in 1934 Moscow ordered communist parties to postpone class struggle and instead to build alliances with socialist and liberal parties. In 1936, the popular front in France won a clear majority in elections, leading to the presidency of socialist Léon Blum. Wang Ming pushed that policy in China, publishing an article calling for a united front on August 1, 1935. His comrades in China adopted the new Comintern line, but insisted that the Nationalists must be excluded from any united front, understandably enough given that the Nationalists had driven them from central China all the way to their base at Yan'an, a desolate region in the northwest. But when the Communists in collaboration with local militarists took Chiang Kai-shek prisoner in December 1936, Moscow ordered them to arrange his release and accept the Nationalists into a united front.

Now that front was in danger. A Japanese victory in China would have left the Soviet Union threatened not just by Germany, well known to want new *Lebensraum* to its east, but also by a Japan with the resources of a subjugated China at its disposal. In 1936, a small number of clashes took place between Soviet and Japanese units along the Siberian–Manchurian border. A defeat of China's united front would have ramifications for European popular-front movements as well. The Kremlin meeting decided that "a new force familiar with the international situation should go and help the central committee of the Chinese Communist Party."[3] Step forward, Comrade Wang Ming.

Popular Front

Three days after his meeting with Stalin and Dimitrov, Wang Ming was on his way. Following stopovers in Urumqi in Xinjiang and Lanzhou in Gansu, he arrived at the Yan'an airstrip on November 29. When the airplane carrying Wang Ming approached, some residents worried that a Japanese bombing raid on the Communist capital was about to get underway. Their anxiety subsided when they saw Communist leaders rush toward the airfield. A message from Moscow had notified the Communist top brass about the impending arrival of the delegation.

After Wang Ming and his travel companions, who included a new Soviet representative, climbed out of the Soviet plane, Mao Zedong addressed them: "welcome sages descending from Kunlun Mountain, welcome esteemed international friends, and welcome comrades returning from Moscow. It is a delight to have you in Yan'an. As the saying has it, 'good fortune comes down from the sky.'"[4] In martial arts fiction and popular legend, sages hone their magic on Kunlun

Mountain before descending into the world. After Wang Ming replied modestly that the delegation did not deserve the honor bestowed on it, he and Mao Zedong embraced in comradely fashion.

The pleasantries over, Wang Ming set to work. On December 9, the Politburo, meeting in an expanded format to allow Wang to attend, began a five-day conference. The negotiations for a united front with the Nationalists, begun after Moscow's intervention in December 1936, only led to a formal agreement in September 1937, even if, from the start of hostilities, the Communists had expressed their support for it in principle. Even so, the Communists kept up a harsh critical line, condemning the Nationalists for their reluctance to arm the people, their failure to release political prisoners and their refusal to dismiss pro-Japanese officials. They called for a national assembly to "adopt a genuinely democratic constitution, decide on a policy to resist Japan and save the nation, and elect a national resistance government."[5] Their aim was to become "the core of nationwide resistance";[6] that is, to replace the Nationalists. They kept most of their forces in Yan'an, and those that took to the field did so behind Japanese lines to wage guerrilla warfare in mountainous regions. Useful, of course, but of little help to Chinese forces fighting the Japanese in Shanghai.

Wang told his colleagues that they must change: "Some comrades do not understand the united front ... If we do not unite with Chiang Kai-shek, objectively that is the same as aiding the Japanese."[7] He insisted that "everything must serve the united front."[8] Politically, that meant that the CCP should take seats in a unity government. Militarily, Communist forces should accept integration into the Nationalist order of battle and obey a single command. Wang also insisted that the Yan'an government be integrated into the Nationalist state. Having the backing of Moscow, Wang won the day and senior CCP leaders made self-criticisms. Speaking on the third day of the meeting, Mao admitted, "we have not sufficiently recognized the change in the KMT after the outbreak of war."[9] He agreed that "it is in the interest of everybody to have the KMT and the CCP collaborate. Our attitude toward the KMT must be aboveboard, unselfish, accommodating, and magnanimous." In accordance with Stalin's instructions, leadership arrangements stayed the same, with the exception that Wang Ming was put in charge of united-front work.

Then it was off to Wuhan for discussions with Chiang Kai-shek, who had indicated to Stalin that he would welcome Wang Ming's return. Wuhan, the central China transport hub known as the "Chicago of the East," had become the new center of resistance after the Battle of Shanghai and the fall of Nanjing on December 13, 1937.[10] Wang Ming and his colleagues, including future premier Zhou Enlai and future marshal Ye Jianying, stayed at 89 Middle Street, not far from the quay lining the Yangzi River in the Japanese concession, which the Japanese had evacuated.

China was in shock and Wuhan was in chaos. If Chiang Kai-shek gave out to be "supremely confident that ultimately China would come out on top,"[11] many others believed that China should cut its losses and sue for peace.[12] Chiang Kai-shek met with the CCP delegation for the first time on the evening of December 21. This was a good time for the Communists to negotiate with the Nationalists, not only because the latter needed all the help they could get but also because the Soviet Union was the only realistic source of foreign aid. It would deliver. In the first two years of the war, the Soviets supplied no less than 348 bombers, 542 fighters, eighty-two tanks, 2,118 vehicles, 1,140 artillery pieces, 9,720 machine guns, and 50,000 rifles, plus ammunition and pilots for the airplanes. But collaboration also came with risks. The Nationalists could feed Communist forces into the maws of the advancing Japanese with predictable results. The risks did not run just one way. For the Nationalists, the danger was that the Communists would break out of their confinement at Yan'an. Still, a Japanese victory would be fatal for both.

At this first meeting, Wang Ming talked in general terms about the war, relations between the two parties and the international situation.[13] Chiang Kai-shek indicated his goodwill: "we want to relax the restrictions on the Communist Party so that it can do its very best for the War of Resistance."[14] A committee was formed to draft a common platform.[15] But the discussions stalemated soon and in February Nationalist negotiators turned tough. Punning on the Chinese word for guerrillas, "to roam and attack," they mocked Communist troops for "roaming without attacking."[16] Articles appeared in the Wuhan press that criticized the Communists for running a "feudal separatist region" at Yan'an. *Wipe Out*, the *Wuhan Times*, *Blood Road*, and *Resistance and Culture* trumpeted the slogan "one leader, one ideology, one party."

Faced with this attack, Wang Ming and Zhou Enlai returned to Yan'an for consultations. The Communists decided that they would agree to the creation of an armed force of "several tens of divisions" operating under "a unified command,"[17] leaving open the possibility of Communist units operating independently outside this structure. But they refused to fold their party into the Nationalists. They also continued to call for a joint government "dedicated to serving the spirit of Mr. Sun Yat-sen," the late founder of the Nationalists.

Chiang Kai-shek declined this proposal but instead did three things. The first was to reorganize the Military Affairs Council, creating a political department in it and offering its vice directorship to Zhou Enlai, a way of pulling Communists into his government without recognizing them as equals.[18] The second was to establish a Three People's Principles Youth League. It borrowed the Communists' proposal for an alliance in Sun Yat-sen's name but restricted its members to youths. Finally, Chiang convened an Extraordinary Congress of the Nationalist Party. Meeting from March 29 until April 1, it adopted a proto-constitution for the duration of the war and declared that the aim of the war was not merely the defeat of Japan but also the completion of the task that Sun Yat-sen had set for China's revolution before his death in 1925, namely, leading the country to become a modern democratic republic.

The Communists fell into line. Wang Ming, Zhou Enlai and Ye Jianying had their misgivings,[19] but their fellow Politburo members in Yan'an believed that the path of greater wisdom lay in supporting Chiang Kai-shek.[20] The alternative was to risk popular condemnation for refusing to work with the Nationalists at this time of existential crisis. Zhou Enlai agreed to accept the office Chiang Kai-shek had created for him.[21] Other Communists joined his political department, including the novelist, historian and archaeologist Guo Moruo.[22] An embryonic Chinese popular front had come about.

Wuhan's Spring

"History, grown weary of Shanghai, bored with Barcelona, has fixed her capricious interests upon Hankow," wrote the famous

British writers W. H. Auden and Christopher Isherwood, who were in the city that momentous spring.[23] Hankow – or Hankou, to give the city its Pinyin transliteration – was one part of Wuhan. They were right. A new generation of young foreign journalists, who had sought to kick-start their careers in China during the depression, rushed to Wuhan. They included Edgar Snow, famous for his book *Red Star over China*. Its Chinese translation, *Mao Zedong's auto-biography*, electrified educated Chinese youths after its publication in November 1937. Others included Agnes Smedley, Michael Lindsay, Harold Timperley, Tillman Durdin and Freda Utley; their China reporting soon made them household names. The photojournalist Robert Capa came straight from Spain. Joris Ivens, the Dutch documentary maker, traveled the fronts in China to record footage for *The 400 Million*, a documentary on the fighting in China in 1938 that Frank Capra used later for the US War Department propaganda film *Why We Fight*. Across Europe, large demonstrations were held in major cities against Japanese brutality, which played into widespread fears of aerial bombardment, brought to a high pitch by German bombing of Guernica in April 1937 during the Spanish Civil War. In the spring of 1938, the world's focus was on Wuhan.[24]

So was China's. Journalists such as Zou Taofen, Tao Xisheng, Ding Wen'an and Xie Bingying; public intellectuals such as Liang Shuming and Hu Shi; and military leaders including Chen Cheng, Bai Chongxi, "Christian General" Feng Yuxiang and Jiang Baili were there. Evacuated government officials from Nanjing joined them. One was Chen Kewen, who served in the Executive Branch. He arrived in Wuhan on November 28, finding the mood in the city a mixture of despair, defeatism and decadence. Reports of military casualties, local officials abandoning their posts, corruption and nepotism filled him with pessimism.[25] Hundreds of thousands of refugees made it to the city, some arriving by ship, others by train or bus, but most on foot. Each could tell a tale of hardship, disease, and death. One memoir by a woman then still only a schoolchild recounts that the first thing her family had to do was to purchase one coffin and reserve another for her very ill baby sister and mother. The reservation could in the end be canceled, to her understandable relief.[26] The *Manchester Guardian* reported on the arrival of a group of 150 persons at a refugee facility run by a woman missionary.

"A boy of fourteen led the way, staggering along under two loads on a carrying pole, representing everything the family had."[27]

The city's mood recovered over the next few months. Political and military leaders addressed public rallies. Chiang Kai-shek did so standing on a high platform in front of national and party flags, dressed in a tight-fitting military uniform and speaking into a microphone so that his words could be broadcast through loudspeakers and occasionally over the radio. Chen Kewen attended one of the regular Sun Yat-sen memorial meetings at which Chiang spoke. These gatherings followed a set liturgy, including the reading of Sun's Testament and the audience's triple bow to Sun's portrait. Chen described Chiang in his diary as tired but resolute. "Such a supreme commander will lift the spirit of the broad masses."[28] On another occasion, Chiang kept an audience of a thousand people spellbound. Chen Kewen had tears in eyes. Chiang is not known as a good public speaker, but he shone in Wuhan.

Many other famous people addressed audiences across Wuhan. They included General Chen Cheng, who co-ordinated the defense of the city. So did countless young students and activists, not just in Wuhan but across China. They spoke from improvised stages or just from atop soap boxes. Left-wing artists and writers giving *actes de présence* included playwright Tian Han. He had written the lyrics to *The March of the Volunteers*, which became hugely popular during the war and now is China's national anthem. When Chen Kewen heard a column of soldiers marching through Wuhan belting out "Arise, you who refuse to be slaves / With our flesh and blood let us build a new Great Wall," two of its lines, his spirits rose.[29]

In April, Nationalist and Communist organizers in Wuhan put together a propaganda week. Their good fortune was that on April 7, Chinese defenders at Taierzhuang on the north China plain drove back General Isogai Rensuke's 10th Division. Wuhan erupted. "A million and a half Chinese in this temporary capital tonight celebrated China's first decisive victory," the *Washington Post* reported.[30] Guo Moruo described the scene he witnessed that evening:

> Some 400,000 to 500,000 persons paraded with torches ...
> At Yellow Crane Tower, the people were so closely packed together that ferries could not unload their passengers.

The flames of the torches lit up both shores of the Yangzi River. The sound of the songs we sang, the firecrackers we set off, and the slogans we shouted rent the air. Wuhan has come back to life.[31]

The Yellow Crane Tower, one of the most famous in China, stands on a hill near the Yangzi River.

The propaganda week consisted of a week of lectures, parades, rallies and performances in schools, universities, markets, theaters, cinemas and factories. It concluded with a massive parade on April 13.

> Government and Kuomintang [Nationalist] officers, schools, factories, and public institutions were also represented. Military and boy-scout bands headed the parades, which carried portraits of Sun Yat-sen and Chiang Kai-shek. Demonstrators performed tableaux such as "The Bombing of the Idzumo," the Japanese flagship at Shanghai, "Japanese Atrocities," "Down with the Traitors," and "The Final Victory is Ours."[32]

Cinemas showed talks in which General Chen Cheng spoke about China's resistance.

Spectacles such as the April parade were one face of Wuhan's still largely spontaneous popular front. Another one, away from the public eye, was surprisingly effective military collaboration. Communist forces expanded rapidly from somewhere between 30,000 and 40,000 troops at the start of the war to some 160,000 by the time of the fall of Wuhan. From their base in Yan'an, they marched first into Shanxi Province to support warlord Yan Xishan against the Japanese and then into Shandong and Hebei, where they established new base areas. The Nationalists provided funds for nine Communist divisions, coming to some 18 million yuan during the first three years of the war, besides uniforms, arms, ammunition, medicine and food.[33]

General Ye Jianying played an important liaison role. In January 1938, for instance, he messaged Yan'an, passing on a request by Chiang Kai-shek for Communist forces to cross the Yellow River into the Taihang mountains to block a drive west by Japanese units.[34] In February, Yan'an told him to discuss with the Nationalists planned Communist deployments into Henan, Anhui, and Hebei. In a telegram of March 17, Mao Zedong asked Ye to suggest to Chiang that he secure Yellow River crossings so that forces engaged in the Battle for Xuzhou, which was then raging, could retreat if that became necessary. The same month, Communist commander-in-chief Zhu De wanted him to ask the Nationalists for 700,000 rifle rounds, 300,000 rounds for machine guns, and 500,000 grenades on the grounds that Communist forces were down to their last twenty rounds per rifle. In a telegram of June meant to tell the Nationalists that Communist troops were actively fighting the Japanese to secure more Nationalist supplies, Zhu claimed that from September 1937, they had waged 638 battles, causing 34,734 Japanese casualties and a loss of 25,986 Chinese.

Unsurprisingly, the Communists were not always fully frank. On May 20, Mao Zedong wrote to Wang Ming, Zhou Enlai and Ye Jianying that after Xuzhou had fallen, "Wuhan will be in danger. Then Chiang Kai-shek will approve the deployment of our forces south so that they can operate in the enemy rear in Henan, Anhui, Jiangsu and Shandong." He told them that two divisions would then be ordered into these provinces, but added, "do not mention this to Chiang Kai-shek until an appropriate moment."

The Communists and the Nationalists used the momentum generated by the propaganda week to put some institutional foundations under the united front. The political consultative conference brought into being by the KMT's Extraordinary Congress met for the first time on July 7, 1938, a year after the war had broken out. In line with Wang Ming's approach of participating in the united front while criticizing the KMT's right wing, its meetings were, as the *New York Times* reported, "marked by clashes between communists and right wing leaders."[35] The *New China Daily* of the Communists lamented that it "is not a sovereign people's representative."

Nonetheless, "sentiment for the subordination of party differences to the cause of unity against Japan predominated." Unsurprisingly so. Already, over a million Chinese lay dead.[36] Japan saw fit to drive home the point. On July 12, eighteen Japanese bombers raided Wuhan, causing 500 casualties.[37] Overall the Communist press was positive: the consultative conference "connected all parties and factions, all provinces and regions, and representatives of all people ... It has the right to discuss and decide on all important domestic and international government policies ... it is an appropriate organ for representing the people's will during the war."[38] Three of the conference's eight Communists joined its twenty-five-member standing committee.

The Three People's Principles Youth League was established on July 9, 1938, in Wuhan. It drew a following from young government and military personnel as well as university and school student bodies. The practical work it undertook at this time included managing way stations for young refugees, sending youth parties to war zones to offer support to the wounded, organizing aid to families with sons at the front, and conducting propaganda drives. Later, the Nationalists attempted to turn it into an organization to control young Chinese.

In Wuhan, Wang Ming was a very busy man. He headed the Communist organization in the city, which supervised Communist activity not just in Wuhan but also all along the Yangzi River and in south China. He gave lectures at public rallies and universities, attended memorial meetings for famous war casualties, and oversaw a Communist membership drive. Besides conducting negotiations with the Nationalists, he gave countless interviews and produced articles for the Wuhan press, such as "Our views on the defense of Wuhan and the third period in the War of Resistance,"[39] "The Chinese War of Resistance and world peace,"[40] and "On the movement for women's liberation."[41] Wang was in his element. This was his moment.

Had Wang Ming rated his work since his return to China, he could have given himself a good report. Communist policy had changed fundamentally. He and his colleagues were working flat out in Wuhan to give substance to the united front. The Nationalists had adopted a political platform around which all anti-Japanese groups could unite. He had not succeeded in creating a joint government, but Communists held official positions in the Military Affairs Council. When he had met Dimitrov and Stalin, they had told him that Communist forces should not engage in "direct attack, but should irritate the enemy, to draw it into the countryside and to attack it from the rear."[42] Some 160,000 were now doing exactly that. Not a bad result for half a year's work.

Wuhan Abandoned

But Wuhan's spring had already passed its high point. On June 15, in a long article, Wang Ming and Zhou Enlai asked the question, "Can Wuhan be defended," to which they replied, "Yes! Recall the glorious experiences of the defense of Madrid by the Spanish people."[43] They pointed to China's new unity, its army of several million troops and even greater number of militias, the revolutionary tradition of Wuhan's workers and citizens, and China's large size and huge population as reasons to have confidence. Unfortunately for Wang, staking the future of the united front on the defense of Wuhan proved a huge mistake.

The Nationalist decision not to defend the city was fatal. In June, Chiang Kai-shek had called for that, but in late July he let it be known that "China will no longer make great sacrifices to hold a position or a city."[44] The *Manchester Guardian* reported that

> everyone with knowledge of the true conditions knows that the morale of Chinese armies is lower than it was during the fighting for Suchow [Xuzhou]; that the strongest boom Matung [the Madang Barrier] on the Yangtze has fallen; and that the vast majority of the Chinese people are not yet mobilized.[45]

The Nationalist Army was in a bad state. "Half of it is stricken with malaria and about 15 per cent with dysentery."[46] This was not an army fit to withstand a siege for months on end. Far better to withdraw into China's vastness to recoup strength than to lose all in one last heroic act.

Wuhan emptied out. Women, children, refugees and wounded soldiers had already been ordered out of the city in early June.[47] By early October, the Wuhan municipal government had evacuated 300,000 refugees. They were passed on to other provinces and put to work on vast reclamation projects.[48] The crated contents of the Palace Museum traveled in a ship "so full that women could be found in the smoking rooms."[49] On July 17, remaining government personnel were told to be ready to depart the city on ten days' notice. The Executive Branch co-ordinated, as best as it could, the departure of offices, businesses and industrial plants to "the great rear." Wuhan's cinemas, theaters and restaurants soon stood empty.

Chiang Kai-shek left the city on October 25, when the sound of Japanese guns, just ten miles away, could be heard in the city.[50] On October 26, Japanese troops marched in and "the first of a long line of warships of all sizes steamed up river and moored off the bund [quay]." The remaining Chinese forces had departed in good order, having "removed everything portable from the city which might be of service to the Japanese – factory machinery, pontoons, and even sewer covers."[51] Nationalist destruction units dynamited strategic buildings. "Flames stabbed the sky as unchecked fires spread a trail of ruin and ashes for the invader to seize."[52]

The fall of Wuhan came at a bad time for popular-front communism internationally. Léon Blum had refused to throw France's weight behind Spain's Republicans, fearing that his own country would split down the middle, possibly leading to civil war. He fell from power on April 10, 1938. By then, Franco's victory in Spain had become a matter of when, not if. Already in April, his forces had split the Republican-controlled eastern half of Spain into two. Convinced that he would win, Franco refused a Republican offer of peace negotiations and insisted on unconditional surrender. The Republicans attempted a counteroffensive in the summer, but French and British attempts to pacify Hitler in Munich in September 1938 crushed Republican morale. On March 31, 1939, it was all over. Stalin drew his own conclusion. In September 1939, he signed a non-aggression pact with Germany, the notorious Molotov–Ribbentrop pact. Popular-front communism was dead.

Dead Man Walking

After the Second World War, Dimitrov became president of Bulgaria. Wang Ming would die in 1974 in Moscow, far from power, angry at his fate and demonized in Beijing. According to Beijing-endorsed histories of the CCP, Wang Ming fell from favor at a Central Committee meeting that took place in Yan'an from September 29 to November 6, 1938. Supposedly, the cause was a new Comintern directive by Dimitrov that "decisively canceled Wang Ming's self-appointment as the Comintern's plenipotentiary," as Mao Zedong's CCP biographer Jin Chongji puts it.[53]

Wang Ming became a dead man walking, not in 1938, but in 1941. The circumstances of Dimitrov's instruction have never been truly clarified. In 1979, after Deng Xiaoping came to power, he allowed a period of open debate within the CCP about Mao Zedong's role in history. Senior CCP official Wang Jiaxiang, who had transmitted Dimitrov's instruction, published a piece in the *People's Daily* in which he set out his version of events. Given its importance, he must have done so after consulting widely. According to Wang, Dimitrov told him that the Communists should continue the united front with the Nationalists, keep up criticism of the KMT right wing, and support resistance against Japan in the name of implementing Sun Yat-sen's Three People's Principles. Dimitrov also told Wang Jiaxiang that he approved of Chinese Communists serving in the Nationalists' military but not in its government, and that he believed that the CCP leadership should rally around Mao.[54] None of this contradicted his instructions to Wang Ming in November 1937 in any way.[55]

The year 1938 simply was not the time. To have shown anything but wholehearted support for the united front as the defense of Wuhan crumbled would have strengthened the hand of Nationalists who believed that further resistance was pointless. Wang Jingwei, the Nationalist deputy leader, had long held doubts about the wisdom of continuing the war; he concluded that only the Communists could profit from the War of Resistance. On December 21, 1938, he flew from Chongqing to Hanoi and began negotiations with the Japanese. He would fail, but that was by no means certain at the time.

Mao Zedong spoke out more enthusiastically about the united front at the 1938 Central Committee meeting than at any time before or after. He insisted that relations should be much closer, endorsed Chiang Kai-shek as the united front's supreme leader,[56] and waxed lyrical about past Nationalist achievements. He predicted for them "a great future," including after the war. Midway through the meeting, Wang Ming and Zhou Enlai left Yan'an to continue negotiations with Chiang Kai-shek in Chongqing, handing them a letter signed by both Mao and Wang. That does not suggest a leadership bust-up.

This does not mean that Mao and Wang saw eye to eye on everything. In July, Wang Ming had refused to publish Mao Zedong's *On Protracted War* in Wuhan. *On Protracted War* was many things, including a powerful argument about the importance of base areas for revolution in a country as large, populous and rural as China.[57] It was also a rejection of Wang Ming's call for making a stand at Wuhan: "we must avoid waging disadvantageous battles. When we cannot defend a position, we must resolutely abandon it."[58] But that issue was settled. Mao criticized Wang Ming's slogan "all through the united front," but added, "Wang Ming has made great contributions in the history of the Party. He has worked very hard for the realization of the united front ... We must be generous toward him."[59]

All this changed in the autumn of 1941. Until then, Wang Ming continued to have a high reputation among Yan'an intellectuals. He was a member of the Politburo and served in various prominent positions. He was respected as the "embodiment of Marxism–Leninism" and "honored at almost the same level as 'Chairman Mao,'"[60] as highly regarded PRC historian Gao Hua puts it. In January 1941, though, the Nationalists had destroyed a Communist division in central China in their worst clash during the Second World War. The Communists did not declare a formal end to the united front, but they ceased further collaboration, refusing, for instance, to attend consultative conference meetings. Mao now struck.

At a Politburo meeting that autumn, Mao tore into Wang Ming. At first, Wang gave as good as he got,[61] but soon Mao crushed him: "Wang Ming thinks we are too leftist, but on the contrary we think he is too rightist ... Comrade Wang Ming committed many errors during the Wuhan period."[62] He then turned sarcastic:

> Your dogma is useless, or to put it more crudely, "it isn't worth shit." We can see that dog shit can be used as fertilizer and human shit can be used to feed a dog, but dogma cannot be used as fertilizer or fatten up a dog, so what use has it?[63]

Days later, Wang Ming was ill. In 1974, Wang stated in Moscow, where he lived from 1956, that "starting from October 4, I had at least one meal at his [Mao Zedong's] place daily. On October 8, I felt a searing pain followed by a loss of blood, dizziness, and heart weakness. After examining me, the doctor said that the symptoms looked like poisoning."[64] Peter Vladimirov, the TASS agent in Yan'an, backed up this claim in a diary published in 1975, also in Moscow. PRC historians now argue that Wang Ming had indeed been very seriously ill and remained so for the next three years, as a result not of intentional poisoning but of medical incompetence by which Wang suffered from a mercury overdose.[65] Dimitrov tried to intervene when news of Wang's plight reached him,[66] but Mao rejected his proposal to fly Wang out of Yan'an for medical care, arguing that Wang "has engaged in diverse antiparty activities."[67]

In 1971, on the fiftieth anniversary of the CCP's founding, Wang Ming wrote *Fifty Years of the CCP*. Wang produced the memoir when relations between the Soviet Union and the PRC were at a nadir as a result of the Sino-Soviet split. Moreover, in 1971 Henry Kissinger made his way to Beijing to meet Zhou Enlai, the first step in the USA–PRC rapprochement that isolated the Soviet Union strategically and fissured the Communist world for good. Wang Ming's *Fifty Years* was but one blow in the Soviet's China-bashing of this time. Wang Ming went so far as to charge Mao with having been pro-American all along. That was nonsense. But Wang Ming's memoir does contain a grain of truth (and he certainly had cause for complaint).

Wang recounted in the memoir how, on April 1, 1944, Mao Zedong visited him on his sickbed and apologized for his failure to visit him during the previous two years. This meeting took place as what is known as the Yan'an rectification campaign was nearing its conclusion. Mao's aim in the campaign was to compel all Chinese Communists not only to bow to his authority but also to accept his view of their party's past. Here Mao followed in the footsteps of Stalin. Seeking to put an end to divisive ideological debate in the Soviet Union, Stalin commissioned the *History of the Communist Party of the Soviet Union (Bolsheviks): Short Course* in 1935. If Stalin had relied on trials, in the rectification campaign Mao had all CCP members read a set of Communist texts, a good number his own. They discussed these, wrote confessions of their own lives and ideological errors, and assessed each other's conduct and thinking in self-criticism and mutual-criticism sessions. Mao may have been ruminating on the idea when, at the 1938 Central Committee meeting, he said, "the whole period from Confucius to Sun Yat-sen, we must give it a general summary and we must inherit this valuable heritage."[68] But he only acted on it after 1941.

At their bedside meeting, Mao first told Wang that one purpose of the rectification campaign was to purge Lenin, Stalin and the Comintern from the CCP's history. That is a one-sided way of putting it, but Mao's main claim as an ideological innovator was that he was uniquely able to apply the general truths of Marxism–Leninism to the concrete circumstances of China. Mao then, Wang claims, praised Wang's contributions, especially his pioneering promotion of the united front. But Mao worried that if the CCP's version of the *Short Course* recognized this, then Wang would have led the CCP for fourteen out of the previous twenty-five years, leaving just eleven for Mao himself. Would Wang, Mao asked, agree to let Mao be seen as having had responsibility for the united front?[69] Wang replied that with recent history still living memory, few would accept this version of events.

During the rectification movement, Mao turned Wang Ming into the example par excellence of a dogmatist, someone who had been unable to adapt Marxism–Leninism to the Chinese context, and so had led the Party into grievous mistakes. Meeting after meeting was dedicated to denunciation of Wang. Mao achieved his goal in April 1945 when the Central Committee endorsed the "Resolution on certain historical problems." It turned Mao's view of the past into an indisputable orthodoxy and condemned Wang for having implemented an erroneous political line for fourteen years. He was made to produce a letter declaring that he supported the verdict.

The argument that the autumn 1938 Central Committee meeting was an important turning point in the history of the CCP was no more than part of the effort to give Mao's ideological triumph a long, deep history; it was an invented tradition. Instead of being the hero of the hour, Wang Ming's fate in China's revolution was to be Mao Zedong's punchbag. But perhaps Mao Zedong's victory was not completely total. Wang Ming claimed that Mao wanted to have "-ism" after his name.[70] Rather than Mao Zedong-ism, though, in April 1945 the Seventh Party Congress adopted a Party constitution that made Mao Zedong Thought, not Mao Zedong-ism, the Party's guiding thought. It is tempting to think of it as a faint trace of lingering resistance to Mao. But, more likely, it resulted from a pragmatic decision not to step on Stalin's oh-so-sensitive toes. Mao wanted to sinify Marxism–Leninism, but still needed Stalin's help in the coming civil war.

The day that Wang Ming met Stalin and Dimitrov, November 11, 1937, had been Armistice Day, solemnly commemorated around the world, including in colonial Hong Kong and the British concessions in China, even during the War of Resistance right up until Pearl Harbor. In 1938 in London, one person interrupted the commemorations at the Cenotaph, attended by royals, political and military leaders, and the great and the good. During the traditional two minutes of solemn silence, one person cried "hypocrisy" and "you are preparing for war."[71] *The Times* assuaged its readers; the man was not of good mind and had only just escaped from an asylum. But he was, of course, not wrong; countries were rearming for a war that all feared but that seemed more inevitable with each passing day.

Wang Ming and Dimitrov were not wrong to link Madrid and Wuhan. Popular-front communism enthused millions across Europe, China and elsewhere during the depression in the 1930s. The refusal of Western governments to give it their support was understandable, given that the cost of the First World War was still felt everywhere and therefore appeasement seemed worth the effort. But it also derived from a deep red scare. The result was the defeat of the most powerful force then resisting the ascent of Germany, Italy and Japan. Its failure would result in the emergence of nationalized communisms, which shaped the post-Second World War world profoundly. It is often wise to wait in a crisis, but this time it was not. And so an opportunity was lost.

Chapter 3 – 1940s

In 1972 Japanese prime minister Tanaka Kakuei visited China at the time of the normalization of diplomatic relations between China and Japan. He repeatedly apologized for Japan's invasion of China during the Second World War. When he met Mao, China's leader, accustomed to making flippant remarks, told him to stop apologizing because without the Japanese invasion the Chinese Communists would still be in the hills. The Japanese did do the Chinese Communists a good turn. In the years between 1937 and 1945, Japanese forces made mincemeat of Chinese Nationalist armies. They drove Chiang Kai-shek's regime all the way to Sichuan in west China. The Nationalists would stay the course and eventually emerge as victors, but wartime corruption, military failures, administrative disintegration, the recruitment of village poor at gunpoint, harvest seizures, and factional rivalries ravaged the government's status with large sections of Chinese society. Mao was right: victory in 1949 was the result of Communist good fortune.

But only in part. Winners must also make their own luck. In 1942, Mao made the bold step to transform the Chinese Communist Party into an organization with iron discipline, with a unified political and military strategy, and with a strong leader – Mao himself. Mao drew on the positive examples of Lenin and Stalin, understandably given that Lenin had made the Bolsheviks successful in 1917 and Stalin was leading the defense of his country against the Germans with by now clear success. But he also looked at the Nationalists as a negative example. Their generals frequently failed to co-operate, Chiang Kai-shek's orders were implemented only if they were convenient or advantageous, bureaucratization drove everyone insane, and the Nationalist Party was widely seen as staffed by the well-connected and the obedient rather than the energetic and competent.

For many youths living under Japanese occupation or under the Nationalists, the Communist base in Yan'an was an inspiration: a new, better future was in the making there, so it seemed. They made their way to the Communist capital, committing their lives to securing that future for their country. When Mao in 1942 set about *transforming the CCP through an ambitious rectification campaign, many of these youth were excited and hoped the Communists would thereby address their own faults as the Nationalists had not. But when it became clear that Mao's goal was to build the Party into an all-conquering fighting machine, some worried that the command to toe the party line and uphold its prestige regardless of realities was both misleading and dangerous. That was not the future they wanted. Wang Shiwei, a Communist, a theorist, and a translator of Marxist classics, spoke up for these patriotic youth and revolutionary writers. Mao was caught short and his new rectification campaign was briefly derailed. Wang made a biting critique of the Party's faults and offered a cosmopolitan vision of a revolution open to the best the world had to offer for all working people. Wang's literary revolt would not last long, but the legacy for intellectuals in China lives on today.*

THE 1940s

3 Wang Shiwei's Rectification: Intellectuals and the Party in Yan'an

TIMOTHY CHEEK

Comrades, in this struggle is there anything wrong with your bones? Is it true that you dare not speak up to the VIPs (especially your own boss) and would rather pick on the small fry? Understand, this is the soft bones disease, an unhealthy approach. We must have the moral courage of the strongest and most unyielding bones in order to deal with it.[1]

So declared Wang Shiwei's "Strong Bones, Soft Bones," a poster stuck to the wall of the busy south gate of Yan'an, the Communist capital. It ridiculed Mao's campaign to instill upright behavior, discipline, and obedience in the home of the Chinese Communist Party in 1942.

Mao read it and Wang got his attention. But Wang was not alone. Further essays appeared in the Party press by this cantankerous Party theorist and fellow left-wing writers who had fled to Yan'an from the garrets of Shanghai at the outbreak of the Anti-Japanese War in 1937. While the Party had recovered from the disasters of the 1930s and was expanding its base areas in rural districts behind Japanese lines across north China, all was not well in the Communist capital. Wang was but one dissident voice among the Party's literati – Ding Ling, the well-known woman writer, was a senior editor in the Party's press and led the criticisms of the problems and fault lines in the Party's rule – but Wang Shiwei was the most biting and the most persistent. He disagreed with Mao but had read more of Marx and Lenin than Mao (having translated a fair bit of them). This was Communist dissent. By March 1942, the uproar caused Mao to halt his campaign to deal with these nagging intellectuals and then to lay down the law in his "Talks at the Yan'an Forum on Literature and Art."

Wang's story began in the hothouse student groups at Peking University in the 1920s and then the Shanghai literary world of the 1930s, traveled through the working committees of the Communist think tanks in Yan'an in the early 1940s, and exploded on the pages of Yan'an's *Liberation Daily* in 1942. It reached a crescendo in an appalling public castigation of Wang that June, followed by Wang's new incarnation as negative role model. His Marxist cosmopolitanism became Trotskyite heresy and his efforts to mobilize youth were rewritten as a treasonous campaign by an anti-Party "Gang of Five." Intellectuals were put on notice: you serve the revolution Mao's way, or no way.

Yan'an, 1942

Wang Shiwei's story unfolds in the barren northwest of China to which the Communist forces had fled in the mid-1930s and where Wang Ming and Mao had crossed swords at the Sixth Plenum of the Party's Central Committee in the early days of the Anti-Japanese War. The place was Yan'an, a dusty prefectural town in the impoverished province of Shaanxi and some 300 kilometres north of the ancient capital, Xi'an. In 1936 the American journalist Edgar Snow described the area: "North Shaanxi was one of the poorest parts of China I had seen ... The fields are mostly patches laid on the serried landscape between crevices and small streams." A nineteenth-century German traveler observed,

> We are here at the very center of the loess region. Everything is yellow. The hills, the roads, the fields, the water of the rivers and brooks are yellow. The houses are made of yellow earth, the vegetation is covered with yellow dust ... even the atmosphere is seldom free from a yellow haze.[2]

The Communists under Mao found a refuge in this remote area and from 1936 built a workable local administration. This was in part supported by a new United Front between the Communists and the Nationalists following the Xi'an Incident of December 1936 in which one of Chiang Kai-shek's generals had kidnapped him to impel him to make peace with the Communists and fight the

Japanese who had occupied China's Manchurian provinces. The United Front brought peace, recognition and financial support to the Shaan–Gan–Ning Border Region headquartered in Yan'an. The Communist forces – civilian and military – grew mightily from some 30,000 to perhaps 400,000, with additional base areas springing up across north China. The outbreak of full-scale war with Japan in the summer of 1937 brought patriotic youth to Yan'an from the major cities of eastern China. Driven from their homes, distrustful of corrupt local governments, disillusioned with the unfulfilled prom- ises of Chiang's Nationalist Party, these became revolutionary youth bringing education, professional skills, and enthusiasm to Yan'an. Wang Shiwei and other older intellectuals joined them.

By 1942 the heady days of the early war years had passed. The United Front had broken down and with it came the end of financial subsidies from Chongqing and the return to economic blockade. Worse, the Communists' most ambitious campaign against the Japanese, the Hundred Regiments offensive of August 1940 – like the Vietcong's Tet offensive against the American mili- tary in Vietnam some two decades later – bloodied the enemy but produced vicious reprisals, which the Communists called the "Three All" policy of "burn all, kill all, destroy all." The results were horrific. The population under Communist administration shrank by about half, from something like 44 million to 25 million, and the Communist army, the Eighth Route Army, was reduced from 400,000 to 300,000 or less. In Yan'an food and materials became scarce; the bloated bureaucracy started to look like a needlessly privileged elite.[3]

In addition to these administrative challenges, the Party faced a political crisis. Mao's leadership was not secure. He had sidelined Wang Ming (see Chapter 2), and he had cornered his military rival, Zhang Guotao, but he had yet to win the hearts and minds of the Party – the other leaders and the rank and file. With the deteriorating conditions in Yan'an, the revolutionary intellectuals – key to staffing the Communist bureaucracy, developing its ideology, mobilizing the masses, and providing the skills of modern profes- sionals – were showing increasing signs of losing their admiration for this "people's revolution." Grumbles grew louder. Were the Communists, now in power in one place, going to go the despicable way of the Nationalists and descend into bureaucratic corruption?

Mao's answer to these problems – all these problems: administrative, political, economic, and ideological – was rectification. Formally a political movement (*yundong*) to identify, expose, and eradicate the "three evil workstyles" of subjectivism, sectarianism, and stereotyped Party writing, it came to be called *zhengfeng* or "rectification of workstyles." It would emerge as a comprehensive social, political, and military campaign to promote a change in worldview, habits, and commitments – ideological remolding or "thought reform." Mao's focus at first was the top leadership – to discredit Wang Ming and his approach to the United Front and so secure Mao's own pre-eminence and then the broader leadership to discipline rowdy Red Army officers, socialize clannish Party leaders from various provinces, and weed out bad apples. But Mao was checked from an unexpected source – his revolutionary intellectuals. As soon as he opened the campaign, Mao was dismayed to find that his top Marxist theorists and the famous left-wing writers who had brought such a revolutionary sheen to Yan'an turned on him and his top leaders, accusing them of "degeneration," hypocrisy, and corruption. Wang Shiwei became the loudest and most memorable of these critical voices.

Wang Shiwei was a product of China's new culture movement. Born in 1907 in Kaifeng, Henan, he became a fiction writer and a translator. He entered Peking University in 1925 and soon joined the fledgling Chinese Communist Party.[4] As with so many early Communists, Wang's search took him in and out of local Party organizations as government security services broke Party cells and arrested suspected Communists. At a loose end, Wang came to find the ideas of Leon Trotsky more compelling than those of Comrade Stalin. By the early 1930s Wang was writing short stories and translating Marxist texts from English in Shanghai, while bouncing around east China in various short-term teaching jobs. He translated European literature (German Romantics, Thomas Hardy, and Colette's *Les herbes*) as well as Marx, "Lenin's Will," and parts of *Trotsky's Autobiography*. Beyond earning his literary chops as a left-wing writer, these years developed two enduring traits in Wang Shiwei. First was his theoretical sophistication and considerable knowledge of Marxism–Leninism and the critique by Trotsky of the "degenerated workers' state" of the Soviet Communist Party under Stalin. Wang came to know Wang Fanxi and other Chinese

Trotskyists, though he never joined their organizations. Second, Wang was a fanatical idealist. His novel, *Rest* (*Xiuxi*), from 1930 was set in the form of letters sent to him by a classmate who was driven by economic distress and disgust with the "filth" and "darkness" in society to seek rest in suicide.[5] Wang's writing style in *Rest* would characterize his professional life: indignation at injustice, inflexible opinions, and passion bordering on hysteria. His later friends in Yan'an would describe Wang as something of a revolutionary puritan, upright, easily outraged, and quick to expose and denounce corruption.[6]

Rectification: Mao's Way

The early months of 1942 in Yan'an were awash with announcements of the new education campaign, Rectification. Mao Zedong prepared his Party colleagues with the "Main Points of Propaganda of the Propaganda Department of the Central Committee" of January 26, 1942.[7] The "Main Points" set as the campaign's goals the eradication of the "errors of subjectivism and sectarianism" among Party cadres who had caused the CCP's correct line to be implemented badly. Guidance would be provided by decisions of the Party and speeches by Central Committee leaders – especially Comrade Mao Zedong. All would have to make "genuine self-criticisms." The job of Party propaganda was to mobilize the Party faithful to take stronger efforts in that direction.

And what was to be corrected? Thoughts, ideas, assumptions, attitudes held among the diverse population of Party cadres old and new. Mao told his audience at the opening of Yan'an's Party School on February 1 that the shortcomings in the Party had resulted "from the fact that there are certain things in the brains of some of our comrades that are not quite correct, not quite proper."[8] Mao's solution to these thought problems was ideological education to subdue "three evil" styles – subjectivism in study (favoring Wang Ming's Russian Marxism over Mao's local expertise), sectarianism in organizational life (not doing what the leadership tells you to do), and formalism in Party writing (that is, boring dogmatism that won't mobilize anybody).

Mao made clear the primary source of correct thinking in the same speech to the Party School: theorists (*lilunjia*). Mao asked,

"What kind of theorists do we need?" His answer was people who could "give scientific explanations and theoretical elucidations of China's economic, political, military, cultural, and other problems." This form of intellectual elitism ran deep in Mao's thought. He would write in 1945, "The mastery of ideological education is the principal factor in consolidating the Party and in carrying on its great political struggles."[9]

This is why propaganda mattered to the Party. It was a way to transform minds and souls. And this is why Mao and the Party needed intellectuals. Educated people able to understand political theory and to write and to popularize Party policies were essential for mobilizing the rank and file, as well as the local population, to carry out the Party's vision. Mao had every reason to expect that he would find that talent in Yan'an in its various institutions – the new Party School, the Kangda Military Academy, the Lu Xun Arts Academy, the Central Research Institute, and Yan'an's press, particularly the Party's own newspaper, *Liberation Daily* (*Jiefang ribao*). Naturally, Mao presumed that *he* was the chief theorist who would provide the content for the Party's propagandists.

Revolutionary Artists' Agenda

Mao had high hopes for revolutionary intellectuals, but he was to be bitterly disappointed.

The revolutionary writers in Yan'an responded by proposing their version of rectification. Almost all of the speakers were Party members themselves and all had chosen to come to Yan'an to support the revolution they thought the Party was leading. They believed in literature as an exposé of society's ills no matter where those ills were, including inside the Party. Mao presumed to teach the masses; the revolutionary artists appointed themselves political ombudsmen. They tried to divert Mao's initially limited political aims to broader social and spiritual aims. Both groups sought to attack the same three "evil work styles": subjectivism, sectarianism, and stereotyped Party writing. Same campaign, different dreams.

Ding Ling was the leader. She was the head of women's organizations in Yan'an in 1941 and edited the literature section of *Liberation Daily*. This was a central platform for the writers' agenda for rectification in spring 1942. Ding Ling called for the revival of *zawen* (the "polemic essay"), a form of political criticism made famous by novelist Lu Xun (1881–1936), who was already honored by the Party leadership as an exemplary revolutionary intellectual. In the October 23, 1941, *Liberation Daily* Ding Ling wrote, "I think it would do us most good if we emulate Lu Xun's steadfastness in facing the truth, his courage to speak out for the sake of truth, and his fearlessness. This age of ours still needs *zawen*, a weapon that we should never lay down."[10] Ding Ling started the intellectual rebellion, but Wang Shiwei became its intellectual model and in short order its martyr.

Wang was a dedicated cosmopolitan. Mao was a nationalist. Wang held that the new revolutionary consciousness from Europe also needed new foreign forms – the modern novel, spoken drama (as opposed to traditional sung opera), and translations. Form was inseparable from content, and modern equaled Western:

> For example, if the communication tools of modern culture – automobiles, trains, steamboats, airplanes ... are separated from form, what content can they possibly have? "Old National Forms" would have to be carts, sedan chairs, junks, paper kites, sickles, hoes, and such! But how can the essential content of this modern culture – speed, carrying power, precision, efficiency, etc. – be combined with such "Old National Forms"?

However, Wang felt the Chinese could make them their own. "I believe that whenever a people are able in their own way to master something and make it serve them, then essentially it has already become 'national,' no matter if it came from the outside or was originally possessed (today it's an import, tomorrow it's our own)."[11] In May 1942 Mao would legislate a different view: writers were to use national forms in general and peasant literary styles in particular. To do that, Mao would insist that intellectuals had to get out of their book-lined studios and live with the masses.

Wang Shiwei had the courage of his convictions. In February 1942 in a Yan'an literary magazine, *Grain Rain (Gu yu)*, Wang published a short theoretical essay, "Politicians, Artists." Speaking clearly and reasonably, Wang proposed a vital, independent and useful role for Communist writers as society's caring but relentless critics of evil. "Politicians, Artists" set up revolutionary artists as the active loyal opposition, the public censor, the ombuds-man of revolutionary society itself. Mao would call artists soldiers in the revolutionary ranks. Wang put artists on the same level as politicians like Mao, claiming Stalin's ideal of the "engineer of the soul" for artists:

> Our revolutionary work has two aspects: to reform society and to reform people – people's souls. The politician is the strategist and tactician of the revolution. He is the unifier, organizer, promoter, and leader of the revolutionary force; his duty is primarily to reform the social system. The artist is the "engineer of the soul" whose duty is primarily to reform people's souls (mind, spirit, thought, consciousness – here all one thing).

Wang summed it up, "The work of the politician and the work of the artist are mutually supplementary and interdependent." Wang offered this as a contribution to Mao's new rectification. "Correct use of self-criticism and mutual criticism is the necessary method for consolidating the strength of our camp." But Wang's self-criticism and mutual criticism were not humble studying of Mao's speeches. They were an invitation to bravely call out the abuses of power and corruption that he and other writers had seen in Yan'an. Mao wanted artists to mobilize the masses with praise of the Party; Wang felt that exposing the faults of current Party leaders and institutions was a surer road to revolutionary success.[12] He set out to show just how in his own *zawen*, "Wild Lilies," in March.

Wang Shiwei's "Wild Lilies"

Ding Ling led the public presentation of the writers' agenda for rectification with her own *zawen*, "Thoughts on March 8th," in the literary supplement of *Liberation Daily* that she edited. She called out the double bind for women in Yan'an, cursed as self-seeking if they eschewed family for public work and mocked as stay-at-homes if they married and had children. Others followed suit with criticisms of high-handed bosses, trying living conditions, and disillusionment with the professed ideals of the leadership. Wang, however, was the most critical and insistent among these critical writers. His set of four *zawen* essays, "Wild Lilies," published on March 13 and 23 in *Liberation Daily*, took Yan'an by storm.

The title "Wild Lilies" itself was a barb in the style of Lu Xun. Mao's taste for beautiful women, especially young actresses from Shanghai, was common gossip in Yan'an. And, of course, Mao had married one such actress, Lan Ping ("Blue Orchid," aka Jiang Qing) in 1939. "Wild Lilies" must have made its Yan'an readers smile, with its ironic imagery. In the preface Wang gravely offers a local "national-form" tonic from the hills around Yan'an, the plain and bitter-tasting wild lily. Readers could well contrast it, and the woman to whom it was dedicated – Li Fen, a revolutionary martyr – with their peasant leader's taste for dramatic beauty. Indeed, in these essays Wang emerges as something of a revolutionary puritan. He deplores the frivolity of *Spring in the Jade Hall* (a Beijing opera being performed in Yan'an) and the "swirling steps of golden lotus dance" as inappropriate in the face of the suffering in Yan'an and on the front lines in the war. An early reply to "Wild Lilies" confirms, in fact, that leading comrades in Yan'an did regularly enjoy Saturday night dance parties.[13]

In the first two *zawen* Wang defended the complaints of the youth in Yan'an and justified and commended their outspokenness. Wang showed he could swear along with the best of peasant leaders, in what was clearly a parody of Mao Zedong's renowned colloquial style and salty peasant language. Wang reported the conversation of two students talking about their unit leaders:

> "You're dead right! All this bullshit about loving your own class. They don't even show ordinary human sympathy ..."
>
> "How right you are. They don't care about other people, and people don't care about them. If they did mass work, they'd be bound to fail."[14]

Wang declared, "Young people should be treasured for their purity, their perceptiveness ... what others do not wish or do not dare to say, they say with great courage," and his message is pointed: "we should use these 'grumblings' as a mirror and examine ourselves."

The last two *zawen* of "Wild Lilies" focus on one theme: the Party's distance from the masses. Its leaders are so self-indulgent about the "inevitability" of personal imperfection in class society that "we indirectly encourage darkness to the point of directly manufacturing darkness." Most essentially, the Party maintained a hierarchical system of ranks that, in Wang's view, would betray the revolution. It is here that Wang made his critique of "the three classes for clothing and five levels of food" which Mao would still remember years later. "The ill and the young get only two bowls of congee a day," said Wang,

> while on the other hand we see VIPs in flourishing health and enjoying completely unjustified privileges; such a situation leads subordinates to think that their superiors belong to a different breed of humanity; not only is it difficult to feel affection for them but also, when they think about it, they become uneasy . . .[15]

Mao read "Wild Lilies" – and Wang's other essays put up on wall newspapers in Yan'an – and he was not impressed. A public attack on the current Party leadership's ability to do mass work was not what Mao had in mind for rectification. Around March 25, young intellectuals in the Central Research Institute had posted pages from one of their wall newspapers, *Arrow and Target*, onto a piece of red cloth and hung them on the south gate – a busy area in Yan'an. Along with the articles in *Liberation Daily*, this caused quite a stir. In 1945 Mao recalled the challenge Wang's writings had presented the leadership:

> At that time, the differences in viewpoints in the Party reached to such an extent: there was that Wang Shiwei who wrote an article in Yan'an titled "Wild Lilies." Many people enjoyed reading it. In the spring of 1942 during the Rectification movement at the Central Research Institute there was a wall newspaper, and this wall newspaper was very popular . . . even I went to have a look.[16]

Mao conceded that Wang's criticisms of the comfortable lifestyle of Party leaders had found a sympathetic ear among youth and rank-and-file Party members but insisted that the rectification and production campaigns had resolved Yan'an's moral and material problems.

In March 1942 it was not clear how Mao and the Party leadership were going to carry out this political education and institutional mobilization with these slings and arrows of outrageous intellectuals distracting their intended audience. The solution was three months of increasing struggle, from push-back in the press in April (along with personal pressure put on Ding, Wang and the other intellectuals) to a series of public fora in May in which Mao held forth on art and literature and a gruesome series of mass struggle sessions in late May and June. What emerged was literary rectification focused on "Wang Shiwei the Trotskyite" as a negative example for others. Behind the scenes, the rectification continued through the summer and into the autumn as inner-Party meetings moved on to a Stalinesque purge of spies and traitors (real and imagined) under the rubric of criticizing Wang Shiwei's "Anti-Party Gang of Five." This campaign became the template for Party rectification campaigns for the next two decades, culminating in the Cultural Revolution.

Diary of Struggle

Everything changed in April 1942. On April 1 all newspapers in Yan'an were reorganized to fit with the Party's rectification movement, and the next day a speech by Mao was published reiterating the Party's agenda for rectification study. It was aimed at Ding Ling, Wang and the other Party intellectuals who had, with their "grumbles," derailed Mao's focus on attacking his political competitors. In response, Mao sidestepped the content of the writers' criticisms and attacked their methods: "There are a few people who speak from an incorrect standpoint, that is, the concept of absolute egalitarianism and the method of covert attacks."[17]

First came "persuasion." One of Mao's secretaries, Hu Qiaomu, was tasked with "moving" Wang to reform. No luck. The institute's vice president, the noted philosopher Fan Wenlan, said he went to see Wang three times and wrote twice without success. "The Institute's Party committee entrusted five comrades," Fan reported later, "to talk with Wang to help him realize his faults, but Wang cursed them throughout the meeting ... none of them succeeded in waking him up." This was followed in May by Mao's public persuasion of the Yan'an intellectuals in his "Talks at the Yan'an Forum on Literature and Art." Mao's "Talks" would become the seminal definition of the role of revolutionary artists under the CCP. Indeed, in 2014 Xi Jinping reaffirmed Mao's calls for "socialist artists." Mao's themes are now familiar – literature must serve the workers, peasants, and soldiers; content should be Party-directed; and form should suit elementary readers' needs. At these meetings, Mao told the assembled writers and artists that they had failed to meet this challenge; "they have been heroes without a battlefield, remote and uncomprehending." Grandly, Mao offered a solution, his own "self-criticism" and testimony:

> At this point, let me relate my own experience in how feelings are transformed. I started off as a student at school, and at school I acquired student habits, so that I felt ashamed to do any manual labor such as carry my own bags in front of all those students who were incapable of carrying anything for themselves. I felt that intellectuals were the only clean people in the world, and that workers, peasants, and soldiers were in general rather dirty. I could wear clothes borrowed from an intellectual, because I considered them clean, but I would not wear workers', peasants', or soldiers' clothes, because I thought they were dirty. When I joined the revolution and lived among workers, peasants, and soldiers, I gradually became familiar with them, and they got to know me in return. Then and only then the bourgeois and petty bourgeois feelings taught to me in bourgeois schools underwent a fundamental change. Comparing intellectuals who have not yet reformed with workers, peasants, and soldiers, I came to feel that intellectuals are not only spiritually unclean in many respects but even physically unclean, while the cleanest people are workers and peasants; their hands may be black and their feet soiled with cow dung, but they are still cleaner than the big and petty bourgeoisie. This is what I call a transformation in feelings, changing over from one class to another.[18]

Mao concluded his auto-parable with a practical lesson:

> If our workers in literature and art who come from the intelligentsia want their work to be welcomed by the masses, they must see to it that their thoughts and feelings undergo transformation and reform. Otherwise, nothing they do will turn out well or be effective.[19]

Lest the writers continue in their unfortunate misunderstanding of his message, Mao emphasized that *zawen* (critical essays) are not appropriate for Yan'an; such a sharp tool is fit only for enemies. "If we treat comrades with the ruthless methods required against the enemy, then we are identifying ourselves with the enemy." Mao is exclusive. An act of criticism without Party permission is an act of heresy. Proletarian art, Mao holds, must be subject to the will of the proletariat, especially its leader, the Party. Any other view is the same as the Trotskyite formula "politics – Marxist, art – bourgeois."[20]

Next came coercion. Beginning May 27 the Central Research Institute held a public struggle forum to denounce Wang Shiwei and to make the point of what was and what was not acceptable thinking and writing under the new dispensation. A remarkable "Diary of Struggle" was published in *Liberation Daily* by one of its journalists, Wen Jize.[21] It appeared almost immediately in the Party's biggest newspaper to provide an object lesson on how to carry out ideological struggle. For over two weeks this forum met, going from the general – Party democracy, discipline, and rectification – to the specific – exposing Wang Shiwei as the model of what not to do. Central to rectification study was self-criticism, and so institute leaders led the way criticizing themselves. Fan Wenlan admitted that he had not led the institute well during the early months of rectification; he had been too lax. Criticism, however, quickly moved on to Wang Shiwei. Li Yuchao from the Political Research Office declared, "There are many deviationists among us, but the case of Comrade Wang Shiwei is fundamentally different . . . one can see that his mistakes are consistent, severe, and not accidental." But, others at the meeting demurred, "we can only say that there is a quantitative difference with Wang's mistakes. There is no qualitative difference." By the next day's entry, for May 28, the discussion continued and Wen Jize concludes, "The debate over these two opinions has not yet been resolved."

Debate in the forum consisted of a few minority voices offering some defense of Wang followed by lengthy rebuttals. Presented as persuasion of the "masses" of cadres in the institute and other Yan'an schools, the forum offered participants a simple choice: accept your sin of unintentional deviation which you can redeem by rectification study or risk being condemned like Wang

Shiwei. In fact, no serious rebuttal of the *content* of Wang's criticisms of the Party appeared in the "Diary." This coercive persuasion ran over the next week, including a day off on Sunday, May 31, to study Wang's offending articles, and later proper guidance in readings from Lenin, Stalin, and Mao. Days of meetings offered increasingly faltering resistance and stronger exposition of the solution. Wen Jize declared the great value of studying Lenin on Party organization and literature and Stalin's *History of the CPSU*: "All these passages are about experiences and lessons derived from crushing the oppositional conspiracies in the CPSU [Communist Party of the Soviet Union]. These texts constituted an arsenal to fight against the Trotskyite thought of Wang Shiwei."

Then came Wang Shiwei's day in court. On June 4 he was brought into a large meeting to be cross-examined. "Even every window sill was filled," notes Wen. Wang spoke:

> "Just now, Comrade Li Yuchao said I was a Trotskyite, but I myself do not know ... If you had read my article on national forms of literature published in *Chinese Culture*, you would know that I stand firmly behind the United Front. How can I have Trotskyite thought?
>
> [Accused of stating that there were Trotskyists in the Soviet Union and that they were not all bandits:] "I remember everything I have said. Yes, I said that I hated the Trotskyites who organized against Stalin. But I am deeply moved by their alliance with the CPSU against fascism."
>
> [Wen:] "Everyone was outraged by his unrepentant attitude and his blatant propagation of the theories of the Trotskyite bandits. The chair was asked to stop Wang Shiwei from straying from the subject and to reply clearly to the questions.
>
> "One comrade stood up and asked him, 'Why did you say that people have ignored the crimes committed by Stalin during the purge of the party in the USSR? You made this statement.'"
>
> [Wang:] "I believe that during the purges of the CPSU, many enemies could have been turned to comrades. Stalin's character is too brutal." [Wen:] "The slander of Stalin aroused righteous indignation of the whole meeting."

Wang was unrepentant. Walking out of the meeting with Wen Jize, Wang said, "Only I can rectify my errors." Wen only gave a cold laugh.

Finally, the denouement: the confession of Ding Ling and the conviction of Wang Shiwei the Trotskyite. On June 11, the last day of the forum, the Party leadership produced its trump card – Ding Ling. She denounced Wang Shiwei and described his baleful influence on Yan'an life. She also made a public self-criticism:

> I did not study well in the rectification of the three evil work styles movement. But now I've suddenly begun to be clear about quite a few of the issues that used to confuse me. I have the experience of "turn around, and you will see the bank of the river" … a feeling of suddenly realizing the whole truth. I walk forward with steady and sure steps.[22]

Luo Mai (*nom de guerre* of Li Weihan), the Central Research Institute's director, and Fan Wenlan, its vice director, closed the meeting with the lesson for going forward. This was all about the broader rectification movement. "Over the past eighty days and more [from the second week in March]," Luo concludes, everyone has learned "the importance of studying the rectification documents and continuous self-examination." Nonetheless, he thought, Wang Shiwei still had time to redeem himself, as had Ding Ling. Fan Wenlan continued on the theme of Wang's refusal to accept the grace offered to him by the Party: "We tried to pull him out of his shit pit (*maokang*) and save him, but he wanted to drag us down into it." Fan summed up the lessons of the whole anti-Wang struggle, "from now on determine to resist liberalism and to preserve discipline … be even better at reading the rectification documents and strictly examining ourselves."

Wang's "Anti-Party Gang of Five"

Mao's version of rectification was implemented across the major institutions in Yan'an – the media, research institutes, government offices, and security services. This rectification movement continued into the autumn of 1942 and extended over the next two years to other base areas controlled by the Party. Rectification was publicly paired with Yan'an's production campaigns that aimed to cut bureaucracy, develop economic self-reliance, and send cadres to live and work with the peasants. But there was a third shadow partner, an inquisitional purge of Party cadres not publicly advertised but known as the "Rescue Campaign." Wang Shiwei lived as a negative model throughout these Party efforts at popular mobilization, organizational discipline, and paranoid security.

Party propaganda in the newspapers and the reformed literature that Ding Ling and others turned out extolled the virtues of Yan'an and of Mao's way, and depicted stalwart peasants resisting feudal landlords and invading Japanese under the dedicated leadership of humble, capable, and friendly Party cadres. *Yangge* local drama cast the Party's message in attractive traditional form for north China peasants. It was a literature that "led the peasant from his place in the wings, where he waited to perform briefly as buffoon or potential bandit, to the center of the stage as a dramatic figure in his own right."[23] Meanwhile, *Liberation Daily* continued to promote the virtues of rectification for the Yan'an cadres still subject to training. Zhang Ruxin, reflecting on the rectification movement in the Central Research Institute in October 1942, offers this enthusiastic summary:

> In the initial stage erroneous tendencies appeared and we exposed Wang Shiwei's anti-Party activities. Afterward, the erroneous tendencies were corrected. This period is merely six months' time, but it is undoubtedly comparable to a few years in terms of its content and effect on our comrades.[24]

Zhang's message is inspirational, his purpose motivational: personal redemption and liberation to join together in making a new world. Wang Shiwei showed the wages of sin, so let's all walk toward the light together! It was a message widely repeated in the Party press, and as we shall see, many intellectuals found this a system they could serve.

Internal Party documents tell a different side of the same story. At a joint forum of the institute and the Central Committee's Central Research Office on October 31, Yang Shangkun, a top leader appointed to the Central Study Committee in the summer of 1942, gave a telling account: "Activities of the Trotskyite Wang Shiwei and Liberalism in the Party."[25] Yang's speech appeared in *Party Life*, an internal publication limited to Party members. Here we meet the "Anti-Party Gang of Five" led by Wang Shiwei.[26] Comprising two couples Wang knew in his translation work, one of whom were simply his neighbors in the cave next door, one could be forgiven for wondering just what threat five translators and eggheads posed to the revolution. Not so, says Yang. Wang organized a non-Party-sanctioned organization and, therefore, in Yang's view, an anti-Party organization. The gang's members "adopted a two-faced means to coax the Party" by using "close relationships" and sentiment to mobilize "those whose standpoint was unsteady and who were dissatisfied, plus those who did not feel emotionally well due to certain illnesses." Yang concludes that this was Trotskyism in thought and deed aimed "to destroy the CCP."

Yet, why wasn't this anti-Party gang exposed earlier? How could they have gotten so far? Yang's answer: "I think it's because of the weakness in our inner-Party life, mainly the pervasive liberalism (a lack of political awareness, a political flu, and a lack of steadfast standpoint on principle)!" The disease could only be cured by a strict regimen of ideological study and political obedience. Untreated, this "influenza" would poison a person. Yang hammered home his point: "To undermine the Party ideologically is certainly the most vicious counterrevolutionary ploy." Wang's ideas were "ideological poison." Fighting this poison, says Yang, "fits Comrade Mao Zedong's admonition of improving political awareness at the beginning of the rectification movement."

Yang Shangkun's stern message to cadres pales in comparison to that of Kang Sheng, head of the Party's secretive "Social Department" (its secret police). Kang reviewed Wang Shiwei's case in a secret briefing to a training class at the Central Party Security Academy in August 1943 that has never been officially published.[27] Kang's brief was intelligence work, his purpose, security – the elimination of spies and traitors. Kang sets out to explain how, through rectification over the past year and a half, he and his subordinates managed to trick anti-Party elements into exposing themselves. Kang opened his lecture with Mao's call for rectification in February and the June 1942 meeting that denounced Wang Shiwei but he quickly moved on to more and more startling revelations. Kang "revealed" a broader conspiracy underneath Wang's anti-Party gang of five: now it has six members! The new "leader" turns out to be a certain Yu Bingran, a scholar at the Political Research Department. And there were more, many more, traitors and spies, dozens of anti-Party publications, all across Yan'an. Kang reports with satisfaction that he and his troops have laid these demons to rest.

For Kang, this was a battle of cunning based on basic (and base) human instincts for self-preservation. Rectification in Kang Sheng's hands was "exposure" – tricking or terrifying suspects into incriminating themselves and others. He recounted how he uncovered these unsuspected traitors – allowing the "masses" first to criticize Mao's secretary, Chen Boda, so that in the process a few would "expose their Trotskyite thought" (i.e., voice criticisms of the Party leadership that could be compared with Wang Shiwei's). Then Kang lent on them until the next was revealed. This "Ideological Rectification," Kang gloated, followed "the Leninist strategy of winning over the majority and attacking the minority so as to destroy them one by one."[28] Kang was not boasting idly. The cadre-screening and spy-hunting campaign that he headed from 1942, which became the notorious Rescue Campaign by 1943, ruined the lives of thousands of Party cadres.[29]

Wang himself went to jail to do "reform through labor." He no longer appeared in public. However, since the Nationalists in Chongqing had already made a stir about "intellectual repression in Yan'an," when outside journalists visited Yan'an in 1944 Wang Shiwei was brought out. Ding Ling accompanied Wang, who spoke for an hour, denouncing his "Trotskyite errors." Asked about his literary works from the 1930s, Wang replied derisively, "No, now I only have interest in politics; in the future I want to join political work." The journalists concluded that Wang's mind had been damaged by the "Wild Lilies" affair.[30] Wang Shiwei was executed in the spring of 1947 in a remote valley of Shanxi province in the Communist's Jin–Sui base area during their retreat in the face of attacks from Nationalist forces in the emerging civil war. Wang, as an unrepentant prisoner, was too much baggage.[31]

Wang's execution was a mistake. Even Mao acknowledged this in 1962, claiming that the decision was made by the security service and not the Party Center.[32] The real tragedy occurred in the rectification movement itself through its coercive educational mechanisms. The mind of an articulate and productive Marxist theoretician was destroyed. Nonetheless, other intellectuals in Yan'an, and in other base areas, found ways to live within the new system.

Rectification outside Yan'an was less intense and happened later in some other base areas (such as Jin–Cha–Ji, due to ongoing fighting with the Japanese).[33] In most areas, the excesses of Yan'an's "Rescue Campaign" prompted the Party to pull back by late 1944. Ding Ling went on to win the Stalin Prize for her novel on land reform, *Sunrise over the Sungari River*, and a host of intellectuals rose to staff institutions of the new People's Republic after 1949. Yet the shadow of Yan'an's rectification would return. Ding Ling was cut down in 1957 in a similar rectification and purge, the Anti-Rightist Campaign and a generation of Party intellectuals succumbed to the Cultural Revolution, a rectification campaign gone viral.

Wang Shiwei was finally rehabilitated in 1992. Wen Jize, the journalist who chronicled Wang's show trial in 1942 in "Diary of Struggle," spent more than a decade in the post-Mao period trying to get the cantankerous old Party intellectual rehabilitated.[34] In fact, the post-Mao reform leadership of the Party took a dim view of these ideological campaigns.

> From the criticism of Wang Shiwei during the Yan'an era to the criticism of Hu Feng later on, to the criticism of the "Three Family Village" during the Cultural Revolution, all these experiences tell us that the conclusion of cases made on the basis of carrying out movements (*yundong*), beating with sticks, turning ideological issues into political issues, and then punishing by organizational means have little staying power.[35]

Wang Shiwei's memory in China also owes much to the efforts of the redoubtable journalist Dai Qing. She pushed Wang's case in public in the late 1980s, contributing to public opinion in favor of his rehabilitation inside China.[36] Wang Shiwei lives on today as a negative model, not of intellectual heresy or "Trotskyite thought," but as an example of intellectual integrity and perhaps reckless courage, but certainly as a warning of the abuses of power that have stained the story of Chinese communism.

Chapter 4 – 1950s

After the CCP had undergone Mao's rigid rectification in Yan'an from 1942 to 1944, it became a less diverse but more disciplined Party. Under Mao's leadership, the Party moderated its rural reform policies and above all stressed its nationalist commitment, appealing to patriotic sentiments in a country that was trapped in a brutal battle with Japan. When the Second World War came to an abrupt end with the atomic bombings of Hiroshima and Nagasaki in the summer of 1945, the CCP was a Party ready and fiercely determined to reach for its place in the sun.

In the ensuing civil war between Chiang Kai-shek's Nationalist Party and the CCP, now very much under Mao, the CCP eventually gained the upper hand. The speed of the Communists' victory surprised everyone, including the Communists themselves, who did not imagine total victory until 1948. The Nationalists fled to Taiwan. In the era of the Cold War, the US and other Western countries now had to face the fact that China was "lost" to communism.

Mao Zedong had a different view, famously claiming that the "Chinese people have stood up." Official Party histories until today maintain that the Party was carried to victory on the cusp of a broad popular uprising, but such a narrative is difficult to substantiate. Even if the CCP enjoyed sympathy among certain groups in the population, such as urban workers, students, and progressive intellectuals, the Party hardly had the support or even the acceptance of a majority of the population living overwhelmingly in the impoverished and disaster-stricken countryside. CCP victory was made possible as much by the disintegration of the Nationalist forces and the sustained support of the Soviet Union as by the strong Party and army that the Communists had forged during a decade of war. Many in China viewed the CCP with little more than curiosity. The lack of popular acceptance was also one of the reasons why Stalin and the Soviet advisers constantly urged the CCP during the civil war to form a "coalition government" with the so-called "democratic parties" in China and to act within the existing political structures and institutions. The Communists were not destined to conquer the nation, the Soviets did not want it, and even Mao did not expect it at first. Yet in power they were, ready or not.

The new socialist Chinese state that came into being on October 1, 1949, consciously self-fashioned itself as new. Its policies aimed at a profound transformation of society. Ambitious state initiatives sought to reconfigure business ownership; landholding; marriage; the organization of work and daily life; the very understanding of one's self, one's community, and one's past. The new People's Republic of China was above all new: A "New China" (xin Zhongguo) in a new era. The Party established a new calendar (different from that of the Republic) and "leaned to one side," building new international alignments with the socialist world centered in Moscow. An enthusiasm for everything new was carefully cultivated.

Yet this project of remaking China soon ran into difficulties. The PRC had inherited difficult circumstances from the past: bombed-out cities, broken dikes, land-hungry peasants, industry in tatters, and refugee movements across the country. It was also a richly diverse, multilayered and varied society: there were capitalists, Christians, Buddhists, Muslims, liberal intellectuals, artists, movie stars, and other followers of value and faith. They were skeptical of communism and they defied Party initiatives. Beyond new campaigns and productions there were older memories and aspirations, institutionalized or diffused, open or underground, holding sway. The "Old China" held on in bits and pieces. The "New China" struggled to be born. In the 1950s the CCP had to contend with the China in existence despite growing Party power and the expanding reach of the state. The arts, media, and movies were a key part of the Party's program to promote New China. But the most famous artists were all formed in the "old society"; the challenge, reflected in the life of the film heroine Shangguan Yunzhu, was to make them into Red Stars.

4 THE 1950s
From Fallen Star to Red Star: Shangguan Yunzhu
ZHANG JISHUN*

Introduction

At six o'clock on January 10, 1956, Mao Zedong received over seventy of Shanghai's celebrities and high-ranking cadres at a banquet in the newly constructed Sino-Soviet Friendship Building. Among the invited guests was the famous actress Shangguan Yunzhu. She would remember the following scene five years later, as if it had been yesterday (Shangguan, May 5, 1961):

> I was too excited to remember what I replied to Chairman Mao, but I clearly remember what he taught us that day: he wanted us to unite and to further develop strength to advance socialism. Until today, I still hear the echo of his speech. I will always remember Chairman Mao's instructions.

Although this kind of event was nothing unusual in the Mao era, it had an extraordinary effect on Shangguan Yunzhu's life. While she had become a star in the 1940s, she was now to experience the unpredictable turmoil of the revolution. Having been received by Mao changed her fate from being considered a "backward element" shunned by the revolution to gaining the status of an "old star," someone who could be (re-)educated. Shangguan Yunzhu worked in the film industry for twenty-five years and played leading roles in only about thirty movies. Yet her life provides many more entry points into crucial moments of history. During the first ten years of rule of the Chinese Communist Party (CCP), Shanghai's popular culture was changed to further the revolution, with the authority of the Party infiltrating the film industry. This proved to be both harmful and beneficial for Shangguan Yunzhu. Her circumstances reveal the ambiguity and complexity of the CCP's urban revolution and unveil the urban as it was negated and concealed in the Party's revolutionary narrative.

This story also hints at the bond between Shangguan Yunzhu and old star Lan Ping (better known as Jiang Qing, Mao Zedong's fourth wife). It is common knowledge that the mainstream discourse of the revolution, which was established during the Yan'an period, did not lack opposition to the popular culture of modern cities. Mao Zedong despised intellectuals and declared that, if not transformed, they would remain much "filthier" than workers and farmers whose "hands are dirty and whose feet are smeared with cow dung."[1] Shangguan Yunzhu was thus obviously "unclean," Jiang Qing too. While we all know Mao Zedong married a movie star from Shanghai, somehow this fact does not have the same meaning in our understanding of PRC history that similar behavior of other leaders has elsewhere. In this chapter, it is suggested that this hints at the way "metropolitan modernity" is hidden in the discursive construction of the Party's rural origins and characters, and the inextricable link that exists between Yan'an and Shanghai.

From a Small-Town Married Girl to a Shanghai Celebrity

Shangguan Yunzhu's birth name was Wei Junluo. She was born in 1920 in Changjing, a small town in Jiangsu Province. When she was sixteen, studying at Suzhou Leyi Girl's School, she married her art teacher, and in January 1937 their son was born. In the fall of the same year, the Japanese army attacked the Jiangnan area. Having suffered through an air raid, Wei Junluo and her family left her hometown to escape the chaos of war. After nearly a year of wandering from place to place, they found a home in the French Concession in Shanghai. Her husband, Zhang Dayan, was hired at a middle school and Wei Junluo started working at a photograph studio as a cashier.

The shopkeeper of the photograph studio had originally worked as a photographer at a movie company. He still had many acquaintances from that time, so there were many celebrities and intellectuals among the regular customers of the studio. Watching these glamourous people, Wei Junluo started dreaming of a life in the movie world. The shopkeeper–photographer saw a business opportunity in Wei's beauty and decided to display a photograph of her in his shop window to attract further customers. For the young mother, who had left her small-town home to escape the war, it was this small display window that opened her way to become a star.

In 1940 Wei Junluo enrolled in the Huaguang Theater School to study drama. Through hard work, her talent for performing quickly unfolded. Before long she had taken to the stage and joined the Xinhua Film Company's acting course to study film. Here she was discovered by director Bu Wancang and it was he who gave Wei Junluo her stage name, Shangguan Yunzhu. In 1941 she starred in the movie *The Displaced Girls* and began to make a name for herself. Within only two years, she played in eight movies, realizing her goal of dedicating her life entirely to the art of performance.

Her husband Zhang Dayan, however, did not want a wife who was a star and continuously in the public eye. He wanted a housewife content with her place in the home, and this caused insurmountable conflict between them. They signed their divorce papers in May 1943. Shortly thereafter, Shangguan married a man called Yao Ke. Yao Ke had graduated from Soochow University after the beginning of the Second Sino-Japanese War and had studied performance in the United States. After his return to China, he wrote many screenplays and became renowned in Shanghai's entertainment business, and his support enabled Shangguan to find a foothold in it. In 1944, they had a baby girl whom they named Yao Yao. The relationship, however, was short-lived. Returning to Shanghai from a performance tour in autumn of 1946, Shangguan discovered that Yao Ke had had an affair and she ended the marriage.

During 1941 and 1942, Shangguan experienced Shanghai's fall because of the outbreak of the Pacific war. Many left-wing movie stars had already left for Chongqing or Yan'an, and a large number had gone to the strongholds of the Communist New Fourth Army in central China. The Communist Lan Ping, who had been very active in Shanghai's movie world, went to Yan'an in 1937. The next year, she married Mao Zedong there and became Jiang Qing, wearing the uniform of the Eighth Route Army and meticulously taking care of Mao's daily life. But Jiang Qing was unable to forget the metropolitan city of Shanghai. She supported ballroom dancing in Yan'an, attending a dance once a week, and thereby reliving scenes from Shanghai's entertainment and social circles.

During the Japanese occupation of Shanghai, Shangguan Yunzhu's nascent film career was interrupted, but she remained behind and spared no effort to advance her career. After the war, she played leading and supporting roles in many movies and became known as one of Shanghai's most beloved and charming female stars.

In 1947 Shangguan joined the Kunlun Film Company, which had close connections with the CCP. Portraying attractive urban characters in a series of left-wing movies enabled her to form political and social ties which would prove crucial in the upcoming era of the CCP.

Shangguan Yunzhu was very smart and good with people, gentle and considerate, and also she had a strong sense of justice and was generous. She never showed weakness. Even after she was famous she would treat her colleagues with caution.[2] As a public figure, Shangguan was subject of much celebrity gossip, with small newspapers regularly reporting on her two marriages and her private life. Shangguan had lacked the opportunity of a good education, but she managed to raise her daughter Yao Yao to become a cultured and disciplined lady, according to the standards of Shanghai's upper-class families prior to the Mao era. In Shanghai's glamorous movie world, Shangguan was indeed a pop-culture idol. But it was in the Mao era that she became a legend.

The Spouse of a Corrupt Element

In May 1949, Shangguan and her friends welcomed the arrival of the People's Liberation Army (PLA) to Shanghai. With the support of the CCP government, the nearly bankrupt firms of Kunlun, Wenhua, and other private film companies experienced a revival. Shangguan appeared in the movie *Spring of Peace* and two others at the time. The Communist Party fundamentally transformed society in Shanghai, and it was impossible for movie stars to distance themselves from this transformation. Shangguan responded to every call of the government, promptly changing her fashionable wardrobe for Lenin-style clothes, which had been popular in the Yan'an era, and she was seen to be active at political and social events.

Coinciding with these historical changes, Shangguan's love life also experienced change. She became involved with Cheng Shuyao, who was appointed first vice general manager of the Lyceum Theatre in Shanghai after the PLA took over the city. In 1950, Shangguan played the leading role in the epic drama *Song of the Red Flag*, the first play performed after the establishment of the PRC, which reflected the life of industrial workers. This play was quite a sensation. It was performed in the Lyceum Theatre in Shanghai nonstop, 159 times in all. In the second-floor rehearsal hall of the same theater, in the same year, Shangguan and Cheng Shuyao married. Friends from both inside and outside the theater world came to congratulate them.

In May 1951, Mao Zedong launched a critique of the movie *The Life of Wu Xun* (Sun Yu, 1950). The protagonist, Wu Xun, was a farmer in Shandong who begged for alms and collected money to establish a school offering free tuition. Mao criticized the movie because "it was enabling a subservient attitude toward the reactionary feudalistic rulers." Jiang Qing, the "first lady," was an active advocate of this critique, which was to be the first instance of thought reform in literature and the arts in the 1950s. Artists at private movie companies were the first to be attacked. Shanghai's film industry was the birthplace of Chinese movies. It matured and flourished in the Republican era prior to 1949, creating the "golden age" of Chinese movies. But in the chaotic political climate of the 1950s, the entertainment business entered a severe economic depression. Although private companies were able to complete some movie projects, the movie output of the state-owned Shanghai Film Studio was zero in 1951 and only one movie was produced in 1952. The merging of the privately owned movie companies with the state-owned Shanghai Film Studio progressed swiftly and by January 1953 work at Shanghai's private movie companies came to a standstill. All their professional workers, including Shangguan and her colleagues, were turned into state employees and put on a state salary.

During these cultural and political movements, Shangguan did her utmost to reinvent herself. She learned to write self-criticism, personal history, and ideological reports, and she developed the mind-set required by the (political) "system." Yet, although Shangguan worked ferociously on drawing closer to the revolution, something unexpected happened. During the "Three Antis" campaign (anti-corruption, anti-waste, anti-bureaucracy), a political movement that began at the end of 1951, her husband, Cheng Shuyao, was accused of corruption. Previously, Cheng had been hired as a bookkeeper for a fund-raising activity at a garden party organized for the People's Liberation Army. The allegations were based on the fact that the accounts of this event were not in order. Shangguan was certain that her husband would not commit such a crime, so in order to free him she spent her savings clearing his "corruption debt." She thought this money would lessen his punishment, but on the contrary it was taken as a confirmation of his guilt. From then onward, he was associated with corruption. He was dismissed from his vice manager's position at the theater and put under supervision for a year.

Shangguan too was considered guilty because of her association with Cheng. The cadre who led the Three Antis campaign at the film studio questioned her relentlessly. While some people directly accused her of being the "spouse of a corrupt element," others said she was "very cunning." One of the leaders of the film studio asked the director Shen Fu to "help" Shangguan and advised Shen to tell her, "if she wants to continue to be an actress, she must confess right away. Ask her whether she wants to continue to act in the future?"[3]

"Do you want to be an actress or not?" For Shangguan, no other question could have greater destructive power. There was no doubt that with the mark of being a "spouse of a corrupt element," her political and artistic life would be ruined. In order to continue her career, she was willing to sacrifice her family so she proposed to Cheng that they divorce. But Cheng did not comply with her request. He asked his younger brother to come from Beijing to persuade Shangguan to stay married, but she reacted with anger and accusations. All of her old friends tried to convince her to stay, but to no avail.[4] After the divorce, their daughter Yao Yao stayed with Shangguan and their son Deng Deng was raised by his father. The family was torn to pieces.

Following the revolution of 1949, divorce cases were intended to reduce political pressure. However, political pressure did not relent after Shangguan's divorce and the door to the movie world remained shut. Although her connection with the "corrupt element" was legally cut, she was still placed on the Party's "political ranking" list within Shanghai film circles and categorized as a "backward element." Not long after her divorce, her former secret love affair with vice director He Lu was uncovered and strongly criticized by the Party's organization. Private affairs of these kinds between men and women were considered a "life-behavioral problem" according to the Party's standards.

A Teachable Role Model

From 1953 onwards, movie production started to come back to life and some of the "old stars" made appearances in revolutionary movies. Nonetheless, a great number of directors and actors were still without work. Despite their defeat and retreat, the artists of the privately owned movie industry were unwilling to give up their right to create, so they chose to closely follow the Party. The need to improve politically according to the Party's standards was increasingly urgent. By 1955 more than forty famous playwrights, directors and actors at Shanghai Flm Studio had expressed their desire to join the Communist Party.[5] Shangguan did not have very high hopes of rehabilitation, but she longed to be on-screen again one day.[6]

At the beginning of 1955, Shangguan received an unexpected chance to play a leading role in the movie *Return to My Unit*. She was to play the character of Fu Ruohua, a head nurse in the guerrilla force during the fight against the Japanese invasion of the island of Hainan. While under siege by the Japanese forces, she led a group of wounded and sick soldiers out of the encirclement and, with no food or medicine, overcame hardship to reunite them with their unit. This kind of revolutionary movie was absolutely nothing new for the film industry of New China, but for Shangguan it was a way out of her predicament. She broke out of the circle of urban women, consisting of concubines, dancers, and housewives, and created a precedent for female stars of the "old society" by portraying a revolutionary female warrior.

In the movie, Fu Ruohua might have successfully led the group of sick and wounded back to their unit, but that did not mean that Shangguan had also made it into the "progressive" or "middle-left" political ranks. Within the studio, many people still held prejudices against her as a "backward element." Even when Party members deemed Shangguan's depiction of Fu Ruohua "acceptable," they nevertheless criticized the studio's leadership for its choice. "Her thoughts and consciousness are so bad and her lifestyle is such a mess. Why are you giving her such a role to perform?"[7]

When the shooting of *Return to My Unit* neared its end, the Party began loosening political restrictions for intellectuals. In December 1955, the Central CCP and the Shanghai Municipal CCP had the Party organization within Shanghai Film Studio investigate the circumstances of intellectuals within the studio. The focus was on inspecting whether the work, thought and life of intellectuals were in line with Party expectations. In the investigative report, Shangguan's comeback was noted for a particular purpose. It showcased the Party's inability to unite intellectuals outside the Party, acknowledging that Party policies were not handled well during the time of the Three Antis campaign.[8]

On January 11, 1956, news of "Chairman Mao inviting Shangguan Yunzhu to dinner" spread like wildfire through Shanghai Film Studio. Returning to the studio, "she told anyone she ran into that 'she would never have dreamed' of this." But many people had objections. The Party secretary of the studio wrote in the report for the Municipal CCP:[9]

> After she had dinner with Chairman Mao, the head of the actors' group went to the branch secretary early the next morning and asked, "Why did you send Shangguan Yunzhu to see Chairman Mao?" After the branch secretary had explained, he asked further, "Will the loss outweigh the gain?" ... Our Party members talked with each other and said, "Well, now Shangguan Yunzhu is cocky!" And, "She is so proud of herself, but the reason why Chairman Mao sought her out is that she was a backward element" ... From that point forward, one could see the seriousness of the factionalist trend among the cadres and Party members of our company.

> This factionalist trend did not change a bit because Chairman Mao himself met with Shangguan Yunzhu and talked to her. On the contrary, it was even intensified and spread around unchecked.

In a meeting of the Shanghai Municipal Committee regarding the issue of intellectuals, the Party secretary of Shanghai Film Studio made her position very clear: "We will turn Shangguan Yunzhu into an example for others. That she was won over and reformed will be a teachable role model for our whole Party and our whole cadre."[10] This was a significant stroke of luck for Shangguan, who later stated that she was truly understanding of "the leadership not having given her any acting roles from 1952 to 1954" because "we did not have much work in those three years, and many people did not get a role, so it is only natural that I would not, too."[11]

From being a "backward element," Shangguan Yunzhu was transformed into a "teachable role model." Her meeting with Mao changed her political fate and set her on what she believed to be the right path.

Chairman Mao in Our Midst

Shortly after Mao Zedong entertained Shangguan Yunzhu, she was placed in the first batch on the list of "Shanghai's high-ranking intellectuals," which turned her into one of the "most celebrated artists."[12] *The Story of the Southern Island*, formerly *Return to My Unit*, received much praise and was awarded second place among the excellent films of 1949 to 1955 by the Ministry of Culture in March 1957. An article, "When I was Fu Ruohua," detailing her personal experience shooting the movie, was published in the magazine *Popular Cinema*. In July 1956, Shangguan was part of the Chinese film delegation which was sent to the ninth Karlovy Vary International Film Festival in the former Czechoslovakia. When she returned, she wrote fifteen *Travel Sketches of Europe*, which were published as a serial once a month in the best-selling *Xinmin Evening News*. Shangguan joined the China Democratic League. On November 23, 1956, she published an article in a special discussion column of *Wenhui Newspaper*, appealing to the leaders to find a feasible solution for actors who had no acting roles – a "long-standing issue" – so that "these countless buried jewels could shine again."

At the end of 1956, Mao suggested letting "a hundred flowers bloom and a hundred schools of thought contend," in literature and art. This was the start of the Hundred Flowers movement (1956–1957), during which citizens were encouraged to express openly their opinions of the government. The movement was about to reach its zenith when Mao Zedong encouraged Chinese cinema to catch up with Japan's annual output of art movies. To Zhao Dan (the star of the film about Wu Xun) he said, "*The Life of Wu Xun* was once criticized, but that doesn't matter now. If a work is not good, you can rewrite it and it shall be good in the end."[13] Inspired by Mao's encouragement, the film artists put all their energy into the creation of socialist movies.

In 1957 Shangguan played a surgeon in the movie *Loyal Partners*, which portrayed scientists in the New China. However, when the movie had just started to be shown in the cinemas, in May, Mao Zedong launched the Anti-Rightist Campaign, in which "anti-CCP and anti-socialist" rightists, mostly intellectuals, were criticized and attacked. As before, Shanghai Film Studio found Shangguan on the front line of a political campaign. In the studio, more than forty filmmakers were branded as serious rightists, among them Shangguan Yunzhu's old friends Wu Yin, Wu Yonggang and Xu Changlin. Director Bai Chen, who had helped Shangguan to win the revolutionary acting role of "Fu Ruohua," was also labeled a rightist and sent to a farm in rural Anhui to be "reformed through labor." One of the most tragic cases during this period of severe criticism was Shi Hui, a talented actor and director, who committed suicide by drowning himself in the sea.[14]

In the midst of this struggle, Shangguan and other celebrities Mao had received remained protected, as if shrouded in his splendor. Shangguan was, however, labeled a rightist by the Party Committee of Shanghai Film Studio because she had written an article complaining about the lack of opportunities many actors and actresses received to make movies. The committee even organized a meeting targeting her, but in the end she was protected because "although her right-wing thinking is seriously wrong, she is still teachable."[15] Having escaped the fate of a "rightist" by a hair's breadth, Shangguan was immensely grateful to the Party and to Chairman Mao. On December 23, 1957, Shangguan expressed her feelings in a speech at a meeting which Minister Zhou Enlai had organized for writers and artists:[16]

> I am a person who did much wrong and is unworthy of the Party's nurture and care and of the prime minister's many personal instructions ... The prime minister's words caused me to once again personally experience the Party's grand spirit to rescue a person who made a mistake.

She also said, "The leadership approved of me going to the country-side to improve myself through labor, and I am determined to transform myself properly, to completely eliminate my severe bour-geois individualism, and to firmly establish the idea of serving the working people."

In 1958, Shangguan and her colleagues were sent to the countryside by Shanghai Film Studio to do manual work and to undergo reform thought in labor. Actor Wang Danfeng, who lived with her on the outskirts of Shanghai during re-education, remembered that "she treated the farmers very kindly. In the village, old and young all called her 'Auntie Shangguan,' just like one of their own relatives."[17]

From 1958 to 1960, Shangguan starred as the lead in only one movie, *Floating Far Away* (1959), but she made many guest appearances. Although her relationship with vice director He Lu was public knowledge, it was not serious, and she managed to avoid criticism for so-called "behavioral issues."

At the end of the 1950s, Shangguan once again received the highest honor of having an invitation to dinner with Chairman Mao. On April 5, 1959, Mao Zedong went to Hangzhou, where he remained until April 12. During this period, Shangguan was accom-panying her cousin Yan Yongjie, who had come to relax and do some sightseeing in the city. Yan Yongjie was the wife of Tan Qilong, the Party secretary of the CCP Provincial Committee of

Shandong Province. At a ball organized by the public relations office of the provincial government, Shangguan and Yan Yongjie met not only Mao Zedong and his wife Jiang Qing, but also Liu Shaoqi's wife Wang Guangmei and others. The following day, Mao sent someone to bring Shangguan and Yan to his residence to have lunch. Mao Zedong treated them with warm hospitality, and Jiang Qing accompanied him. During the opulent meal, Mao mentioned that factionalism existed not only within literary circles but also existed within each of them. He explained that this was the reason why Shangguan was suffering such injustices. After the meeting, the director of the Public Security Bureau of Zhejiang Province asked them to keep this private meeting a secret, since literary and arts circles are complicated and they hoped to avoid any unnecessary misunderstanding.[18]

Shangguan and Jiang Qing did not talk much at this private meeting. Jiang Qing's political ambitions were relatively low-key before the year 1958 – moreover, she was not in the best of health, traveling to the Soviet Union several times for treatment. After 1958, however, Mao increasingly guided and praised his wife on political matters.[19] The fact that at this lunch Mao had raised the subject of factionalism within the literary and artistic circles of the Party would later become Jiang Qing's trump card when she first entered the political stage and fiercely criticized those she labeled "blacklisted literary figures and artists of the 1930s." However, Mao and Jiang are thought to have been drifting apart in this period, with Jiang Qing enjoying a privileged existence, including watching classical Western movies. She was said to be a great fan of Hollywood actors and actresses, including Ingrid Bergman, Gary Cooper, Greta Garbo, and Vivien Leigh, and she often had their movies shown in small screening rooms.[20]

On May 1, 1961, Shangguan celebrated International Labor Day together with thousands of other people in China. In the intermission between afternoon and evening performances as part of the celebration for this festival, Shangguan, her colleague Bai Yang, and Wang Danfeng received notification from the municipal Party committee asking them to participate in an important meeting and they realized that Mao Zedong had invited them once again to meet him. In an article published on May 5, 1961, Shangguan described this fortunate moment excitedly:

Chairman Mao illuminated all of us like a red sun. He shook our hands very kindly and greeted us. Those tremendous hands that had the power to turn around heaven and earth, to radically transform the world, I was then already holding them in my hands for the sixth time. Every time this gave me more power and encouraged me.

In the same article, Shangguan expressed her feelings of honor and gratitude for meeting Mao in person: "'He is a mighty leader but also a member of our big revolutionary family and he dwells among us.' This is a sentence from 'Chairman Mao in Our Midst,' the poem I have enjoyed reciting the most in the last three years."

The Fall of a Red Star

In 1962, large photographs of twenty-two movie actors and actresses were showcased in the halls of every cinema in China. Shangguan Yunzhu's photograph was among them. Shangguan's work onstage reached another high point. She played a widow in *Early Spring* (Xie Tieli, 1963) and then a declining "queen of the Yue opera" in *Stage Sisters* (Xie Jin, 1964). These are considered masterpieces of tragic female characters in the movies of the Mao era.

For Shangguan Yunzhu this glamourous moment was, however, also the turning point in her career and life. In December 1963 and June 1964, Mao Zedong wrote two harsh "instructions" that denounced culture and artworks in the PRC as counterrevolutionary and backward. He criticized literary and artistic circles for not carrying out the Party's policies and having fallen to the edge of revisionism. The film industry became the first target, and *Early Spring* was publicly criticized. Not long thereafter, *Stage Sisters* met the same fate.

It was on the eve of the Cultural Revolution that Shangguan went to the countryside in Jiangxi to join the Four Cleans campaign (1963–1966 – the goal was to clean up thought, politics, organization, and the economy) at the end 1965. In February 1966, Shangguan returned to Shanghai and was diagnosed with breast cancer, and the cancer soon spread to her brain, leading to temporary memory loss. Returning home after surgery, she could not rest and recuperate. Red Guards and rebellious groups frequently searched her apartment. Her daughter Yao Yao announced that she would cut ties with the family, staying at her college dormitory without returning home. Shangguan was dragged to Shanghai Film Studio, publicly humiliated on site, severely beaten and finally detained in a so-called "cowshed." An "Investigation Committee for Shangguan Yunzhu" and a "Special Investigation Committee for Shangguan Yunzhu" constantly interrogated her and extorted confessions. Facing this extreme pressure and humiliation, having no means of curing her illness or relieving her pain, watching her family be torn apart, and seeing no possibility of continuing the career that had given her life meaning, Shangguan abandoned all hope.

Before dawn on November 23, 1968, Shangguan Yunzhu is believed to have jumped out of the fourth-floor window of her own home. She was forty-eight years old.

Ten years later, Shanghai Film Studio organized a memorial ceremony for Shangguan Yunzhu and publicly "rehabilitated and exonerated" her. At the conclusion of the "final reinvestigation" of her case, it was acknowledged that she "was fortunate to have been received by the Supreme Leader Chairman Mao seven times." Her friends composed texts commemorating her. In one, actress Qin Yi depicted this unforgettable scene:

> After her second operation, she was unable to speak. However, she did not yield to the disease but, with tenacious willpower, practiced making sounds and learned to speak again. Once, with tears in her eyes, she stared at a picture of Chairman Mao for a long time, her mouth quivering, and exhausting all her energy, she finally shouted with a hoarse voice, "Chairman – Mao!"[21]

Conclusion

Shangguan Yunzhu's life in the 1950s reveals some internal tension in the CCP's revolution, the tension between the proletariat revolutionary ideal and the modernity of the Republican era. Even though she was criticized as an "old star" of the "old Shanghai," a "spouse of a corrupt element," and a politically "backward element," and was finally engulfed by the Cultural Revolution, Shangguan's acting talent and her creative adaptability were still appreciated in the new regime. Her career after 1949 suggests that the stars of an earlier period were indispensible to the film industry in the People's Republic of China. A new country not only requires revolutionary force but also needs educating and persuading. Therefore, old stars like Shangguan were chosen and even sometimes welcomed to play leading roles in new formalistic revolutionary performances on-screen to convince their audience. It is certainly possible that the "Supreme Leader" encouraged her to play revolutionary roles in order to set an example of a "well-educated" old star with political value. But it is also undeniable that even during the revolutionary era, Shangguan Yunzhu was still one of the most brilliant female Shanghai stars. On- and off-screen, she stood out. She had countless fans and revolutionary leaders were no exception. Her charm was beyond revolutionary criteria and sometimes immune from political judgment.

If one observes Shangguan Yunzhu and Jiang Qing in Yan'an, it becomes clear that metropolitan modernity, hidden in the Party's political and cultural mainstream discourse, never actually disappeared. It is not possible to analyze here Mao's decision to marry a movie star nor to analyze the nature of their private relationship. But it is somewhat ironic that Mao Zedong admitted Jiang Qing into his life, considering that she personified the modern metropolitans and intellectuals he hated. This link between rural Yan'an and urban Shanghai is also present in the relationship between the Communist Party, which established itself in the countryside, and metropolitan modernity. On August 1, 1957, Mao Zedong instructed that the struggle against the rightists must be deepened. In the dark of the night, however, when he could not sleep, he read two poems by Fan Zhongyan, a poet of the Song Dynasty, and made the following annotations:[22]

Poetry has two styles: the subtle and concise style (*wanyue*) and the powerful and free style (*haofang*). Both are inspiring and should be read ... I am more interested in the powerful and free style, but do not give up on the subtle and concise style ... The two poems by Fan Zhongyan lie between the *wanyue* and *haofang* styles, but on the whole, they are still of the subtle and concise style. They are both bleak and elegant and do not let the reader tire of it ... Human emotions are complicated. Although we have preferences, our moods are still complicated. What is called complicated is the unity of opposites ... After I show this to Jiang Qing, Li Na (daughter of Mao and Jiang) shall have a look.

The Chinese Revolution was as complicated as human emotions, if not more so. Shangguan Yunzhu's ups and downs in the 1950s and 1960s may give us a glimpse of such complications.

Chapter 5 – 1960s

Two of the moments in this book meet in the Cultural Revolution. Shangguan Yunzhu lept to her death in 1968 (Chapter 4), and Wang Guangmei, wife of China's president, Liu Shaoqi, was denounced and paraded in front of a mass criticism rally in 1967. Both were woeful examples of the violent excesses of Mao's effort to revitalize the Party and China's revolution in the 1960s.

As will become clear in this chapter, the distinction between perpetrator and victim, between Party and cadre, is not so very clear. Wang Guangmei suffered in the Cultural Revolution, yet her Peach Blossom Experience *– a report of her Party work team's visit to rectify the local leaders in a village – supported the sort of revolutionary violence and mass criticism sessions that, in the end, were turned on her. How did the Party come to such a state of affairs?*

In 1958, the Eighth Central Committee of the Communist Party of China congratulated itself on a decade of success. This was not without some reason. China in 1949, when the Communists had taken power, was war-ravaged, with a broken economy and a starving population. The Party had restored order and basic health, albeit at times violently. The life of Shangguan Yunzhu reflects that the Party had some success in building its image of a New China and garnered the talents of a number of artists and intellectuals. Yet the sclerosis of the Soviet system, the institutional corruption, the lack of personal freedoms, and the depressed consumer culture began to take their toll. The limits of Party power to remake China were showing.

Mao refused to acknowledge this and led China on three great waves of "continuing the revolution" to save the CCP from the fate of the Russian Communists under Khrushchev, whose "revisionism" was replacing revolution with consumer goods. All three efforts failed. In early 1957 Mao turned to urban intellectuals to trim the bureaucratism of the Party, but the criticism from intellectuals turned out not to be limited to and aimed at local leaders, but rather was systemic and aimed at the Party itself. This spring of "a hundred flowers blooming" turned into a brutal purge that summer and fall of intellectuals – and even of loyal Party members – who had headed the call to criticize Party bureaucratism. This became the Anti-Rightist Campaign of 1957–1958 in which thousands of intellectuals were packed off to prison camps. Next Mao turned to the peasants and his "Great Leap Forward," an ill-conceived forced production campaign that resulted in the largest famine in modern history. Between 1958 and 1960 tens of millions of farmers died. One lasting impact of the Leap was the reorganization of rural land and agricultural production into collective people's communes. Finally, Mao's last revolution is best known as the Cultural Revolution of 1966–1976, but it began with the Four Cleans campaign in 1964 – exactly the scene of Wang Guangmei's Peach Blossom Experience. *Through all these radical campaigns, and despite the growing casualty list, the authority of Mao and the Party kept leaders like Wang Guangmei willing to follow Mao's ideas and blunted the attempts of any to resist. Mao had succeeded in reuniting China when all doubted it could be done. Now, not even his comrades could stop him as he drove China to the brink.*

5 THE 1960s
Wang Guangmei and *Peach Garden Experience*
ELIZABETH J. PERRY

Introduction

In the spring of 1967, China's former first lady, Wang Guangmei, was paraded onto a stage before a jeering crowd of half a million people to suffer public humiliation for her "bourgeois" crimes. Despite her repeated protestations, Wang was forced for the occasion to don a form-fitting dress festooned with a garland of ping-pong balls to mock the elegant silk *qipao* and pearl necklace ensemble that she had worn only a few years earlier while accompanying her husband, now disgraced president Liu Shaoqi, on a state visit to Indonesia. William Hinton describes the dramatic scene at Tsinghua University in Beijing, where the struggle session took place:

> A sound truck had crisscrossed the city announcing the confrontation, posters had been distributed far and wide, and over three hundred organizations, including schools and factories, had been invited. Some had sent delegations, others had simply declared a holiday, closed their doors, and sent everyone out to the campus. Buses blocked the roads for miles and the sea of people overflowed the University grounds so that loudspeakers had to be set up beyond the campus gates ...
>
> At the meeting Wang [G]uangmei was asked to stand on a platform made of four chairs. She stood high enough so that tens of thousands could see her. On her head she wore a ridiculous, wide-brimmed straw hat of the kind worn by English aristocrats at garden parties. Around her neck hung

a string of ping-pong balls ... A tight-fitting formal gown clung to her plump body and sharp-pointed high-heeled shoes adorned her feet. The whole outfit was grotesque ...

The masses ... shouted angry slogans, "Down with cow-devils and snake-gods! Carry through the revolution to the end!" These shouts from tens of thousands of throats rolled through the campus and surrounding district like sea waves. They pounded the plump figure of Wang [G]uangmei in her straw hat and her ping-pong ball necklace until it seemed she could no longer stand, but stand she did and the meeting went on ... The mass confrontation with Wang [G]uangmei marked the high point of the repudiation of capitalist-roaders in Peking.[1]

Shortly after this event, which was among the largest and most spectacular of the countless struggle sessions to occur during Mao's Cultural Revolution between 1966 and 1976, Wang Guangmei was packed off to prison. It would take a sea change in the Chinese political landscape before she was finally released twelve years later. Wang Guangmei's tribulations reflect the brutality of the most tur-bulent decade of Mao's tumultuous rule, a period marked by wave after wave of state-mobilized mass campaigns. But Wang was no innocent bystander in this vicious chapter of PRC history. Renowned for her intellect and acumen as well as her elegance, she was a key protagonist in the political conflicts of the 1960s that culminated in the cruelty and chaos of the Cultural Revolution.

Background

Wang Guangmei was born in 1921 into an affluent and educated family in Peiping (as Beijing was known between 1928 and 1949). Her father, who had studied business administra-tion at Waseda University in Japan, served as a government official under various pre-Communist Chinese regimes. Her mother, schooled at a progressive academy for girls in Tianjin, encouraged her three sons and five daughters to aspire to a high level of peda-gogical and professional achievement. Inspired by her childhood heroine, Marie Curie, Wang Guangmei dreamed of becoming a scientist. She attended Furen University, a German Catholic institution in Peiping, where she studied the science of optics and cosmic rays. An outstanding student, Wang Guangmei was the first woman in China to earn a graduate degree in atomic physics. After completing her MA at Furen, she received offers of admission to doctoral programs at Stanford and the University of Chicago.

Instead of going abroad to pursue a PhD in physics, however, Wang decided to accept the invitation of an acquaintance in the Chinese Communist Party (CCP) underground to serve as an interpreter for the CCP mission to the Executive Headquarters, the organization in Peiping that was established at the end of World War II by General George C. Marshall as a vehicle for negotiating a cease-fire to the civil war between the Nationalists and the Communists. When that work wrapped up after a few months, she requested and received permission to proceed to the Communists' revolutionary capital of Yan'an. Fluent in Russian and French as well as English, she worked for several months as a translator in the Foreign Affairs Department of the CCP. Then in the spring of 1947, Wang, like thousands of other young intellectuals whose patriotism and idealism had led them to Yan'an, was dispatched to the countryside as a member of a land reform work team charged with mobilizing revolution in villages under Communist control. Thanks to her computational skills, Wang was assigned the job of compiling the registers that recorded the seizure and transfer of land and other property from landlords to poor peasants.

The Jinsui base area in northern China where Wang Guangmei spent the next year was known for exceptional bloodshed in the land reform campaign. Several high-ranking CCP leaders – including her future husband, Liu Shaoqi, as well as Mao's personal henchmen, Kang Sheng and Chen Boda – were sent there from Yan'an to correct initial errors of "peaceful land reform." Thanks to their forceful intervention, Jinsui's originally nonviolent style of land redistribution was superseded by a particularly vicious approach. The richest landlord in the county where Wang lived and worked, Niu Youlan, was a strong supporter of the revolution who had been personally hosted by Mao in Yan'an and had written glowingly of the Communist movement. Niu had even turned over his sizable estate to the Party to use as its local headquarters. In the fall of 1947, however, Niu was made the prime target of a struggle session attended by over 5,000 people. Playing on the fact that the character for the surname Niu (牛) also means "cow," his accusers subjected Niu Youlan to bestial treatment normally reserved for livestock. They branded his flesh with a burning-hot iron, forced a metal ring through his nose, and had his son (a revolutionary activist who became vice minister of finance in the PRC) lead him around on a rope. Niu Youlan died in detention just a few days later.

Wang Guangmei herself was not directly involved in mobilizing peasants to engage in land reform struggle sessions, in part because her educational background qualified her for office work but also because she was utterly unable to communicate in the local dialect. Her fluency in three foreign languages was of no help in deciphering the northwest Shanxi dialect. She was assigned an interpreter, who recalled that getting the peasants to understand Wang's standard Chinese proved even more challenging than getting them to attack landlords!

Despite the formidable linguistic barrier, Wang deemed her land reform experience extremely valuable. Having been raised as a cosseted urban intellectual, she would later credit her year on a rural work team with instilling lessons in personal discipline and practical politics that she could never have obtained from reading books in the sheltered comfort of her Peiping home. Wang's time in the countryside brought other life-changing opportunities, too. Liu Shaoqi, whom she had met briefly at dance parties in Yan'an, showed a personal interest when they encountered one another again in Jinsui. The following year, in August 1948, the couple was married in the interim Communist capital of Xibaipo. Although Wang Guangmei was Liu Shaoqi's fifth wife, and twenty-three years his junior, she immediately became a partner in work as well as life. Wang joined the Communist Party and took on an important political role as Liu Shaoqi's personal secretary.

After Liu Shaoqi was named president of the PRC in 1959, a position that put him in charge of government operations, Wang Guangmei accompanied her husband on a series of high-profile state visits to Afghanistan, Pakistan, Burma, and Indonesia. She joined him on domestic expeditions as well. In the spring of 1961 Wang accompanied Liu for a month on a work team dispatched to his native province of Hunan to investigate rural conditions in the wake of the terrible Great Leap famine that had claimed tens of millions of lives. On this occasion, Liu urged his wife to get close to the peasants by conducting house-to-house visitations. She found herself frustrated again by being unable to communicate in the local dialect. She did, however, take note of Liu Shaoqi's warning that grassroots cadres were trying to conceal information from the work team and that to get at the truth it would be necessary to organize mass struggle sessions among the villagers rather than simply convene group discussions or listen to summary reports from officials.

Wang Guangmei remembered these admonitions two years later when Liu Shaoqi suggested that she venture down to the countryside again to participate in the Socialist Education Movement (or Four Cleans campaign, as it was more commonly called), a state-mobilized anticorruption campaign that was then gearing up. Liu did not volunteer a reason for suggesting that his wife decamp to a rural village without him, but he was sixty-five years old and in poor health. Like others in the top leadership, Liu was heavily dependent on daily doses of sleeping pills; he had already suffered several serious falls while under the influence of the drug.[2] Wang suspected that her husband was grooming her for a day when he would no longer be around, so she might be capable of taking independent political action.

Peach Garden Experience

With three young children to worry about in addition to her husband's declining health, Wang Guangmei was initially reluctant to be separated from her family in Beijing. Other members of Liu Shaoqi's staff advised against the idea, as did Premier Zhou Enlai. Liu continued to insist, however, and eventually Wang felt she had little choice but to comply. Having participated in rural work teams in the past, she began to look around for a suitable Socialist Education work team to join. This time she was determined to select a location where she could understand the local dialect well enough to communicate directly with the peasants. She set her sights on the surrounding province of Hebei. It promised the dual advantage of an intelligible patois and proximity to Beijing, enabling her to return home quickly in case of need. Before finalizing things, she sought Chairman Mao's blessing. At a dance party in Zhongnanhai, she told Mao of her plan to go to a village in Hebei for an extended period to "squat on a point" (蹲点) and implement the Four Cleans. He responded, "Good!"[3]

Thus reassured, Wang met with the Party Secretary of Hebei Province to decide on the destination for her sojourn. He suggested joining a work team bound for a village in Funing County, one of two counties designated as provincial "test points" for conducting the Four Cleans campaign. Wang was familiar with Funing, having visited it on several occasions when staying at the nearby seaside resort of Beidaihe, where the top leadership repaired each summer to escape the Beijing heat. She readily agreed to the recommendation.

Despite these amenable arrangements, Wang was seized with doubts when she headed off on her mission. She would later recall:[4]

> As I walked away clutching my suitcase, I glanced back and saw Shaoqi still standing there in the doorway of the office. Knowing that I would be gone for a year, I felt uneasy. Since marrying Shaoqi, we had never been separated for such a long period. I had never left the family for such a long period. He was old and in failing health. He worked day and night. If I wasn't there, who would care for him? There would be no one to remind him to dress properly. He was prone to catching cold! What if he got up in the middle of the night and took a fall? Would the children's education not disturb his work? Who would take charge of all the household affairs? But things had already reached this point and it wouldn't do to delay any longer. I had to grit my teeth and, while looking back again and again, walk on.

Although she did not fully realize it then, Wang Guangmei's decision to participate in the Four Cleans presaged her debut as an influential actor on the Chinese political stage. Posing under a pseudonym as a cadre from the Hebei security bureau, Wang spent the next half-year "squatting on a point" and practicing the "Three Togethers" (三同) of living, eating, and working with the peasants of Peach Garden Brigade. According to her account, the dearth of televisions in China at the time meant that neither the 1,000-plus villagers nor most of her fellow work team members were aware of Wang Guangmei's real identity. Only a handful of cadres from the Hebei provincial security bureau who were responsible for ensuring her personal safety knew that the deputy head of the Peach Garden work team was actually China's first lady.

Initially Wang Guangmei found daily life in Peach Garden trying. While the local dialect was basically intelligible, other features of mundane existence were more difficult. The morning chore of fetching water from the village well proved especially challenging. She dropped both buckets down the well on her first attempt to maneuver a shoulder pole. But Wang eventually adjusted to the rigors and routines of rural life, and the villagers for their part began to open up in response to her probing inquiries about cadre improprieties.

After a few weeks of investigation, she determined that Peach Garden was plagued by two "black winds" of cadre malfeasance. First, cadres often resorted to striking and beating the peasants to enforce compliance. Second, they (along with most of the villagers) were addicted to the illegal practice of gambling. Further investigation revealed that local cadres had abused their positions by embezzling public resources for private gain. The work team convened a series of mass meetings at which cadres were instructed to confess their wrongdoing. After being subjected to the public humiliation of "flying swallow" treatment (in which both arms were roughly yanked behind their backs to resemble a bird in flight), the chastened officials admitted their errors and agreed to return or repay stolen goods and money. This process was known as "taking a bath." The "fruits of struggle" were then distributed among the villagers at large. Seeing the financial benefit of cadre "baths," some villagers suggested convening a "mass bath" as well. At these sessions, ordinary villagers confessed to petty thefts and other infractions. Tools, kitchen utensils and other stolen objects were remitted to the collective and in many cases reunited with their original owner.

Midway in the work team's Peach Garden sojourn, team members returned home to celebrate the lunar new year holiday. On this occasion Wang Guangmei again took advantage of a gala at Zhongnanhai to seek Mao's guidance. While dancing with the chairman, she expressed disappointment at the peasants' reluctance to expose the full extent of cadre misbehavior. Mao advised her not to be so detached and impassive and suggested that she should convene a huge struggle meeting with thousands of people and enough excitement and fanfare to "mold public opinion."[5]

Buoyed by this encouragement, Wang returned to Peach Garden Brigade determined to press forward with a militant crusade.

Drawing on her own experience during the land reform campaign, she stressed that the work team's primary task was an all-out mass mobilization of ordinary villagers to engage in struggle against "class enemies." Revolutionary techniques that had previously pitted peasants against landlords in an often bloody process of land redistribution were now to be deployed against Communist cadres themselves.

Because the land reform campaign in this part of Hebei had been conducted with minimal violence and loss of life, Wang suspected that it had failed to thoroughly identify class enemies. The work team therefore mobilized the youth in Peach Garden to research and write up family and village histories intended to reveal concealed property. Five landlord households and two rich peasant households were found to have escaped detection in land reform. More alarming, still, these "hidden class enemies" were accused of exercising influence over the local cadres and the Party branch. Although central Party guidelines at the time held that more than 95 percent of village cadres were reliable, the Peach Garden work team forced thirty-nine of the forty-six cadres in the brigade (85 percent) to submit to mass criticism. When the Party branch secretary complained about the work team's harsh procedures, he was declared to be a "counterrevolutionary enemy of the people." The secretary and deputy secretary were both removed from office, expelled from the Communist Party, and sentenced to hard labor. County-level cadres challenged this verdict, but Wang Guangmei did not back down. To add insult to injury, she falsely accused the former Party Secretary of keeping a mistress and smeared his wife as a prostitute who consorted with village bachelors. A new leadership team was selected by the work team; at Wang's recommendation, the militia captain was installed as the new Party Secretary.

Shortly after Wang had completed her five-month stint in the countryside, she was asked to report on her experience at a gathering of central-level Party cadres. Her riveting account of the Peach Garden saga earned her other speaking engagements – not only in Beijing, but in Hebei, Shandong, Anhui, Jiangsu, Shanghai, Henan, Hubei, Hunan, Guangdong, Guangxi, and Yunnan as well. Recordings of the talk, which took a full six and a half hours for her to deliver, circulated even more widely. Considering this positive reception, Liu Shaoqi – who had recently been tasked with command of the national Four Cleans campaign headquarters – proposed that his wife transcribe and revise her talk as a written document which he then edited. On September 1, 1964, after getting the green light from Mao, Wang Guangmei's report – entitled *General Summary of One Brigade's Experience in the Socialist Education Movement* and commonly referred to simply as *Peach Garden Experience* – was distributed as an official Party central document to all Party committees and millions of work team members around the country. At the time, Mao was so impressed by Wang Guangmei's report that he recommended it as essential reading to his own wife, Jiang Qing.

Composed in the context of a nationwide campaign to combat corruption by reviving the revolutionary spirit, *Peach Garden Experience* provided a how-to manual for stirring up conflict and division in Chinese society. Key to this process was the identification and cultivation of allies at the grass roots who could be counted on to attack designated "enemies of the people" and enforce central Party priorities. While practicing the "Three Togethers" of working, living and eating with the villagers, the first job for an outside work team was to "strike roots and forge links" (扎根串连) – or develop a network of its own supporters among the masses who were not beholden to the local power structure. These grassroots allies, or "roots," would reach out to like-minded members of the community to create a web of activists or "backbones" committed to carrying out the dictates of the higher-level Party and government authorities to whom the work team reported. They would in turn mobilize other villagers to participate in large-scale, emotional "speak-bitterness" struggle sessions at which "class enemies" were criticized and punished for their misdeeds. A major challenge for the work team was to "control the temperature" (掌握火候) so that these "class struggle" meetings could reach a blistering temperature without, however, boiling over and out of control.

Wang Guangmei opens *Peach Garden Experience* with a bold characterization of the Socialist Education Movement as a "great revolutionary campaign" marked by a "sharper, more arduous and more complex class struggle than land reform." She credits her previous time on a land reform work team as valuable experience, but criticizes land reform work teams for not having understood the basic patterns and principles of mass movements. Drawing on her education as a scientist, she explains,

> In the past, I studied natural science and have always felt that social science was more difficult than natural science ... Thermometers indicate whether someone has a fever and other instruments measure other conditions ... but there is no instrument to gauge the temperature of a mass movement ... The art of leading a mass movement lies in knowing what to stress at what stage in the boiling process.

The first challenge, she notes, is to figure out with whom to "strike roots." Unlike Beijing opera, "where the actor's gestures, costume and makeup reveal immediately whether he is good or bad," the outside work team cannot make an instant determination. The work team cannot depend on local cadres for information; it must conduct its own painstaking investigation. Moreover, a brigade work team need not limit its operations to the village level; it should investigate cadres at commune, district, and county levels as well. She concludes her report by depicting the Four Cleans as the antidote to Soviet revisionism; instead of Khrushchev's policy of "peaceful evolution" she prescribes class struggle.

In interviews many years later, Wang Guangmei emphasized that the lodestar behind all her activities at Peach Garden Brigade was Chairman Mao's admonition in 1962 to "never forget class struggle!" Her contribution was to develop a systematic method of "all-out mass mobilization" (放手发动群众) which established a direct connection between work teams and ordinary people that was beyond the purview of local Party and government officials. Work teams were not only expected to enlist mass involvement in policy implementation; they were instructed to investigate and intimidate recalcitrant cadres in the process. With outside work teams authorized to replace the local power structure, their numbers and influence expanded commensurately. In 1964, virtually every college upperclassman and countless cadres and activists were assigned to these large and powerful entities. When Liu Shaoqi declared that a requirement for higher-level Party promotion would be a successful record of "squatting on a point" and "striking roots and forging links," ambitious Party members volunteered in droves for Four Cleans work team assignments.

Work team members underwent a lengthy training program in the policies and methods of the campaign before being dispatched to villages, factories and schools around the country. The struggle techniques detailed in *Peach Garden Experience* were a cornerstone of this instructional curriculum, eagerly studied and imitated by the more than three and a half million people (including more than one and a half million cadres) who participated in Four Cleans work teams. But Wang Guangmei's recipe for mobilization had detractors as well. And soon its fate became entangled in high-level political conflicts that caught Wang by surprise.

In January 1965 Mao Zedong began to voice complaints about the composition and conduct of the Four Cleans work teams. As the person overseeing the campaign, Liu Shaoqi (and by extension his wife) would suffer the consequences of Mao's growing dissatisfaction. At a central Party meeting in the Great Hall of the People, Mao launched an unexpected broadside against the tactics being employed in the Four Cleans campaign: "More than ten thousand people descending on one county, wasting time studying documents, not relying on the masses, acting secretively, striking roots and forging links, too detached and impassive, engaging in scholasticism, engaging in human wave tactics ... Why do we need all these work teams anyway?"[6]

Tsinghua University

As the Four Cleans gradually ebbed only to be overtaken by the sudden onrush of the Cultural Revolution, the question of work teams continued to concern the central leadership. Mao's growing reservations notwithstanding, work teams had been the Chinese Communist Party's standard method of campaign governance since the days of land reform. Following the familiar CCP playbook, the Politburo Standing Committee in June 1966 approved a decision to send work teams to schools and universities to manage the increasingly unruly Red Guard student movement that had emerged with Mao's call for a Cultural Revolution. Unlike the Four Cleans, however, the Cultural Revolution work teams were dispatched in haste, with minimal higher-level direction or advance instruction. In just over a week, thousands of Party officials were assigned to hundreds of teams with unclear missions. The result on the ground was chaos and confusion.

At Tsinghua University the work team immediately removed the popular president and Party secretary, Jiang Nanxiang, who was also serving as China's minister of higher education. It proceeded to suspend all university officials and Party branch members from their posts, pending investigation and criticism. Refusing to acknowledge any genuine "leftists" among the Red Guards, the work team generated a hostile backlash from the incensed students.

Liu Shaoqi deputized his wife to investigate the chaotic situation at Tsinghua, where, as it happened, his daughter Liu Tao was also a student. After spending a couple of days reading the big-character posters of handwritten student and faculty criticisms posted across campus, Wang took up residence in a guest house near the university. Commuting to campus by bicycle each morning, and operating under a pseudonym, Wang served for more than a month as senior adviser to the Tsinghua work team. The Tsinghua work team was notable for conducting the most thoroughgoing purge of any university in the country. Only fourteen of the 206 top officials were spared labor reform; the majority were forced to perform grueling manual labor from morning to night with signboards hanging from their necks identifying them as members of a "black gang" of counterrevolutionaries.

With the university administration having been completely displaced by the work team, Wang's chief concern was to curb Red Guard extremism. She presided over several all-school assemblies where work team members squelched attempted protests by student rebels.

At the end of July, however, Wang Guangmei had the rug pulled out from under her when Mao declared his opposition to Liu Shaoqi's method of conducting the Cultural Revolution, accusing the work teams of having suppressed the student movement. Work teams were quickly withdrawn from all schools and universities, and Wang – after a brief stint serving potatoes in the college cafeteria as penance for her mistakes – retreated to Zhongnanhai. Radical Red Guards at Tsinghua, now feeling fully vindicated in their opposition to the work team, demanded that Wang Guangmei return to campus for a public reckoning. Premier Zhou Enlai intervened to delay the confrontation, but eventually the Tsinghua rebels – with higher-level assistance – resorted to deception to lure Wang back to campus.

Framed as an epic ideological and political struggle against the corrosive forces of "revisionism" that threatened to undermine Mao's socialist project, the Cultural Revolution also had a more personal and less heroic underside. Just as Mao begrudged the expanding power of Liu Shaoqi following the disastrous Great Leap Forward, so Mao's wife, Jiang Qing, resented the outsized influence that Wang Guangmei enjoyed after the nationwide distribution of *Peach Garden Experience*. The Cultural Revolution presented an opportunity for Jiang Qing to turn the tables on her rival. In December 1966 Jiang went to Tsinghua to visit Liu Shaoqi's daughter, Liu Tao. Presenting herself as the appointed emissary of "Uncle Mao," Jiang informed Liu Tao that Liu Shaoqi and Wang Guangmei had both been deemed "counterrevolutionaries" and that she herself would have to choose between filial piety and Mao's revolution. To ease the choice, Jiang Qing arranged for Liu Tao to meet her birth mother, a previous wife of Liu Shaoqi, who was only too happy to fill Liu Tao's head with ugly stories about her father in his younger years. Once persuaded to sacrifice her father and stepmother for the sake of the revolution, Liu Tao helped her radical classmates at Tsinghua concoct a pretext to decoy Wang Guangmei from her Zhongnanhai home.

On January 6, 1967, Liu Shaoqi's security guard received an agitated phone call saying that Liu's younger daughter Liu Pingping had been hospitalized after breaking her leg in a serious traffic accident on the way home from school. Shaken by the news, Liu Shaoqi and Wang Guangmei hesitated over how to respond, knowing it was unsafe for either of them to venture outdoors at a time when radical Red Guards had vowed to seize them and subject them to struggle meetings. Before long, however, a frantic follow-up call warned that the hospital required Wang Guangmei's signature for the emergency surgery to proceed; time was of the essence if Pingping's leg were to be saved. Wang rushed to the hospital, where she was captured on the spot by Red Guards who spirited her back to Tsinghua for interrogation.

The first struggle session directed against Wang Guangmei turned into a fiasco when Wang's deft ability to deflect the Tsinghua rebels' questions allowed her to gain the upper hand. Refusing to answer unwelcome queries on grounds of national security, she repeatedly shot back, "This matter I can only discuss with

Chairman Mao or the Central Committee. I cannot reveal state secrets." But three months later, Wang Guangmei was sent back to Tsinghua – this time with the approval of Chairman Mao and Premier Zhou – to face a much more intimidating round of criticism. By then the Red Guards had done their homework, with the help of Jiang Qing and others in the top leadership determined to destroy Liu Shaoqi and his wife.

The crowd of half a million spectators who gathered on the Tsinghua campus in the spring of 1967 to taunt the absurdly attired former first lady included some who had journeyed over a hundred miles. Cadres and villagers from Peach Garden Brigade who had suffered at the hands of Wang Guangmei's work team three years before were among her most vehement accusers. In preparing for the mass struggle meeting, Tsinghua rebels had made repeated trips to Peach Garden to gather incriminating evidence of Wang's "counterrevolutionary" activities. In the process, they learned that the work team's decision to favor some Peach Garden cadres at the expense of others was not the result of unbiased investigation. It turned out that Wang's choice of Peach Garden as her "squatting point" was not simply due to the intelligible local dialect. Both Wang Guangmei and Liu Shaoqi had visited the village back in 1958, while attending a summer gathering of the CCP leadership at the nearby beach resort of Beidaihe. When Peach Garden became part of the newly established East Wind Commune a month later, the couple donated a Soviet-made movie projector to the commune, in return for which Liu's entire family was granted honorary membership. While ordinary villagers may have failed to recognize China's first lady when she returned on a Four Cleans work team, that was not the case for the cadre whom the work team elevated to Party Secretary at the expense of his local rival. He was the very person who had arranged for the exchange of the movie projector for commune membership. Now his persecuted adversary had a chance to even the score.

Other elements of the Tsinghua struggle session had a backstory as well. Wang's outlandish getup was the product of sartorial suggestions from Jiang Qing herself. As it happened, Jiang had offered Wang Guangmei some fashion tips prior to her 1963 trip to Indonesia that the first lady cavalierly ignored. The form-fitting silk gown, floppy straw hat and florid ping-pong necklace that she was now forced to wear was not only a mockery of her state-visit finery; it was vengeful payback from a nemesis of her own.

Denouement

When Wang Guangmei's agonizing day at Tsinghua finally ended late that night, she was returned to Zhongnanhai only to be jailed in a small room. Initially Wang Guangmei attempted to defend her activities at both Tsinghua and Peach Garden as a faithful reflection of Mao Zedong Thought, but she was eventually worn down by successive rounds of harsh interrogation and public humiliation. On August 5 a final mass struggle session, this time together with Liu Shaoqi, was conducted inside the leadership compound. Liu and Wang's youngest children later recalled,

> We three children had been ordered to attend ... We stood at the back of the crowd and were seized with sorrow and fury as Mommy and Daddy were brought into the hall by several burly men who pushed down their heads and forced back their arms into the "jet plane position." They hit and kicked Daddy and pulled on his thinning white hair to make him look upward for a photograph. Then they dragged both Mommy and Daddy into a corner of the hall just a few steps from us and made them kowtow in front of two huge cartoon-like drawings of Red Guards. Daddy's nose was discolored and his face was swollen from having been beaten. His shoes had been trampled and he was in his bare socks. But suddenly Mommy broke free and clasped Daddy's hand. Daddy ignored the kicks and punches and held on tightly. They stood tall, hand in hand, gazing at each other. That was Daddy and Mommy's final farewell.[7]

After a few more months held captive in Zhongnanhai, where she was assigned to hard manual labor transporting bricks, Wang Guangmei was transferred to the dreaded Qincheng Prison on the outskirts of Beijing. She was falsely charged with having served as a secret agent for the United States while working as an interpreter for the CCP mission to the Executive Headquarters. For the next twelve years Wang endured solitary confinement, under round-the-clock surveillance. The most demeaning aspect, she later recalled, was that a window directly above the toilet in her cell subjected even the most intimate behavior to observation.

It was while in prison that Wang learned of her husband's death three years earlier. A lifeless Liu Shaoqi, suffering from either medical neglect or torture, had been found lying on the floor of a makeshift prison in Henan drenched in vomit and feces. Wang was informed of Liu's demise only because their children had written a letter directly to Mao, inquiring into the whereabouts of their parents whom they had not seen for five years. Mao scribbled a terse note in response: "Father is dead, can visit mother."

Wang Guangmei was finally released from prison in December 1978, two years after Mao's death. For the next three decades, she devoted herself to the posthumous rehabilitation of her late husband's political reputation and to philanthropy. In 1995 at age seventy-four Wang became founding director of Project Happiness (*Xingfu gongcheng* 幸福工程), an NGO to assist mothers living in poverty, which she endowed by auctioning off family antiques that had been returned to her after the Cultural Revolution. By the time of Wang Guangmei's death in 2006, Project Happiness had distributed over 400 million yuan in microloans to more than 170,000 mothers in need across China.

Conclusions

Wang Guangmei was a catalyst to the fiery politics that culminated in the inferno of the Cultural Revolution. But rather than simply point the finger of blame, judging her to be as much a perpetrator as a victim, it is perhaps more instructive to reflect upon the multiple contradictions and paradoxes that Wang's remarkable biography embodies. Raised in an elite family of means, she joined a peasant revolution committed to eradicating the very privileges that she had once enjoyed. Intelligent and well-educated, she sacrificed a promising academic career for the sake of the revolution and of her husband's leadership role in it. A chief architect of "class struggle" under socialism, she was undone in the 1960s by the application of her own destructive tactics. Yet after the Cultural Revolution Wang reclaimed her dignity and purpose, repairing her husband's damaged reputation and drawing on her own inherited wealth for philanthropic ends that befitted a scion of the Beijing elite. Such ambiguities are not unique to Wang Guangmei. They run through the biographies of many of the early revolutionaries. In some respects, Wang's eventful life exemplifies the ironies of Chinese communism itself – a radical rejection of elite tradition that in the end reproduces much of what it ostensibly repudiates.

ADDITIONAL REFERENCES

Guo Dehong (郭德宏) and Lin Xiaobo (林小波), *Siqing yundong shilu* 四清运动实录 (Annals of the Four Cleans Movement) (Hangzhou: Zhejiang University Press, 2005).

Walder, Andrew G., *Fractured Rebellion: The Beijing Red Guard Movement* (Cambridge, MA: Harvard University Press, 2009).

Wang Guangmei (王光美), "Guanyu yige dadui de shehuizhuyi jiaoyu yundong de jingyan zongjie" 关于一个大队的社会主义教育运动的经验总结 (General Summary of One Brigade's Experience in the Socialist Education Movement) (July 5, 1964).

Wang Guangyu (王广宇), "Qinghua pidou Wang Guangmei de yige xijie" 清华批斗王光美的一个细节 (Details of Tsinghua's struggle against Wang Guangmei), in *Yanhuang chunqiu* 炎黄春秋 (2013), no. 5, pp. 15-17.

Wang Haiguang (王海光), "Taoyuan jingyan yanjiu – cong minzhongshi de shijiao kaocha" 桃园经验研究 – 从民众史的视角考察" (A study of *Peach Garden Experience* – from the perspective of popular history) (Shanghai: unpublished paper, n.d.).

Zhi Xiaomin (智效民), *Liu Shaoqi yu Jinsui tugai* 刘少奇与晋绥土改 (Liu Shaoqi and the Jinsuil land and reform) (Taipei: Xiuwei Information Science Press, 2008).

Figure 1. Henricus Sneevliet's passport photograph in 1922. Sneevliet Archive at International Institute of Social History (with permission).

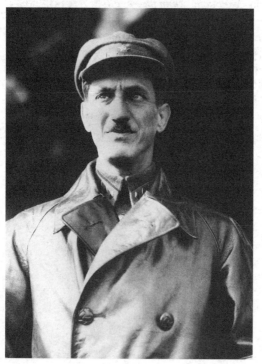

Figure 2. A brooding Mikhail Markovich Gruzenberg, captured by an unknown photographer in spring 1925, described to British readers at the time as "Russian OGPU agent Borodin, AKA Comrade Lung Kwa Wah, sent to enflame Chinese mobs to attack Europeans during war in China." Topical News Agency/ Hulton Image Archive via Getty Images (with permission).

Figure 3. A banner reading "Mobilize the power of the masses to defend Wuhan" hangs outside the headquarters of the France, Belgium, and Switzerland Returned Students Association in Wuhan, June 1938. Historical Photographs of China project, University of Bristol, collection reference Bi-s162 (with permission).

Figure 4. In a photograph produced by a Soviet journalist in 1937, we see the front gates of Kangda, a "prototype of a revolutionised school of the proletariat," the Chinese Anti-Japanese Military and Political College in Yan'an. Sovfoto/Universal Images Group via Getty Images (with permission).

Figure 5. Mao Zedong pauses from his work to pose for a photograph at his desk in the wartime base of Yan'an in 1937 or 1938, the tabletop hinting at hard-won intellectual labor – scattered pens, crushed packet of cigarettes, a battered enamel cup, loose papers, and a stack of well-thumbed books. Sovfoto/Universal Images Group via Getty Images (with permission).

Figure 6. Over a decade later, on October 1, 1949, Mao stands on the Gate of Heavenly Peace in Tiananmen Square and announces the founding of the People's Republic of China. To his left and right we see early members of Sun Yat-sen's Tongmenghui (Revolutionary Alliance) who later joined the Communist Party, Lin Boqu (1886–1960) and Dong Biwu (1886–1975). Arnoldo Mondadori Editore via Getty Images (with permission).

Figure 7. Members of the Central Committee of the Chinese Communist Party (bottom row) receive delegates of the Third Congress of the China New Democratic Youth League at the closing session on May 25, 1957, just before the launch of the tumultuous Anti-Rightist Campaign. From left to right, leaders include Lin Boqu, Chen Yun, Zhou Enlai, Zhu De, Mao Zedong, Liu Shaoqi, Dong Biwu, and Deng Xiaoping.
Sovfoto/Universal Images Group via Getty Images (with permission).

Figure 8. Shangguan Yunzhu (second right) in her starring role in *A Spring River Flows East* (directed by Cai Chusheng and Zheng Junli, 1947). Personal collection of Zhang Jishun (with permission).

Figure 9. A decidedly more proletarian Shangguan Yunzhu in the 1950s. Personal collection of Zhang Jishun (with permission).

Figure 10. Liu Shaoqi, number two leader in the Party, and his wife Wang Guangmei captured by a Soviet photographer during happier times in 1949. Sovfoto/Universal Images Group via Getty Images (with permission).

Figure 11. Wang Guangmei wears her "pearl necklace" (made of ping-pong balls) during a struggle session at Tsinghua University in Beijing, spring 1967, in the Cultural Revolution. Personal collection of Elizabeth Perry (with permission).

Figure 12. In September 1971, protestors carry posters of Mao Zedong down 42nd Street of New York City, demanding China's entry into the United Nations.
Bettmann Archive via Getty Images (with permission).

Figure 13. An off-brand Mao is held aloft over a crowd of Albanian workers "expressing their ardent affection for the Chinese people, the Chinese Communist Party, and Comrade Mao Zedong" in May 1974. Sovfoto/Universal Images Group via Getty Images (with permission).

Figure 14. A sign of the times. Throughout the late 1970s and the 1980s, Western visitors flooded into China, with the Great Wall more often than not marking their obligatory first stop. Here George Michael and Andrew Ridgeley, of the British pop group Wham!, stand on the Great Wall in the spring of 1985 before their concert at the Workers Stadium in Beijing. Peter Charlesworth/ LightRocket via Getty Images (with permission).

Figure 15. Students gather at the monument to the People's Heroes in Tiananmen Square on April 19, 1989, following the death of General Secretary Hu Yaobang, a top leader widely seen as supporting greater economic and political reforms. The portrait of Hu, which echoes the more famous portrait of Mao on the Gate of Heavenly Peace opposite the monument, is paired with a couplet reading, "Where can [my] soul find peace?" (a line from the Nine Songs of Qu, by the ancient poet Qu Yuan, who famously drowned himself in protest at reckless policy); and "With deepest condolences, the Central Academy of Fine Arts" on the left. Unexpectedly, this impromptu memorial would soon transform into a nationwide protest movement, culminating in a violent crackdown in the early morning of June 4, 1989.
Catherine Henriette/AFP via Getty Images (with permission).

Figure 16. Zhao Ziyang, General Secretary of the Party, visits Tiananmen Square on May 19, 1989 – one month after the death of Hu Yaobang – pleading with the students to end their hunger strike and leave the square. Behind Zhao is Wen Jiabao, then director of the Party General Office (and future premier).
Credit: Chip Hires/Gamma-Rapho via Getty Images (with permission).

Figure 17. Leading New Enlightenment figure and Party intellectual Wang Yuanhua in the 1990s.
Personal collection of Xu Jilin (with permission).

Figure 18. East meets West in a 1998 photograph of the desk of United States labor historian and Party member Zhang Youlun, director of the Research Institute of History, Nankai University, in Tianjin. Like many intellectuals of his generation, Zhang spent a formative year as a visiting fellow abroad (in his particular case, at the University of Minnesota in 1983), laying the foundations for the unprecedented intellectual pluralism that has marked the Reform era.

Rita Reed/Star Tribune via Getty Images (with permission).

Figure 19. A bust of Communist hero Lei Feng stands before a newly opened Pizza Hut in Xiamen, 1996, while a street peddler walks past. On the plinth, in Mao Zedong's calligraphy, "Study from Lei Feng."
Robyn Beck/AFP via Getty Images (with permission).

Figure 20. Basketball superstar Yao Ming snaps a photograph of the closing ceremony of the Beijing Olympics in August 2008, an event which continues to carry symbolic significance for the Party up to the present day. Following a wildly successful run on the Houston Rockets, Yao has likewise emerged as a key figure in the Party's soft-power initiatives.
Robert Gauthier and the *Los Angeles Times* via Getty Images (with permission).

Figure 21. Guo Meimei takes a selfie behind the wheel of a Mini Cooper in an image posted on the Internet in July 2011. Claiming to work for a company attached to the Red Cross Society of China, Guo ignited a firestorm of controversy online as an apparent example of corruption in a high-profile nonprofit organization. Guo Meimei's materialist concerns reflected the larger shift toward "depoliticization" as championed by Deng Xiaoping and his supporters at the outset of the Reform and Opening Up period. STR/AFP via Getty Images (with permission).

Figure 22. A widely circulated Internet meme from 2014 features Jiang Zemin and his avatar, an inflatable toad – a comparison which presumably arose due both to superficial resemblance and also to the former General Secretary's penchant for yawning in meetings ("toad" in Mandarin puns with "yawn"). This and other memes (for example, Xi Jinping as Winnie the Pooh) reflect a thriving culture of irreverence toward the Party online – one which in earlier eras was expressed in the even more ephemeral media of jokes and doggerel poetry.

Sup China (with permission).

Figure 23. Taken in late February 2020, at the height of the COVID-19 pandemic in China, a Shanghai street cleaner, wearing a surgical mask, fully absorbed with a cell phone walks past a bus stop, providing an ironic counterpoint to the television screen, which shows the current core leader of the Chinese Communist Party and nation, likewise wearing a surgical mask. The subtitle indicates that viewers should have "respect and gratitude" for Xi and the Party – alongside a timetable for the next two buses.
Yifan Ding via Getty Images (with permission).

Chapter 6 – 1970s

The Cultural Revolution had revealed that the efforts to create a new China had ended dramatically in chaos, internal strife, confusion, isolation and destruction. At the end of the Cultural Revolution decade in 1976, the Party's dreams about a new China were shattered. Under the Party's leadership, China seesawed between new beginnings and hard landings, aspirations and betrayals, experimentation and failure, construction and destruction.

When Mao Zedong died on September 9, 1976, the Party and the country that it had governed since 1949 were deeply exhausted from the overambitious projects of the Mao period. The campaigns and movements left behind a country that was depleted and scarred from the enormous costs of Mao's utopian dreams, its energies sapped. Decades of personality cult, however, had spread Mao's words and images into every home, every factory, and every school. For better or for worse, Maoism had engulfed the Party and the country entirely. After Mao's death, the mood of the country oscillated between shock and relief, which is captured at the beginning of the following scene.

After 1978 the CCP worked to come to terms with the Mao period. In June 1981, after lengthy discussions, the Communist Party Central Committee adopted a resolution on "Certain Questions in the History of our Party', which concluded: "Comrade Mao Zedong was a great Marxist and a great proletarian revolutionary, strategist and theorist. It is true that he made gross mistakes during the Cultural Revolution, but if we judge his activities as a whole, his contributions to the Chinese Revolution far outweigh his mistakes." This evaluation of the Maoist period allowed the Party to shift its course and pursue a far-reaching reversal as it embarked on a path of opening up internationally and market liberalization.

The legacy of Maoism, however, lived on inside and outside of China. Maoism continued as a global myth, with Mao as its main icon mass-produced on posters, badges, and pamphlets. It continued to radiate to other places and areas, reaching from Latin America to the Himalayas, to Paris, and to West Berlin. Mao had admirers even among well-respected thinkers such as Michel Foucault. A Mao in afterlife and freed from reality became a powerful inspiration to revolutionaries worldwide who formed Communist parties based on his military tactics and mass mobilization techniques. They studied his theories of peasant revolution. With this large presence on the global stage, the CCP after Mao's death had become an unknowing participant in a global revolutionary enterprise between far flung regions, just at the time when the Party began to embrace global capitalism.

THE 1970s
6 The Death of Mao and Life of Chairman Gonzalo
JULIA LOVELL

September 9, 1976, was a hard day for Dr. Li Zhisui. At ten minutes after midnight, Mao Zedong – Li's personal charge for much of the past twenty-two years – died, holding his doctor's hand. The chairman's sickbed immediately became a maelstrom of anxious courtiers. Mao's widow, Jiang Qing, barked blame at the medical team while trying to appoint herself Mao's heir. Mao's former lover-turned-nursemaid Zhang Yufeng wailed about what would become of her, while Mao's favorite nephew paced about the room (he allegedly took advantage of the confusion to lift Mao's Swiss watch).

Events quickly took an ominous turn for the doctor: the captain of the compound's garrison told Li that the Politburo was meeting and that he should anticipate imminent arrest for the murder of Mao: "you won't be able to run away."[1] While Li distracted himself by searching for formaldehyde through the early hours of the Beijing morning – a brisk injection to Mao's leg artery would be required to preserve his body for a week of public mourning in Beijing's still-hot September – some good news broke: the Politburo had exonerated Dr. Li of causing Mao's death. But the relief did not last long. Wang Dongxing – chief of Mao's bodyguards – told Dr. Li that the Politburo had also decided, against Mao's own wishes, to preserve his body for permanent display. Dr. Li protested that Chinese science lacked the know-how to pull this feat off; on a visit to Moscow back in the 1950s, he had learnt that the nose, ears and mustache had rotted off the bodies of Lenin and Stalin in their mausoleums; the same fate had befallen Ho Chi

Minh after his embalming in 1969. Following a chase around sketchy embalming manuals for unproven formulae (and after asking the Institute of Arts and Crafts to secretly construct a wax dummy, just in case), Li's team decided as a temporary measure to inject twenty-two liters of formaldehyde into Mao's corpse. Although Mao promptly swelled up like a perspiring balloon, after about six hours of massage and the judicious application of makeup he looked normal enough to be placed in a crystal display coffin for the official mourning period. As soon as it concluded, Dr. Li and his makeshift squad of embalmers removed the corpse to a secret underground embalming facility, to begin the work of indefinite preservation. At three p.m. the next day, September 18, China fell silent for three minutes; half a million mourners gathered in Tiananmen Square for Mao's memorial. Dr. Li – unsurprisingly – almost fainted with exhaustion during the eulogy.

The Chinese Communist Party (CCP) had lost its "helmsman": the individual who, for thirty years, had been its emblem. Within another three weeks, the post-Mao power struggle broke into the open. As rumors swirled around the inner circles of power about a coup by Jiang Qing, Mao's anointed successor Hua Guofeng on October 6 pre-emptively arrested Jiang and her closest allies – Mao's key architects and supporters of the Cultural Revolution. Chinese urbanites responded to the arrest of this "Gang of Four" with explosive celebrations: firecrackers, wine, and crab dinners – for the Chinese word for crab puns with a term meaning "bully." Much was still to change in Chinese politics over the next five years. Deng Xiaoping, the toughest, brightest veteran survivor of the Cultural Revolution, would return to power in 1977, sidelining Hua and pushing through dramatic transformations: acceptance of private farming and a resumption of education and testing systems based on academic merit rather than political background. But already before this, the key shift in the Party had taken place: the turn from puritanical, ideological radicalism. In his short time at the helm, Hua Guofeng introduced policies anathema to the Cultural Revolution: prioritizing modernization over class struggle, regularizing Party procedure, bringing in special economic zones for foreign investment and sending delegations abroad to study science and technology. Even as the CCP abandoned radical Maoism, however, the revolutionary military ideas and practices that it had broadcast across the globe between the 1950s and 1970s, as part of a bid for leadership of the world revolution, persisted in Communist parties elsewhere – above all in Peru and South Asia. This contrasting story – of Maoist retreat within, and ongoing Maoist Party-building without China – is the focus of this chapter.

~

In the culture, economics and foreign policy of the People's Republic of China (PRC), the headline story of the years following Mao's death seemed to be de-Maoification. During the Cultural Revolution, Mao's works or image had been the safest choice of ceremonial gift. In one story, a married couple received 102 copies of Mao's works as wedding presents. Enough portraits of Mao had been produced for each Chinese person to own three.[2] More than a billion copies of the Little Red Book had been produced.[3] Millions of copies of Mao's works were mouldering in warehouses. On February 12, 1979, however, the Propaganda Department banned the sale of the Little Red Book and – barring a few copies to be held in reserve – ordered all extant volumes to be pulped within seven months. Up to 90 percent of remaindered Mao-era political books were turned into mulch – including the entire run of Volume V of Mao's *Selected Works*.[4]

Even the propagandists of Mao Zedong Thought stopped believing in the message they had been trained to communicate. In 1978, the writers, editors, and polishers of the Foreign Languages Press (FLP) – the organization that churned out the works of "external propaganda" that vectored Mao's ideas and influence across the world – finally had an opportunity to view the world for themselves, including the Western world, which throughout their professional lives up to that point they had been certain China was about to liberate. One early-middle-aged FLP editor – a veteran of the Cultural Revolution's exhausting political and social upheavals – was shocked by everyday life in small-town New Zealand:

> Before I left China, all the propaganda was about how people in capitalist countries were suffering, oppressed – that anything to do with capitalism was bad, and anything to do with socialism was good. But when we actually went abroad, we found it was nothing like that. The culture

shock was very strong. Everything was so different from China – including daily levels of civility. Every day, parents took their children to school, and picked them up at the end of the day. I thought: how lucky these children are. I wept to see it. I'd spent all these years doing external propaganda in China, but I had no idea how people were living abroad.[5]

Chen Xiaolu, son of Chen Yi, Mao's direct contemporary and one of the founders of the PRC, was a participant witness to China's immediate post-Mao transition. In 1966, Chen Yi had the misfortune to be minister of foreign affairs, and as such was attacked by Red Guards in the ministry for his supposed bourgeois capitulations on the global stage. Although Mao and Zhou protected him from the worst extremes of Cultural Revolution violence, he was demoted, sickened, and died in 1972. Chen Xiaolu, meanwhile, joined the Red Guards himself, terrorizing his teachers. On joining the Ministry of Foreign Affairs after Mao's death, he found himself at the coalface of diplomatic de-Maoification in the early Deng era:

[My generation] deeply felt the failure of the Cultural Revolution. I arrived in the UK [on a diplomatic posting] in 1981. After we arrived in the UK, we realized that we were the ones who were suffering. The British standard of living was much higher than ours. It was a real shock that things weren't as we'd been told. We [realized we] had to copy capitalist countries.

Some witnesses to this transition argue that the Chinese people were so used to going along with the political line handed down from above that, when the CCP began to back away from the signature policies of Cultural Revolution Maoism – when it reinstated high school and university exams, when it allowed the communes to break up into private plots, when it permitted sidelines and markets for farmers – most people simply fell in line, without giving the decision much thought. Chen Xiaolu, looking back in 2016, gave ordinary people greater agency:

This political transformation wasn't Deng Xiaoping's alone. It was an issue for all Chinese people, their thinking. They couldn't go on as before ... back then, we felt: we've been fooled for 30 years ... It made us coolly reflect on our society. On our value system.

So had the three decades before 1976 been wasted? "Look," he sighed,

> the road of experience is twisted. People inevitably make mistakes. Countries inevitably make mistakes ... But without the Cultural Revolution, we wouldn't have the reforms. We have this old saying: things turn into their opposite when they reach the extreme (*wuji bifan*). Without the Cultural Revolution, China would have been like the USSR. Without reforms, we wouldn't have China now. How else could we have caught up with the most advanced parts of the world? We're number two in the world ... Without the disaster of the Cultural Revolution, without all those empty things that people said back then, we wouldn't have a unified understanding that it was wrong.[6]

~

Some 17,000 miles away, however, in Peru, the death of Mao and renunciation of the Cultural Revolution garnered a very different response. There, a middle-aged philosophy professor and leader of a Maoist groupuscule – ignorant of the unedifying maneuverings of Mao's court – was horrified: the arrest of the "Gang of Four" and its aftermath were a "revisionist counterrevolutionary coup d'etat that usurped the power of the dictatorship of the proletariat and restored capitalism in China."[7] On learning of Mao's decease, this Peruvian gushed encomia: Mao had been "a titan of the proletariat," the "indispensable leader of the Chinese and world revolutions," "the masterful heir to the great masters of the international working class ... the extraordinary man whose life beat to its very end with the imperishable light of Marxism, with the creative omnipotent force of the masses and the spirit of serving the people."[8] With the Great Proletarian Cultural Revolution, Mao had created the road map to communism: a philosophy of constant, two-line struggle against monsters and bourgeois followers of the capitalist path: "To be a Marxist–Leninist today is to adhere to Mao Zedong Thought."[9]

The name of this passionate Peruvian Maoist was Abimael Reinoso Guzmán (1934–); the name of his group, the Communist Party of Peru – Shining Path (usually abbreviated as Shining Path). In late September 1976, Guzmán dispatched a worshipful message of condolence to the Chinese embassy in Lima ("Eternal glory to Chairman Mao Zedong!") and honored his hero at a memorial meeting.[10] It was his last public appearance for sixteen years. Far from discouraging him, Mao's death convinced Guzmán that the time had come to go underground, to unleash a People's War in Peru – to keep flying the flag of Maoism. "It was now the moment to defend the revolution," he would later observe. "We began [our armed struggle] to defend the revolution."[11]

Throughout the 1980s, the followers of Guzmán's Shining Path – or *senderistas*, as they were known – would organize, sing, fight, torture, and kill in the name of a Peruvian Maoist revolution, waging protracted guerrilla warfare and "two-line struggle" against revisionism, and liquidating markets, inequality, religion, and political dissent. By the early 1990s, the magical realism evoked in the Latin American literary boom had become a black reality for the country. Peru was in the grip of cholera epidemics, inflation running at more than 12,000 percent, and a millenarian cult of Mao in which Guzmán was deified as Peru's "Chairman Gonzalo" and the "greatest living Marxist–Leninist." Between 1980 and 1999, this Maoist civil war killed 69,000 people, annihilated political moderation, gave gangster oligarchs an excuse to bulldoze democracy, and distended the country's cities with at least 600,000 refugees from Maoist and state violence.

Viewed from one historical angle – the emergence of neoliberalism under Reagan, and the CCP's own shunning of the Cultural Revolution in the early 1980s – the Shining Path's project was bizarrely out of its time. It was also ill-suited to Peru. Few of the preconditions for Mao's own revolution in the "semicolonial, semifeudal" China of the 1940s seemed to be present: Peru in 1980 was a democracy; it was largely urban and literate; and there was no colonial invader to fight, no militant social rebellion to capitalize upon, no massive inequality of landownership.

Yet if we consider these events in the context of the historical, political logic of the 1960s and 1970s, when the Shining Path came to life, the movement's doctrines become less surprising. For at that point, thanks substantially to the CCP's energetic global promotion of Mao's revolution from the late 1950s onwards, dreams and plots of Maoist insurgency ran in the bloodstream of the global radical left. However cultish the group would later come to seem, in the 1960s and 1970s many of its ideological underpinnings were fairly standard. Mao's ideas of continuous revolution and political militancy had permeated deeply enough to be satirized in mainstream Western pop culture, in Monty Python's *The Life of Brian* or the Beatles' "Revolution." In Peru, meanwhile, big-talking Maoist militants were ten a penny: "nothing special," as two Dutch agronomists there in the 1970s remarked.[12] In China, confidence in the radical 1960s' Maoist revolutionary model faded with the CCP's own turn from the Cultural Revolution. But in the Peruvian context – in a country scarred by gross socioeconomic and political inequities – and in the hands of particular, dogmatic personalities, these ideas could incubate, then resurge with the same sectarian passion that they had provoked in the 1960s.

This essay focuses on the eruption of global Maoism in Peru, because it was contingent on the death of Mao, because it so deeply affected that country between the 1980s and the 1990s, and because it in turn helped inspire another transformative Maoist insurgency in Nepal after 1996. But there are many other global explosions of the Cultural Revolution which continued to reverberate through and beyond Mao's death: Maoist civil war in India, Khmer Rouge genocide in Cambodia, the Zimbabwe African National Union's (ZANU) victory over white minority rule in Southern Rhodesia, far-left urban terrorism in Western Europe. The militant wing of the Black Power movement in the US – including the Black Panthers – borrowed heavily from Mao's rhetoric and theories of party organization in training its own cadres during the 1960s and 1970s. For the Mao-era CCP has a global as well as a domestic history, which takes in the tea plantations of north India, the villages of Zimbabwe, the rice paddies of Cambodia, and guerrilla refuges amid the high-rises of suburban West Germany, as well as the sierras of the Andes.

~

Abimael Guzmán was one of thousands of Latin Americans – presidents, painters, poets, philosophers, agronomists, labor activists – who traveled to Mao's China in the 1960s and returned full of admiration for its achievements. The globalization of Mao's ideas on revolution and of the Party organization needed to achieve it was no accident, for during this decade Mao and his lieutenants actively aspired to leadership of the world revolution. The PRC under Mao widely exported not only ideology, including hundreds of millions of copies of Mao's Little Red Book, but also harder currencies of revolution – money, weapons and Party training for global rebellions, especially in the developing world. Beijing, and training camps in South and East China, became hubs of drifting revolutionaries, as Mao's China declared itself the global headquarters of insurgency: anticolonial, anti-US, anti-Soviet. There were melancholic Chilean bolero singers, Colombian actors, Venezuelan armchair *guerrilleros*, and the doctrinaire British Maoist Elsie Fairfax-Cholmeley, who allegedly danced in jubilation around the burning ruins of the British legation when it was torched by Red Guards in 1967.

Within this group, Guzmán belonged to a subset (about a thousand strong) of Latin Americans who had received military training, as well as flattering hospitality, in China. They pored over China's "external propaganda" and spread the Maoist word through the continent in travel books, pamphlets, and lectures; in reading groups and classrooms; and at rallies. Like many parts of the developing world, Latin America after the Second World War was looking for political and economic models on both sides of the Cold War – oscillating between reform and revolution, democracy and dictatorship, while the US intensified its meddling in the continent by backing right-wing dictators to contain the spread of socialist ideas. After the Sino-Soviet split, Communist parties in Latin America – as in the rest of the world – began fracturing into pro-Chinese and pro-Soviet factions. Unlike the rest of the world, however, in several Latin American countries – Peru, Brazil, Colombia, Bolivia, and Paraguay – the Chinese factions were about the same size as the pro-Soviet groupings, indicating the strong attraction that the Chinese revolution exercised through the continent.

Across the continent, radicals and leftists absorbed Mao's military maxims; Guzmán was far from the only Latin American dreaming of a Maoist "People's War" in the 1960s. The Mexican guerrilla Florencio Medrano Mederos – a veteran Communist and agitator for land reform who always kept Mao's works within reach – planned protracted war in southeast Mexico.[13] In 1959, the CCP laid on a five-month training course for delegations from twelve Latin American Communist parties, openly proselytizing Mao's revolutionary doctrines: on organizing the peasantry, the mass line, and armed struggle – core elements of the Party's successful revolution in China. The curriculum was monopolized by Mao's works: Marx, Engels, Lenin, and Stalin were nowhere in sight. The lessons were accompanied by instructive tours around the country. "Most returned," one Peruvian participant recalled, "certain that . . . the road traveled by the Chinese Revolution would have to be repeated in the countries of Latin America."[14]

By his early twenties, Guzmán had turned into a reserved, intellectually self-confident young man with a passion for philosophical abstractions and a horror at the poverty that he witnessed around him in urban Peru. In 1962, he was hired as a professor of philosophy by the Universidad National de San Cristóbal de Huamanga in Ayacucho, the provincial capital of the eponymous southern central region of Peru that would become the epicenter of the Shining Path insurrection. This was one of the most isolated and impoverished parts of Peru, a country that in the 1960s was the second-poorest in Latin America. Life expectancy in the Andean sierra surrounding the city in 1979 stood at fifty-one – the lowest in Peru; roads and transportation barely existed.[15] The region was also rank with racism: of whites and *mestizos* (those of mixed European and indigenous background) toward those of darker-skinned indigenous heritage. The harsh inaccessibility of the Andean sierra weakened the presence of the state – and where it was present, its representatives were often abusive and corrupt. Ayacucho's concentration of marginalized ethnic groups thus presented a large potential support base for an ideology preaching Mao's message of radical egalitarianism and rough social justice.

But there was, in theory, a way out of poverty and exploitation. Social inferiority was tied not only to skin pigmentation but also to a lack of education – to be educated denoted high class. Literacy was the key to social and economic opportunities, including for Indians. When in 1969 an ethnographer interviewed 499 peasants in the area, 91 percent believed that "with an education, a man can be whatever he wants."[16] When Ayacucho's university reopened in 1959 after a century of closure, it promised political and social disruption: it represented the only hope of social mobility in a desert of deprivation. As the novelist Oswaldo Reynoso later recalled, "In an area of deep economic divisions, for the first time the children of landowners and professionals shared classrooms with peasants; they drank beer together, they got to know each other. This drove a revolutionary fervor in Ayacucho."[17]

Through the 1960s and 1970s, the university helped turn the region into a political hothouse. After Guzmán joined the university staff, he made an intellectual impact. Schooling first-year students in Marxist materialism, he quickly acquired a committed band of disciples, who nicknamed their teacher "Shampoo." "He washed your brains," remembered one student; "he cleaned your thoughts when confused; he clarified problems, he had an answer for everything." "He cultivated uncertainty and mystery around him," recalled another. "For his supporters, whatever he said was the last word on any subject. He made them so optimistic, so self-confident. That self-confidence is what I remember most about a friend who was later killed in the jungle by the army." Intolerant of dissent, Guzmán was "a fanatic who had the power to fanaticize others."[18]

Young Peruvians – especially first-generation, provincial university students – seemed vulnerable to stridently confident interpretations of the world in the 1960s and 1970s. Uneasy in their new modern, urban surroundings, these undergraduates sought clear answers, and found them in an abundance of textbooks – originally published in Stalinist Russia and circulating widely in Peruvian universities – that taught them the Marxist–Leninist worldview. They learned about the authoritarian transformation of society through revolution and the wisdom of the single-party system. These books, recalled one lecturer, became "a sort of shortcut toward modernity ... the key for the substantial and positive transformation of the world." "Can you imagine what that means to a twenty-five-year-old kid?" asked one anthropology graduate looking back at that time. "It was to learn to handle a secret language, an abracadabra that let me open all the sesames." China's hispanophone propaganda apparatus also reached a receptive audience. Beijing's Foreign Languages Press scattered across Peru the *Works of Mao* and color propaganda magazines, their glazed pages advertising "a peasant-centred version of revolution for semifeudal countries."[19] Radio Peking broadcast the wonders of Mao's revolution not only in Spanish, but also in two indigenous languages, Quechua and Aymara.[20]

What distinguished Guzmán from the average cultish professor, and what gave him his uncompromising ideology and method, was his encounter with Maoist theory in the early 1960s. He began with Mao the can-do insurrectionist – "A Single Spark Can Start a Prairie Fire" was one of the first pieces he read – but it was the arid doctrinal arguments of the Sino-Soviet split that fully won him over. From earlier reading of Stalin, Guzmán had already learnt to appreciate "the transforming capacity of war."[21] But it was the CCP's militant polemics against Soviet "peaceful coexistence" that convinced Guzmán of the global need for revolutionary violence: "The seizure of power by armed force," he underlined, "the settlement of the issue by war, is the central task and the highest form of revolution."[22] Guzmán shared with his fellow Latin American revolutionary Che Guevara a worship of armed struggle; but unlike Che – whom he dismissed as a "chorus girl"[23] – he also venerated (in increasingly abstract terms) "the masses" and the prospect of grassroots organizational work.[24] In 1964, when the Peruvian Communist Party (PCP) split into pro-Soviet and pro-Chinese camps, Guzmán went with the latter, which renamed itself PCP–Bandera Roja (Red Flag).

In 1965, Guzmán traveled to China to see the "seat of Chairman Mao ... the center of world proletarian revolution" for himself. In comparison with some foreign revolutionaries, Guzmán's reception was only three-star. There was no meeting with Mao, only opportunities to glimpse him from afar at a reception or rally. Still, the impact was huge. Almost fifty years later, writing from the most secure cell in the most secure prison in Peru, Guzmán remembered the visit in almost romantic language: "it was one of the most transcendental and unforgettable experiences of my life."[25] Amid the doctrinaire prose of Guzmán's autobiography, his account of China stands out for its emotional intoxication:

> factories, people's communes, barracks, shopping centres, universities, schools, hospitals and clinics, art studios and shows; squares and streets, boiling tumults of energy overflowing with optimism ... politics in command ... building

the new society, socialism, laying the foundations for future communism ... Beijing, historic and legendary Tiananmen Square: the monumental gate of heavy, dark red and Chairman Mao's imposing portrait, the Museum of the Revolution, the Great Hall of the People ... the Great Helmsman's own calligraphy in golden letters ... the immense sea of masses, Marx, Engels, Lenin, Stalin and President Mao guiding the fight; forests of red flags with hammers and sickles, banners, slogans; workers, peasants, soldiers, women, young people, the Chinese people, a million-strong rally roaring "Down with Yankee imperialism!" ... the East is Red, songs and dances reviving the long, massive struggle of the revolution ... Thirty years have passed, what can I say: only that I owe so much ... to President Mao Zedong and to Maoism ... I can never repay this debt. It served me in what I came to do later.[26]

China taught him "masterful lessons ... in the highest school of Marxism the world has ever seen": in underground Party work and the intimate relationship between politics and violence. "When we were handling delicate chemicals they urged us to always keep our ideology first and foremost, because that would enable us to do anything." He graduated from an explosives course with a sense of superhuman power: "they told us that anything can explode ... we picked up a pen and it blew up, and when we took a seat it blew up, too ... anything could be blown up if you figured out how to do it ... That school contributed greatly to my ... appreciation for Chairman Mao Tse-tung."[27]

The debt was more than ideological. Until 1967, Mao's CCP funneled money and perhaps weapons to Bandera Roja for training in different parts of Peru. The Chinese Communists funded a ragtag of Latin American leftists – sometimes with extraordinary casualness. A Chinese diplomat standing outside the Peruvian embassy once accosted a member of another militant left-wing group – an Indian from north Peru – when he was passing by the embassy. Mistaking him for a Peruvian-Chinese, the diplomat immediately offered to support his cause, training dozens of militants for months at a time; the group launched a guerrilla insurgency against the state in 1965.[28]

Guzmán paid a second visit to China in 1967 (he may have also returned in 1975, in which case he could have encountered Pol Pot – the Peruvian later dismissed the Cambodian as a "pseudo-Marxist"). Although Guzmán was not successful in his primary mission – to persuade the Chinese to reinstate their financial aid to Bandera Roja, which had been recently cut off – he would return speaking ever more fluent Maoism: "whoever has not carried out investigation does not have the right to speak"; "he who does not fear being torn into pieces can pull the emperor from his horse"; "power comes from the barrel of a gun"; "the correctness or incorrectness of the political line decides all." He emphasized the need for the "two-line struggle" against revisionism within the revolution, and the status of Latin America as a "zone of revolutionary storm."[29] Above all, he had experienced the Cultural Revolution as "the greatest mass movement in history ... the highest summit of the world proletarian revolution ... crushing the capitalist roaders in the Party." Schooled by China, his worldview became increasingly Manichean: on the one side were the "brave masses"; on the other were "sinister imperialists" and "sewer rat revisionists."[30] He witnessed large-scale purges of erroneous books and people; he began to idolize Mao as "the third stage" of Marxism. In China, he further concluded, "the main form of struggle is war; the main form of organization, the army ... Without a people's army, the people have nothing ... All communists have to understand the truth that power comes out of the barrel of a gun."[31]

In 1970, Guzmán founded his own Communist faction – the Shining Path – on the Maoist model of the Party and spent the next decade planning and preparing for a Maoist armed struggle, around the nucleus of his university and Ayacucho. (The terms *terroristas* and *universitarios* would later be used inter-changeably to refer to Shining Path militants.)[32] A neglectful, even absent, state presence in the rural areas of the region made it possible. Pro-Shining Path professors turned their undergraduate teaching groups into Maoist think tanks, guiding students to research theses about the socio-political power structures of rural communities in the area, which always seemed to end with Maoist analyses of "rural bourgeoisie, rich peasants, middle-income and poor peasants."[33] The easy, militant solutions to Peruvian ills preached by Guzmán appealed to young provincials frustrated by the lack of career opportunities for the newly educated. While the reopening of the university had widened access to higher education, it had not been accompanied by an expansion of graduate employment opportunities. Young provincials would typically undergo great financial hardship and intellectual effort to receive a degree, then discover on graduation that teaching back in the villages they had worked so hard to escape was the best professional option open to them. Guzmán's disciples scattered in a proselytizing network across the sierra, using their remote communities as springboards for the revolution. "They were young, thin, serious, introverted," observed Gustavo Gorriti, a remarkable Peruvian journalist who tailed the Shining Path story between the 1980s and the 1990s, "in general from poor families ... obedient children and siblings, neat, quiet, hard-working ... To see them wrapped in an aura of explosions and inexplicable ferocity was only the beginning of a much bigger surprise for many families."[34]

~

At two in the morning on May 17, 1980, five hooded men – four students and their leader, a teacher – broke into the voter registration office in Chuschi (a market town some 100 kilometers from Ayacucho), bound the registrar, then burnt the local tools of democracy: the voter registry and ballot boxes. This was the first salvo in the Shining Path's insurgency, the Beginning of the Armed Struggle (BAS; Iniciacion de la Lucha Armada, ILA).[35]

In the preceding three months, Guzmán had prepared for military struggle through an intensive series of meetings to establish the correct political line within an iron framework of quotations by Mao, and to "rectify" (purge) those who opposed him. Admittedly, Mao was not the sole influence on Guzmán's bookishly violent revolution. An obsessive reader for at least four decades, he read passages to his disciples from *Julius Caesar* and *Macbeth*, to teach the finer points of conspiracy and treason. He distributed excerpts from Washington Irving's *The Life of Mahomet*, probably for its account of the power of ideology (it likened Muslims to "the tempests which sweep the earth and sea, wrecking tall ships and rending lofty towers") and from Aeschylus' *Prometheus Bound*, as an instructive "example of the capacity of unyielding rebellion." There were military works also: Stalin's scorched-earth speech to the Soviet people in the days following the Nazi invasion in 1941 – a premonition of what Shining Path, and the brutal state response, would do to Peru. Guzmán would directly import this uncompromising model of warfare – in which any human cost was justified in the struggle against the Peruvian state. But the strategy came from Mao: revolutionary voluntarism (through sheer force of will, the masses under the leadership of a disciplined Maoist party could defeat the state); and protracted warfare, surrounding the cities from the countryside.[36]

On December 26, 1980 – what would have been Mao's eighty-seventh birthday – residents of Lima woke to discover dead dogs hanging from lampposts, their heads pushed through posters emblazoned, in capitals, with "Deng Xiaoping." The ritualistic killing of strays to denounce Deng Xiaoping – the man who broke with many of Mao's keynote Cultural Revolution policies – was the symbolic declaration of Maoist war. The grisly dead-dog stunt on Mao's birthday was a passionate declaration of loyalty to Mao. To Mao's global disciples, of whom Guzmán was one of the most fervent, Deng was a traitor – responsible for a palace coup against the Cultural Revolution and, after Mao's death, the architect of China's capitalist revival. To label him a dog was a direct reference back to invective deployed by Mao himself, who denounced his enemies as "running dogs" (of capitalism, imperialism, feudalism, and so on).

Two days earlier, on Christmas Eve 1980, the first human blood was shed by Shining Path: a sixty-year-old farmer and his nineteen-year-old hired help were assassinated by a guerrilla squad at their ranch. Guerrilla terror – more than propaganda or organizational work – was the cornerstone of Shining Path strategy. It intensified the glorification of violence: the killing swiftly became industrial, based on the principle of a "quota" needing to die before the revolutionary utopia could be created. Guzmán claimed that Mao had inspired this call for bloodshed: "Marx, Lenin, and principally Mao Zedong have armed us. They have taught us about the quota and what it means to annihilate in order to preserve."[37]

The aim – to provoke the state into indiscriminate retaliation – was crude but, as it turned out, brutally effective. The more excessive the state response, the more discredited Peru's democracy, and the more disillusioned the populace, would become. Guzmán was prepared to sustain horrendous losses. He told his cadres frankly that they would have to "cross the river of blood": "many party militants would die ... and they would die in the worst possible ways. Their families would be destroyed ... there was very little in Peru's history that prepared it to confront the level of violence that would eventually be unleashed. Dozens, hundreds of thousands of dead."[38] The revolution envisioned by Shining Path resembled ever more closely a death compact. Shining Path melded Mao's optimistic "a single spark can light a prairie fire" with a Christian metaphor of purification through baptism (in rivers of blood).[39]

A good student of Mao, Guzmán was devoted to the practicalities of guerrilla warfare and to the strict discipline set down in the PLA's "Three Rules" and "Eight Points of Attention."[40] "His undoubtedly superior schematic intellect," analyzes Gorriti, who followed Guzmán's thinking through the 1980s, "defined the intermediate objectives along the way and then marked out a detailed route to each one – segment by segment, step by step. In the history of guerrilla rebellions, in few if any did sheer resolve, backed by exhaustive planning, play such a preponderant role."[41] Shining Path meticulously constructed its military machine. At the bottom were local guerrillas and party committees who could provide information and community control. Above this operated a regional force, roaming across several provinces. The best from this middle force formed a national insurgent army, capable of set-piece military operations.[42] The organization armed its militants through extensive raids on mines: case after case of dynamite, kilometers of fuses, myriads of blasting caps. The whole process was unspectacular: simply slow, persistent, and incessant. The ruthlessness of guerrilla operations was matched by indiscriminate state brutality. In 1982, the Peruvian government placed Ayacucho in a state of emergency, and authorized the army to unleash scorched-earth tactics to eliminate the insurgency.[43] The minister of defense, Luis Cisneros Vizquerra, lifted his strategy from Argentina's Dirty War. "If we kill a hundred people and there is one subversive among them, then it will have been worthwhile."[44]

~

1992 was, in the words of Carlos Degregori, a former university colleague of Guzmán's who later became one of Peru's most informed senderologists, "the worst year in the contemporary

history of Peru." The country was a cataclysmic state. Half the
country's population and a third of its territory were under army
control. Tens of thousands had already lost their lives and, at the
start of the decade, Shining Path had declared that "the triumph of
the revolution would cost a million deaths." Lima was the Beirut of
Latin America, shaken by car bombs, blinded by blackouts, petrified
by the public assassinations of community leaders.[45]

Shining Path's strategy remained staunchly Maoist. The
underground Guzmán took to emphasizing Mao's three-stage military plan for state capture from the 1940s: after strategic defense, the
insurgency had moved onto "strategic equilibrium." This second
stage preceded imminent victory: strategic offense. (This three-point
plan would become holy writ to the Nepali Maoists in their own civil
war after 1996.) By closing in on Lima, Guzmán was enacting Mao's
injunction to "surround the cities from the countryside," although
by this point rural militias had mainly chased senderistas out of their
original Ayacucho heartland. On February 15, 1992, after finishing
their plates of barbecued chicken at a community fund-raiser, a
death-squad of senderistas stood up and riddled the local mayor,
Maria Elena Moyano – a critic of Shining Path terror and architect
of ninety-two soup kitchens in her constituency – with bullets, then
dropped lit dynamite into her lap, all in front of her sons. On the
evening of July 16, a Datsun – cherry-red, no number plate – cruised
down a residential side street around the corner from one of the
largest banks in Peru's well-heeled financial district. Its driver and
passengers bailed out of the moving car as it drifted toward an
apartment block, before fleeing the scene in a pre-parked Toyota.
Shortly thereafter, the explosives inside the car generated a blast
300 meters in diameter. The car bomb claimed twenty-five lives
and wounded 155, left some 300 families homeless, and caused
millions of dollars' worth of damage. Andean villagers had been
dying for years; the Tarata bombing was partly so shocking to
Limeños because, for the first time, the carnage took place in a
wealthy white neighborhood.

Guzmán's clandestinity since 1976 made the insurgency all
the more frighteningly elusive. He was "everywhere and nowhere."
At the time, recalled one Limeño policeman, "people thought
Guzmán was like the rain: you can't see where it comes from. He
was like the serpent that slithers by unseen. The campesinos said,

'Ah, he must be a god.'"[46] The government looked to be on the run. One of the first acts of Alberto Fujimori – surprise winner of the 1990 presidential contest against Mario Vargas Llosa, the elite establishment candidate – was to summon the army commanders and tell them that Shining Path was on the point of taking Lima in a major offensive.

But in 1990, after almost a decade of grotesque mishandling, parts of the Peruvian government started approaching the insurgency more methodically. The government established a Special Intelligence Group (GEIN), a counterterrorism unit within the police that actually archived and analyzed intelligence rather than killing, raping, and burning. Under the directorship of a meticulous, old-fashioned policeman called Benedicto Jimenez, agents tailed likely senderistas; they went undercover as ice cream vendors; they (finally) read Mao. GEIN quickly came to one conclusion: Guzmán had to be in Lima. Jimenez and his team eventually homed in on a yellowish, box-like house in Surquillo, a lower-middle-class part of Lima. (It later transpired that Guzmán favored middle-class areas, within a stone's throw of army headquarters, for his refuges.) The house was rented by a talented, twenty-eight-year-old ballet dancer called Maritza Garrido Lecca, from a comfortable, urbane *Limeño* family with easy links to the Peruvian cultural aristocracy – her musician uncle was on chatting terms with the novelist Mario Vargas Llosa. The police had begun to investigate Maritza after arresting her aunt, a former nun-turned-Shining Path finance officer called Nelly Evans, in January 1991. Four clues suggested this was the place: it was far too big for two people alone; Garrido Lecca was in the habit of buying far more bread, meat, and liquor than she and her partner could need; and empty packets of medicine for treating psoriasis(Guzmán's long-term skin affliction) and stubs of Winston cigarettes (Guzmán's favorite brand) were turning up in the trash. The final giveaway was Maritza's purchasing of extra-large men's underpants – her husband was slim.

On September 12, 1992, the police stormed the house. The raiding party found Guzmán – bearded, rotund, wearing thick glasses – and his consort and second-in-command Elena Iparraguirre in a party planning meeting. When one of the officers rushed at Guzmán, Iparraguirre struck the policeman; Guzmán did not stir from his seat but said forcefully, "Calm yourselves. Who are you?" Both leaders surrendered without a shot being fired. When Guzmán was searched, police found on him a Mao button which he claimed, probably falsely, had been personally given to him by the Chairman in China.[47]

~

With Guzmán's capture, the decapitated Shining Path collapsed like a paper tiger. By the end of 1992, nineteen out of the Central Committee's twenty-two members were in jail; Guzmán had been sentenced to life imprisonment. The following year, Guzmán turned his back on armed struggle and told his remaining disciples to negotiate peacefully with the state. Amazed at their god of war's volte-face, his followers accused the state of torture and of brainwashing, until a visibly well Guzmán broadcast the message a second, and then a third, time on national television.

But as Mao's Party and its Cultural Revolution lived on outside its country of birth, so did Abimael Guzmán's ideas live outside Peru: in Nepal, where the expansive zeal of the Cultural Revolution and its aftershocks also produced a fervent Maoist movement. In 1984, the world's remnant Maoist parties, which had straggled on past the fractures of the 1970s and China's own repudiation of the Cultural Revolution, came together in the Revolutionary Internationalist Movement (RIM): Nepali, Turkish, Bangladeshi, Haitian parties, in addition to Shining Path from Peru, and the Nottingham and Stockport Communist Groups from the UK. The organizational drive came from the Revolutionary Communist Party of the USA, under the leadership of a US Maoist called Bob Avakian. Although unimportant within American politics, Avakian and the members of RIM had an evangelical passion for Maoism, going back to the utopian imaginings of the 1960s. "The rise of Deng Xiaoping," remembered Mohan Bikram Singh, a veteran Nepali Maoist and founding member of RIM's first congress, "made communists all over the world anxious. We in RIM believed that Mao needed saving."[48]

From its beginnings in 1984, RIM engaged in heartfelt but turgid debates about revolutionary ideology; light years from the consumerist visions of Reaganite and Thatcherite Anglo-America. Within the US, Avakian and his nucleus of devoted disciples could easily be dismissed as marginal eccentrics. But for ambitious would-be revolutionaries in Nepal – harboring an intense, textual relationship with Maoist ideology since the CCP's propaganda barrage of the 1960s – this organization encouraged them toward civil war; it represented international validation for armed revolution. RIM, Mohan Bikram Singh remembered, proclaimed that "it's the right moment to start armed revolution in Nepal. Armed struggle will then create its own conditions."[49] To this organization, from the perspective of the 1980s, the Shining Path was a glowing example to be emulated. Singh was skeptical and later broke with RIM, but his more impatient subordinates were persuaded – including Mohan Baidya, one of Singh's disciples. In 1986, Baidya split with Singh's party to form his own Maoist faction of the Communist Party of Nepal (CPN). In 1991, while Nepal began a new experiment with multiparty democracy, this faction (calling itself Unity Centre) resolved to launch a "people's war to bring about a new democratic revolution in Nepal." In 1994, they went underground, to prepare for war; in 1995, the CPN (Maoist) was born; the following year, it openly declared war on the Nepali state.[50] "RIM gave us no material support," Baidya later testified. "Its support was theoretical."[51] In Nepal, that was enough – the single spark to light a prairie fire – and the Shining Path was an example that helped inspire and guide Nepali Maoists. Long after Guzmán was captured in 1992, his political and intellectual influence loomed over the Nepali insurgency. In 1996 visitors to Thawang, the village that became the center of the civil war, were surprised to find murals demanding "Free Gonzalo" (Guzmán's *nom de guerre*); Baburam Bhattarai, the Nepali Maoists' ideologue, posed in front of a picture of the imprisoned Guzmán and commissioned a translation of Gonzalo Thought into Nepali in the year 2000. The phraseology of the Shining Path had a clear impact on the Nepali Maoists' own bespoke ideology, "Prachanda Path."

Politically, the Nepali Maoist war had an even greater instrumental effect than its Peruvian predecessor. The armed rebellion was the principal reason for the collapse of the centuries-old monarchy and the establishment of a federal republic in Nepal after 2006. Between 2006 and 2016, two leaders of the CPN (Maoist) served between them three terms as prime minister of Nepal and many other senior party figures held government positions. Although the CPN (Maoist) did not realize its original ambition –

state capture resulting in unchallenged control of the country, as achieved by the Chinese Communist Party – Nepal is now the only country in the world where you can encounter, forty years after the death of Mao, self-avowed Maoists in power.

~

After the death of Mao in 1976, the CCP mothballed the keynote policies of Mao's last campaign, the Cultural Revolution, and focused instead on domestic economic reconstruction. But the Party's global militancy in Mao's late years shaped landscapes of conflict around the world. Radical Chinese politics attracted millions of renegades, rebels, and party builders who influenced the struggles for decolonization and development in Africa, ideological and nationalist conflict in Vietnam and Cambodia, the shocks and after-shocks of 1968 in Western Europe and the US. And Mao's own demise galvanized long-lasting guerrilla wars in Peru and Nepal, which transformed the destinies of those two states.

Chapter 7 – 1980s

A genuinely new China seemed to be possible in the 1980s. That was the dominant assessment of those who came of age, including the authors of this volume, in the period between 1978 and 1989, framed by the beginning of Deng Xiaoping's reforms and the Tiananmen Massacre. Change swept through the country, beginning in the countryside, where the people's communes were disbanded and farmers once again were allowed to work and think for themselves. Then small individual household enterprises began to sprout up, including in the cities, providing minor services that hugely facilitated daily life, such as tailoring, roadside bike repairs, and photocopying, followed by larger enterprises, especially in textile manufacturing and food production. As the market economy grew, urban households acquired refrigerators, bicycles, televisions, washing machines, and video players. People shed their Mao garb and fashion became fashionable again. The vitality, optimism, and energy they encountered impressed any first-time visitor to China.

This was the decade in which the generation of 1978 and 1979 began to make its way into the world. After being closed a decade earlier during the Cultural Revolution, China's still very few universities once more selected students on the basis of academic potential. In 1978 and 1979, special examinations were held for all youths denied the opportunity to attend university by the Cultural Revolution. Those who were admitted in these two years were the brightest of the bright. They had deep experience in the capacity of people to be cruel and, having spent years in the countryside as sent-down youths, they knew the countryside as well. They wanted change and were willing to work hard to get it. This generation would form the real core leadership of the transformation of China over the next four decades.

That nothing was going to be straightforward was also clear. Each wave of reform was met by a period of retrenchment. Banditry, theft, and even kidnapping were growing problems, met by the party-state with public executions in large sports stadiums. If there was enormous dynamism, there also was deep social tension and mistrust, unsurprisingly so because those who had fought each other during the Cultural Revolution continued to have to work together in their still ubiquitous 'work units' under the State Plan – there had been no job market since the 1950s; jobs were assigned by the state and once in a work unit one rarely was moved.

Deng Xiaoping attempted to turn the Communist Party from a tool for revolution, as Lenin had designed it and as Mao had used it, into a system of rule, including by regularizing Party meetings and processes, devolving power to local authorities, and institutionalizing succession of the leadership. Zhao Ziyang was a loyal Party member who knew how to survive within the system and had a special aptitude for getting the countryside back to work. Deng picked him as his successor after sacrificing an earlier protagonist, Hu Yaobang, to a conservative reaction in 1986. Zhao was up against Party conservatives who wanted to maintain much of Mao's strict rule, but Zhao pursued a more humane, inclusive, and participatory form of socialism. Three years later, the same fate befell Zhao Ziyang, demonstrating that Deng's efforts in transforming the Party remained a work in progress.

7 THE 1980s
Zhao Ziyang and the Voices of Reform
KLAUS MÜHLHAHN

On April 15, 1989, the popular Chinese leader Hu Yaobang (1915–1989) died of a heart attack in Beijing. Two years earlier, Hu had been dismissed from his job as General Secretary of the Chinese Communist Party for being too lenient on intellectuals and too tolerant of their demands for a more liberal policy. Within a few days, thousands of students from Beijing campuses spontaneously gathered in Tiananmen Square, in central Beijing, to demand that the Party give him a proper burial. By expressing their approval of Hu and his policies, the students voiced their disappointment with censorship, the limits on freedom, and the absence of political reform, but also with the corruption, nepotism, and inequality that had spread during the years of "reform and opening" under the country's senior leader, Deng Xiaoping (1904–1997). They wanted an official statement affirming Hu Yaobang's views on democracy and freedom, and an admission that the repressive campaigns against spiritual pollution and bourgeois liberalization in the mid-1980s had been wrong. Their demands also included privately run newspapers, an end to press censorship, and the right to public demonstrations, as well as more objective coverage of the student movement in official media. Over the next seven weeks, while Party leaders prevaricated and gave out mixed signals, the number of demonstrators grew to as many as a million. They included citizens from many walks of life. Demonstrations spread to hundreds of other cities around the country. When the students occupying the square declared a hunger strike and their demands grew more radical, Deng Xiaoping decided to impose martial law, to take effect on

May 20. The death of Hu Yaobang thus had triggered what was without a doubt the biggest crisis since the end of the Cultural Revolution and perhaps the most severe challenge to Party rule since 1949.[1]

The demonstrators dug in and Deng ordered the use of force to commence in the early hours of June 4. On the evening of that night, Hu's successor as General Secretary of the CCP, Zhao Ziyang (1919–2005), visited the students at Tiananmen Square. In tears he addressed the student protesters with a loudspeaker in his hand, pleading them to leave the square in a desperate attempt to avoid violence and bloodshed. He uttered the phrase, "We are already old, we don't matter anymore," which became a popular quotation. A few hours later, as tanks rolled into Tiananmen Square and troops killed hundreds, perhaps thousands, of unarmed demonstrators (the precise death toll is still unknown), Zhao resigned from office. He became the biggest scapegoat of the political turmoil that followed the bloody suppression of the Tiananmen protests. The violence provoked widespread revulsion throughout Chinese society and led to international condemnation, as the Western democracies imposed economic sanctions on China. Zhao Ziyang stayed under house arrest until his death in 2005. His political demise was followed by a conservative backlash that lasts until the present. Many supporters of both Hu and Zhao were purged, demoted, or forced to write self-criticisms.

That two General Secretaries were sacked within two years is in itself not really noteworthy in the long history of often violent and unforgiving fights for power, authority, and money-making opportunities within the CCP. While, since 1949, China has been a one-party state in which the CCP monopolized power, the Party rarely unanimously shared the same ideological positions, socioeconomic backgrounds, or policy preferences. Hence there was a constant struggle at the top that was carried out directly or through proxies and policy debates over the economy, political reform, and corruption. Historians and political scientists have often tried to explain these complicated arcane contests by assuming the existence of factions or coalitions based on ideological, institutional, personal, or regional ties.[2] For instance, there were coalitions that represented different socioeconomic and geographical constituencies. Members of the elitist coalition, a socioeconomic group, for example, are considered "princelings," leaders who come from families of veteran revolutionaries or of high-ranking officials. These princelings often lived and rose to power in the economically well-developed coastal regions. An example of a more regional coalition is the Shanghai group in the post-Mao period, comprising officials who rose to prominence in connection to the Shanghai municipal administration under Jiang Zemin (1926–), who would succeed Zhao as General Secretary of the Communist Party of China. Most members of the populist coalition, by contrast, come from less well-to-do backgrounds. They also tend to have spent most of their careers in the rural inland provinces. Yet empirical studies have also shown that those factions or coalitions are rather fluid and unstable, and have no clear-cut membership and orientation. Both General Secretaries sympathized with more liberal policies, but whether they were part of a faction for (political) reform within the Party is doubtful. But that poses the questions of who they were, where they came from, and why they, as powerful, privileged, high-ranking officials at the top, ended up supporting calls for political reform that could potentially undermine CCP rule.[3] This scene focuses on Zhao Ziyang: his rise through the echelons of the party-state in the 1950s, and after 1978 his surprising metamorphosis from a trusted loyal Party official into an unflinching reformer bent on changing the political arc of the PRC. The story of Zhao Ziyang will take us on a journey through the ups and downs of the world of official China, revealing the conflicting views within the Party about the reform of the socialist system in the 1980s.

The Making of a Party Secretary

Zhao Ziyang's political career spanned several decades.[4] Before 1978, Zhao was a loyal Party cadre, who avoided offending senior leaders or veering from the official policy line. He rose quickly through the ranks, building a reputation for understanding agricultural policy and having a grasp of the management of rural communities. Nothing in this story foreshadows his later commitments to reforming the socialist system.

Born in October 1919 in Hua County, Henan Province, to the family of a relatively wealthy farmer, Zhao Ziyang joined the CCP at a young age, entering the Communist Youth League in

March 1932 as a middle-school student and ascending to full Party membership six years later in 1938. During the Japanese invasion, Zhao's home county was governed by the Jin–Ji–Lu–Yu (Shanxi–Hebei–Shandong–Henan) Border Region. Expansion into southern Hebei and eastward into Shandong eventually resulted in its formal establishment as a border region in July 1941. Zhao first served as Party secretary in his native county. Later he became director of the CCP Work Committee (dealing with, among other things, land reform) and subsequently of the CCP Propaganda Department. Zhao remained in the area until the establishment of the PRC in 1949, working for the Party in various non-military positions.

At the end of 1950, Zhao Ziyang was dispatched suddenly to the southern province of Guangdong, where he was to stay for more than twenty years. His arrival coincided with the second phase of the land reform campaign that was launched in June 1950, on the eve of the Korean War.[5] Land reform was unavoidably disruptive. Work teams sent to the countryside fanned resentment and turned local conflicts into class struggle. So-called landlords were humiliated, beaten, arrested, or killed. Local cadres, however, often objected to the violence and destruction that wreaked havoc on local communities. The second phase of the campaign was intended to overcome local defiance and to speed up land reform nationwide.

Zhao Ziyang arrived in Guangdong as part of a large contingent of cadres and officials from the north to break that resistance. While the main aim was to confiscate the landholdings of the landlords and to distribute them among the poorer peasants, the work teams were also urged to safeguard the economically important farms of small and middle-sized landowners and protect the rural economy.

Zhao worked resolutely to carry out central policies and undo local obstruction. He took part in the relentless purge and punishment of local Party cadres when they opposed central policies. In a speech to an enlarged cadre meeting in August 1951, he pinned heavy blame on local cadres for the problems. Due to his steadfast loyal performance, he slowly climbed up the ladder of the Party hierarchy.

In 1958 political debates in China heated up and Zhao Ziyang found it more difficult to follow the Party line. During the initial stages of the Great Leap Forward (1958–1960) that aimed to speed up China's economic development by mobilizing society, Zhao was an early and enthusiastic supporter of Mao Zedong's policy to mobilize China's population to make major and sudden progress in industrialization and modernization. In a *People's Daily* article of May 1958, he asserted his belief in the power of mass mobilization to raise output and touted Guangdong as an example for mobilization and overfulfilling production quotas.[6] However, he also stressed technical aspects such as mechanization for achieving the goals of the Great Leap Forward and insisted on expertise as necessary for China's aspired transformation. With this he rejected outright Mao Zedong's dictum that it would be better to be "red" (i.e., to have a correct political worldview) than to be expert.

A year later, in 1959, it turned out that the forecasts had been far too optimistic and that China, instead of catching up with Great Britain, would descend into a huge food crisis. Almost everything, including foodstuffs, consumer goods, and commodities, was scarce. Convinced that reported fictitious production figures were to be trusted, and that the shortages were only caused by stockpiling, Zhao Ziyang launched several brutal "anti-hoarding campaigns" in Guangdong, which resulted in ruthless purges, accusations, and criticism of local cadres. When it became obvious that the campaigns were not able to discover many stored supplies in the poverty-stricken villages, where in fact most peasants were starving, Zhao Ziyang started to cautiously distance himself from the Great Leap policy. In a speech to the provincial People's Congress in fall of 1959, he stated, "Some comrades are beginning to be affected by blind optimism and self-complacency ... It is necessary to establish the work style of seeking truth from facts and paying close attention to scientific analysis."[7]

At the Lushan Conference in July 1959, when the leading cadres gathered to discuss the Great Leap policy, Zhao Ziyang appears to have initially sympathized with Defense Minister Peng Dehuai in his criticism of Mao Zedong and the Great Leap Forward. In Guangdong, the provincial government took steps to reverse the damages of the Great Leap Forward by expanding individual peasant ownership of land and allowing emigration to Hong Kong.

After Mao Zedong's comeback in the early 1960s and his call for class struggle and attacking "rightists," Zhao Ziyang still avoided opposing the Great Helmsman and quickly fell in line. In a

People's Daily article of April 4, 1964, Zhao praised Mao's thought as a "great intellectual weapon" and as "glorious." In the course of 1963 and 1964 he gave several similar speeches in support of Mao Zedong's proposed Cultural Revolution.[8] He explicitly threw himself behind Mao's past policies and emphasized the need for heightened class struggle and for the intensive study of Mao Zedong Thought. In fact, right up until his fall from power during the Cultural Revolution, Zhao Ziyang was among the most enthusiastic provincial leaders supporting the Red Guard movement. The Red Guards were mostly young students and workers who followed Mao's call to carry out a Cultural Revolution and oppose revisionism within the Party. However, when, with the support of Tao Zhu, Zhao tried to contain the excesses of the rebelling Red Guards in Guangzhou, the Cultural Revolution Small Group acted swiftly. Tao Zhu, who had become a member of the Politburo Standing Committee at the Eleventh Plenum in August 1966 at the outset of the Cultural Revolution, was attacked in January 1967, and labeled "the proxy leader of Liu-and-Deng-roaders" (referring to followers of Deng Xiapong and Liu Shaoqi) and a "Khrushchev-style ambitionist." He was placed under house arrest in early 1967.

Zhao Ziyang fell shortly after him in October of the same year. He was struggled against in a public criticism session and sent to a remote May 7th Cadre School.[9] The name of these "schools" came from the "May 7th Directive" of 1966, in which Mao called the army a "big school" where soldiers engaged in labor and studied politics. Applied to state and Party cadres, this directive was the basis for the relocation of hundreds of thousands of officials to the countryside, where they should work and live among the masses, mostly in rural communes, while also engaging in political study and self-criticism. In 1970, we find Zhao working as a fitter at Xiangzhong Mechanics Factory in Lianyuan County, Hunan Province.

In April 1971, however, Zhao Ziyang appeared to have been rehabilitated by none other than Zhou Enlai (1898–1976), the second-most-powerful man in China. He was given various assignments in the Inner Mongolia Autonomous Region, where he supervised livestock production and agriculture. In March 1972 he was transferred back to Guangdong. Overall, Zhao Ziyang's exile from office was short; he and his family seem to have survived the Cultural Revolution better than many other leaders.

The Guangdong Red Guards had leveled many charges against Zhao, reaching from "taking the capitalist road" to "promoting the black wind of economism."[10] In his own self-criticism, Zhao Ziyang labeled himself a "pragmatist, who tried to act wisely by thinking out some petty measures and ideas."[11] A CIA assessment of 1982 came to a surprisingly similar conclusion.[12] Zhao was described as "an expert administrator who is pragmatic rather than ideological, conveys an image of public service, and assiduously respects the principle of collective leadership." Yet he is also seen as "a study in contrasts ... He is one of the reformers and an architect of their policies, yet he is on good terms with the party conservatives." Zhao Ziyang's often opportunistic behavior is striking. He wholeheartedly supported damaging political campaigns, although he tried to quietly ameliorate their impact and modify them to limit the harm to local communities.

During his early years before his fall in the Cultural Revolution, Zhao Ziyang had mastered the intricate machinations of the arcane political system in the PRC. He rose fast through the ranks mainly based on his achievements and capabilities as a Party administrator and expert on agricultural development. But he also understood how to avoid making enemies, and how to acquire powerful and influential allies and mentors in the Party, making it possible for him to become known to national leaders, including Mao Zedong and Zhou Enlai. There is no evidence that he ever belonged to a coalition or faction. Nor is there any indication that he was even interested in issues such as political reform. That was about to change, however, when he re-entered national politics in the early 1970s and found himself in the throes of the profound political upheavals in the post-Mao period.

Calls for Democracy in Guangzhou in the Final Year of the Cultural Revolution

Back in Guangdong, Zhao Ziyang reassumed his work on the provincial level. Just rehabilitated and back in power, he continued to unwaveringly support all major political campaigns. But then an incident happened that forced Zhao to make a decision and suddenly a new side of Zhao Ziyang as a guardian of public dissent revealed itself.

At the beginning of the 1970s and especially after the failed *coup d'état* by Mao's chosen successor, Lin Biao, in September 1971 when Lin planned to oust Mao but then had to flee China when his plan was discovered, China was exhausted and disillusioned by the political struggles during and after the Cultural Revolution and rejected further political campaigns. The "Criticize Lin Biao and Confucius" campaign and other political movements were hugely unpopular. This was unmistakably signaled by the appearance of a big-character poster on Beijing Road in Guangzhou in November 1974. Big-character posters were handwritten posters that were mounted on walls to express protest against, or support for, Party policies. The poster had a provocative title: "On Socialist Democracy and the Legal System." "Li Yizhe" – its "author" – was a composite pen name of young Guangzhou residents, former Red Guards of the first hour who had belonged to the so-called rebel faction. The content of the poster was explosive as it questioned the validity of the entire Cultural Revolution. By analyzing the "Lin Biao setup" they critiqued the policies of Mao's wife Jiang Qing and others, calling them a manifestation of "socialist–fascism in our country." They also stated, "The socialist system is not yet perfect and much is to be desired. Therefore, it is very important for China and the Chinese people to cope with the inefficiencies in democracy and the legal system of the country." All this climaxed in the central demand of the poster: "People are not fools! ... They demand democracy, demand socialist legality, and revolutionary and personal rights that protect the popular masses."[13]

This was a forceful call for political participation and protection against the frequent arbitrary arrests made in the course of the countless political campaigns. This poster could only appear because, in January 1974, Zhao Ziyang had shielded the authors of the poster, who had made similar pleas in a written petition to Mao Zedong and the Fourth National People's Congress. Zhao even had the petition printed and made available for internal circulation. He also permitted the publication of another article by the Li Yizhe authors as a poster in April 1974.[14] Zhao Ziyang had allowed, if not actively encouraged, the authors to make their arguments, accusations, and demands public.

Although this poster was soon labeled a "reactionary big-character poster," it exerted a wide influence throughout China.

To counter its influence, the Propaganda Department of the Guangdong Provincial Party Committee published articles criticizing it. The "Li Yizhe" group, however, was allowed to answer by composing more posters with their points of view. This fleeting moment of open debate in Guangdong in the wake of the Cultural Revolution opened up space for the exchange of opposing ideas and viewpoints. It lasted more than a year, until it was finally shut down. Soon, however, similar ideas and concerns would be voiced again in Beijing in 1978–1979 during the Democracy Wall movement. Between November 1978 and December 1979, thousands of people put up "big-character posters" on a wall in the Xicheng district of Beijing, to protest political and social conditions in China. In fact, the Li Yizhe group and its audacious essays were important triggers for the 1978–1979 movement that eventually would command worldwide attention.

Why did Zhao Ziyang take this risk and allow a fervent call for democracy in China to become public? Since he has never himself commented about his time during the Cultural Revolution, we have little evidence about his intentions. But two factors likely played a role. Zhao certainly used the Li Yizhe group's writings and posters to attack the radical supporters of the Cultural Revolution in Guangdong and erode the foundation of their support. Deng Xiaoping in Beijing used similar tactics, such as the articulation of public grievances to put pressure on Cultural Revolution leaders, also later called the Gang of Four, consisting of Mao's wife Jiang Qing and three ultra-leftists, to end the Cultural Revolution. At the same time, the fact that Zhao even had the Li Yizhe articles printed also has to be seen as a sign of a certain degree of sympathy with their arguments. Decades later he frequently expressed his belief that only inner-Party democracy can avoid tyranny and dictatorship in China and thus provide remedies for China's centuries-old political ills. The goal was to prevent concentration of power in, and arbitrary use of power by, a single leader.[15]

In other words, Zhao Ziyang's metamorphosis demonstrates how serious and profound reform could come from within the ranks of the Party. In fact, Zhao was hardly alone in this belief. Similar convictions were widespread among Party members, intellectuals, and students in China coming out of the horrors of the Cultural Revolution. This was the well-spring of internal Party reform. Later, in the 1980s, Zhao would again permit similar arguments to be voiced publicly until they erupted in the massive demonstrations for democracy on Tiananmen Square.

Economic Reformer

In October 1975 Zhao Ziyang was transferred to Sichuan, where he worked from October 1975 to February 1980.[16] It was a time of tremendous changes in the nation. The Cultural Revolution finally came to an end as the Gang of Four lost its grip on power. On December 13, 1978, at the end of a month-long preparatory conference for the historic Third Plenum of the Eleventh Central Committee, held in Beijing from December 18 to December 22, Deng Xiaoping (1904–1997) delivered a carefully thought-out, well-calculated speech. It dared a risky break with the Maoist past and ushered in a new era of "reform and opening up." It is time, Deng stated, that the members of the Chinese Communist Party "emancipate their minds, use their heads, seek the truth in the facts, and look to the future together." He criticized Party members who clung to "book knowledge" and "let their flag blow with the wind." Conservatism and the worship of theories had to be overcome in order to make China a "modern and powerful socialist state."[17] At the same time, Deng also made it very clear that pragmatism should never call into question the political leadership of the Chinese Communist Party (enshrined in the so-called the Four Cardinal Principles: keep to the socialist road, uphold the people's democratic dictatorship, uphold the leadership of the Communist Party, and uphold Marxism–Leninism and Mao Zedong Thought). Reforms should target China's flagging economy, not its political system.

Zhao Ziyang, like almost everybody else in the Party, understood that the economy was the top priority. This primacy of economic reform was obvious and logical. Among many other things, the Cultural Revolution had been an onslaught on bureaucratic structures, including the institutions of a centrally planned economy. At the same time, markets were denounced as the capitalist road. As a result, economic development stagnated. China was plagued by high urban unemployment, languishing levels of food production, deteriorating urban housing conditions, falling wages, widespread rural poverty, and sluggish productivity growth. The destruction and damage of the Cultural Revolution had created a widespread longing for policy that would restore economic stability and prosperity. That intention set the stage for modifications and reforms of the centrally planned command economy.[18]

Given the import of agriculture in a country where 85 percent of the population lived in the countryside, the rural economy needed to be improved first. In Sichuan, an important agricultural province, Zhao Ziyang plunged himself into the work of lifting China's agricultural economy out of stagnation. He carefully cultivated rural economic reform, which became his special field. He also began to systematically read economic books and articles, sought advice from economists, and looked for practical ways to restructure the planned economy. With clear encouragement from Deng Xiaoping, who needed to show that reforms can produce positive results, Zhao Ziyang acquired a reputation for pragmatism and bold successful experiments.

As provincial Chinese Communist Party secretary in Sichuan during the late 1970s, Zhao Ziyang moved decisively to reform the rural economy and to dismantle the communes, although the policies were implemented incrementally. It started with moderate and cautious steps such as production-team autonomy, distribution according to work, flexible policies toward private plots and peasant sidelines, and promoting commune and brigade industry.[19] When those experiments produced good results, Zhao moved to revive an earlier policy called the "household responsibility system." Individual peasant households entered into agreements with the collective (commune) that allowed them to till the "collective" land as their own responsibility. They were also allowed to set up small rural firms for the production of agricultural machinery or for the provision of services. In return, the private household paid the collective contracted quotas of its income to meet tax obligations and other fees. This enabled a rapid reintroduction of household farming and the stimulation of private agricultural production. The gradual transition to a rural market economy while retaining collective ownership was sufficient to relieve the shackles of the command economy, which had previously subjected the rural people's communes and their members to the dictates of the state plan. As a result, most people's communes disappeared in the early 1980s.

Zhao Ziyang advocated a return of small-scale "capitalism" – referring to the return of private farming, free markets for certain agricultural products, and partial autonomy for industrial enterprises – as part of his plan to expose the economy to market forces. The results in Sichuan were impressive: grain production grew by 24 percent and industrial production rose by 80 percent in the period from 1976 to 1979. Those policies first adopted in Sichuan Province became a model for other regions and in 1981 were extended to the rest of the country, leading to dramatic increases in agricultural output.

At the same time, rural industry turned into an extraordinarily dynamic force in the Chinese economy. The dismantling of government-imposed barriers to establishing rural businesses was enthusiastically welcomed by rural local governments. It should be noted that these policies were also successful because they largely revived historical institutions such as household farming, rural markets and commerce.

Due to his success in Sichuan, Zhao was rapidly promoted by China's paramount leader, Deng Xiaoping. Zhao was appointed an alternate member of the Politburo in 1977, a full member of the Politburo in 1979, a member of the Politburo's Standing Committee in 1980, and vice premier in the same year. In September 1980, he replaced Hua Guofeng as premier.[20] When Zhao was thrown into the national spotlight, however, he was not particularly well prepared for this difficult job of leading the nation. His main experience had been in managing the agricultural economy, but as premier he had to deal with the much bigger challenges of upgrading China's ailing industries and inserting China into the global economy. These issues were also much more controversial within the Party. Reform in this area would potentially encounter much stiffer opposition.

Zhao proved to be an able politician. He was an imposing figure, wearing Western suits, with swept-back hair and oversized glasses. He displayed straightforwardness and a matter-of-fact attitude, striving for results. Although he often scuffled with conservative leaders, he was trusted and respected across the political spectrum by both conservatives and reformers, backed by his long administrative experience, intelligence, and integrity. He also understood how to generate political support. He established committees, networks, and platforms that allowed for policy input from experts and think tanks, and for expertise and knowledge, including ideas and scholarship from abroad, and even public opinion.[21] He was also willing to school himself and acquire new knowledge. Although Zhao never finished high school, he was a passionate lifelong learner and autodidact. He became a main champion of technological and scientific progress in China in the early 1980s as he was one of the first Chinese leaders to recognize the revolutionary potential of new technologies, including information technology. He knew that China had struggled to keep pace and to support investments in science to help China catch up with the industrialized countries.[22]

As premier, he laid the foundations for the rise of Chinese economic power in the twenty-first century. Zhao's government introduced ambitious reforms into urban areas and the industrial sector beginning in 1984. Zhao relentlessly pursued institutional changes in several important areas, such as enterprise reform or price reform, phasing out central planning and replacing it with market forces. He did so by starting from sectors peripheral to the operations of the system as a whole, while maintaining central control of the elements considered to be crucial.[23] A good example is the controversial dual-track price system which emerged in the 1980s. It allowed the state to loosen control of some commodities at the margins of the system, so that production for market demand at a market price was first tolerated and later officially sanctioned, while still regulating the price for essential items at the core of the centrally planned economy. In a similar way, managers in state-owned enterprises were slowly given more autonomy and allowed to keep parts of the profits. The government also permitted the adoption of various forms of the contract responsibility system, experiments with shareholding, and the development of a significant individual and service economy in urban areas.

Zhao was a leading advocate of the open-door policy that integrated China with the world economy. He championed the designation of special economic zones and open coastal cities as centers for foreign trade and investment. Here China was able to capitalize on a unique global opportunity. At the end of the 1970s, for the US, China became a strategic partner in the Cold War against the Soviet Union and a pioneer of a more flexible version of socialism that could eventually evolve into a liberal society. As a result, the US was prepared to give China trade preferences, such as low customs duties and technology transfers, which were denied to other countries. In July 1979, the coastal provinces of Guangdong and

Fujian were selected as key regions to begin China's new open-door policy. A year later, Zhao Ziyang pushed further by designating the cities of Shenzhen, Zhuhai, Shantou, and Xiamen as special economic zones. The goal was to attract foreign capital, innovative technologies, and foreign expertise to the export-oriented manufacturing and processing sectors. In return, the special economic zones offered foreign investors a level of legal protection that was not available to Chinese companies.[24]

Significant amounts of inward foreign direct investment started to flow into the special economic zones. Overseas Chinese businessmen from Hong Kong and other countries established new enterprises and set new standards for efficient management. The economic success of Guangdong and other coastal provinces in the 1980s, the transformation of Hainan Island into a province and special economic zone with a high degree of economic autonomy, and the "coastal development strategy" in which China's maritime provinces took part in the international division of labor that helped spur national development, all owed much to Zhao.

Zhao also initiated China's bid for a seat in the World Trade Organization. Overall, he was adept at negotiating with foreign countries and integrating China into the world economy. He regularly charmed international leaders. After a meeting in the White House on January 10, 1984, US president Ronald Reagan described him as "a likeable fellow & a very capable one."[25] The economist Milton Friedman praised Zhao at their meeting in 1988 for having "the temperament of a professor."[26]

Zhao's reform policies were largely successful because they had no losers and demanded no sacrifices. They were not contingent on cuts in other sectors such as heavy industry or state-owned enterprises, nor did they require investments on a large scale. The limited and gradual introduction of market-based elements promised to offend no one. Zhao Ziyang's economic reforms therefore began without a vision, but as a by-product of an inevitable economic readjustment. As he confessed in his memoir, "My earliest understanding of how to proceed with reform was shallow and vague ... I did not have any preconceived model or a systematic idea in mind."[27] The economic reforms in China were a partial and gradual reform strategy characterized by gradual institutional adjustments and frequent regional experimentation.

But the development toward market socialism hit setbacks as well. Price reform was especially difficult. Zhao's strategy focused on lifting controls on four main commodities: meat, eggs, vegetables, and sugar. He decided against softening the blow of price reform to the population and refused to consider paying subsidies. Moreover, news of the beginning of a more system-wide effort toward price reform was leaked to the public. Ignoring warnings, Zhao nonetheless plowed forward. By the end of 1988, no more than 25 percent of the prices for commodities were still directly set by the state. The remainder were allowed to vary within a specified band (25 percent), or were determined by the market (50 percent). With hindsight, it was probably a mistake to announce such radical price reform and move so quickly. Combined with actual price rises, the policy drove panic buying and galloping inflation.[28] In 1988, the government was on the brink of losing macroeconomic control.

During his entire tenure, Zhao pushed the Party to replace ideology with economic development (*fazhan*) – a term that became the mantra of Party rule. Development should lead to "wealth and power." From that moment on, economic development became the overriding quest of the Party to which all other objectives were subordinated. But this transformation was not uncontested. Zhao faced tremendous ideological, political, and bureaucratic resistance to his reform proposals, a difficulty compounded by new problems, such as inflation, income disparities, and governmental corruption, that were fueled by the transitional economy. Zhao indeed complained later that his entire time as prime minister, as well as his ambitious political agenda, was obstructed by constant criticism and maneuvering of the so called "Party elders," "old guard," or "conservatives" within the Party.[29] In fact, opposition came from a rather diverse coalition. Some so-called leftists resisted changes in general on ideological grounds, while others agreed with the policy, but found the reforms too radical and too swift. And there were those in power who resisted Zhao simply because they feared squandering their privileges and perks, or losing influence and power.

Political Reform and the Road to Tiananmen

The mood in China in the late 1980s was restless and agitated. There were passionate debates among intellectuals about how China should change and also how its social and political system should be reformed. Calls for political reforms grew louder. More and more voices called for democracy. Writers, scholars, and intellectuals argued that only political reform and democratic mechanisms could stymie the abuse of power and corruption and provide oversight over those in power. Even within the Party, there was widespread acknowledgment that political reform was necessary and inevitable. When, in January 1987, Hu Yaobang was forced to resign as General Secretary of the CCP and Zhao Ziyang was appointed to succeed him as acting General Secretary, Zhao was nevertheless determined to continue Hu's work for political reform. He established a "Central Small Group for the Study of Reform of the Political System" and staffed it with brilliant young hopefuls. Asked at a news conference in October 1987 what his top priority as General Secretary was, he minced no words: "Reforms. Reform of the political system!"[30]

As we have seen, Zhao Ziyang had actually not shown much interest in political reform, which was mainly the arena of Hu Yaobang.[31] A sarcastic intellectual and smart, passionate, theoretical thinker, Hu Yaobang stubbornly and fearlessly pushed for liberalization in the media, academia, and the arts, allowing the 1980s to become one of the most daring and liberal decades in the entire modern period of Chinese history. Back in 1977, Hu Yaobang, then vice president of the Central Party School and supporter of Deng, had encouraged Party officials to promote new thinking. Under his aegis an internal journal was published called *Theoretical Trends*, which in its articles called for overcoming ideological barriers. In May 1978, for example, an article entitled "Practice Is the Sole Criterion for Checking the Truth" was published, which was later reprinted in major national newspapers. After being picked up by Deng Xiaoping, it became the slogan of the reform period. The idea that practice, not political doctrine, was the only criterion for assessing social and economic developments received overwhelming support.[32]

The topic of political reform had been on the plate since 1980, but no leader, even Deng Xiaoping, dared to touch it. Deng in principle welcomed political reforms, but he understood them in a narrow sense as reforms of the political decision-making process. Practically on every occasion he maintained that a Western democratic system was irrelevant for China and hence out of the question. Hence no progress was made until 1986, when Hu Yaobang started to talk about the need for reform of the political system. He defined it as necessary changes to the socialist system in the following four areas: relations between central and local; relations between government and business; division of labor between the People's Congress, the government, and the Party; and the question of democratic control in socialism.[33] Overall, democracy should improve socialism, not make it obsolete. In the late summer of 1986 Deng Xiaoping finally decided to grasp the thorny issue of political reform, but he asked the more cautious and moderate Zhao Ziyang, not Hu Yaobang, to head a "central discussion group for reform of the political system."[34]

Since the mid-1980s Zhao had started to shift his position and began to see corruption and abuse of power by high-ranking officials as a systemic problem and concluded that a flourishing market economy was not compatible with the system of one-party rule by the CCP. He feared that the Party's vested interests would be a major obstacle to continuation of the economic reforms, convincing him that political reform was essential. He now unmistakably began to embrace political reform, including the introduction of democratic checks and balances.

This was made clear by Zhao's proposals and speeches at the Thirteenth CCP National Congress, held in October 1987. On that occasion, Zhao was formally elected General Secretary of the Party. More importantly, Zhao proposed to the Congress a "comprehensive plan" for reform of the political system, the first and only such plan ever presented during the rule of the CCP.[35] Zhao suggested "building up socialist democracy" as the goal of China's political transition from Maoist institutions, defining democracy against the existing political system, which offered few civic rights and little opportunity for popular participation. The most important goal of his policy was separating the Party and the state by removing "Party groups" in every central and then local government department, separating the government and the enterprises, and reducing the scope of the Party's claim to "political leadership." Zhao also advocated *toumingdu* – transparency and press freedom. Concrete measures were outlined and, to a lesser degree, implemented for downgrading the role of the Party in the political, economic, and social arenas. Zhao also proposed establishing a modern system of civil service, enhancing the rule of law, introducing competitive (though still limited) elections to various levels of Party and state organizations, promoting individual rights and civil organizations, and enlarging the participation of Chinese citizens in politics. Down the road, in spite of the deliberate ambiguities and vagueness of Zhao's reform plan, was the idea of democratizing the elections to local people's congresses and making sure that, as indicated in the state constitution, they really choose and elect local governors or mayors.

It is important to recognize that Zhao certainly conceived of such political reforms within a Marxist framework, arguing that the "initial stages of socialism" still needed to include capitalism. Zhao believed that Marx's argument that capitalist practices must be abolished in order to attain socialism had not taken into account the necessity of capitalist enterprise to prepare the ground for socialism in a developing country such as China. To him it was clear that Stalin and Mao had committed fatal mistakes by expecting that a socialist utopia could spring directly from a peasant society. The capitalist stage cannot be jumped over, Zhao argued, hence China needed to go back and "make up this class" of capitalist entrepreneurs. It would be, though, "capitalism under the leadership of the Communist Party," and only a passing stage. While Zhao saw no fundamental problem with the formula "capitalism plus one-party rule," he did emphasize the need for democratic controls during this transition phase.

Zhao's original ideas were ambitious and far-reaching. The official blueprint for political reform presented in October 1987 to the Thirteenth Party Congress was a meek compromise. It featured a hybrid system of limited, controlled pluralism while maintaining the socialist system as a whole, including one-party rule. Yet even this proposal was completely abandoned in the course of the tumultuous Beijing Spring to come, when disagreements and infights within the Party broke out in the open.

In spring of 1989, when the student-led mass protests calling for political reform and democratization arose in Beijing, Zhao disagreed with his Politburo colleagues on how to deal with the protestors' demands: Zhao regarded substantive political reform toward democracy and the rule of law as the answer, while Premier Li Peng (1928–2019), backed by Deng Xiaoping, insisted on an uncompromising hard-line response, condemning the protesters as trouble-makers. This split became public when the leadership decided to send troops to Tiananmen Square, a move Zhao vehemently opposed. After deciding to send in the army to crush the movement, Deng required Zhao Ziyang to support the Party's decision. Zhao's refusal to back down was considered a deliberate attempt to split the CCP and seen as a very serious transgression of one-party rule. Zhao Ziyang was investigated, dismissed from all posts, and put under house arrest. With this, not only was Zhao Ziyang silenced, but the considerable liberal and pro-democratic forces within the Party lost ground.

A Contested Legacy

Under Zhao Ziyang's leadership, the CCP after 1978 consistently capitalized on the pragmatic opportunities generated by a changing world. Zhao, with the encouragement of Deng Xiaoping, promoted new, nonideological thinking and called upon his countrymen to pursue opportunities and improve their lives, relying on their own talents and ideas. The removal of ideological blinkers also prompted daring explorations into Chinese history and culture; the 1980s became one of the most liberal and intellectually interesting periods in the CCP's history. Zhao also created institutional conditions that allowed and incentivized individual initiative, performance, and risk-taking, while maintaining the overall planning system and state-owned enterprises. Of perhaps most consequence was China's opening to Western markets, especially attracting foreign direct investment into what were designated special economic zones. By changing the rules of how the state managed economic transactions and by reducing the burden of extraction, China put its economy successfully on a growth path.

Political reform, however, remained outside of the purview of the majority of the Party leaders. When Zhao Ziyang and his supporters were ousted in the wake of the Tiananmen Square protests, they were replaced by Jiang Zemin (1926–) and later Zhu Rongji (1928–), who became premier in 1993. The new generation of leaders shared two qualities: they had been major leaders of the reform in big cities during the 1980s, and they prioritized stability when facing popular protest. With that, the split within the Party was resolved, and political reform was no longer discussed or advocated within the Party. It became taboo. Moreover, the Party tightened its control over universities, student organizations, the press and publishers, and the arts and literature. In sharp contrast to the repeated political upheavals of the 1980s, China experienced a prolonged period of icy political stability – a counterintuitive outcome that has surprised many observers.

When looking back to one hundred years of CCP history, it should not be overlooked that Zhao Ziyang and Hu Yaobang stand for important traditions within the Party, even if they have been more or less silenced since 1989. Belief in a more humane, inclusive, and participatory form of socialism, and even in a more open, pluralistic, and liberal political system, has always existed and never completely ceased to exist in the Party.

In rethinking Zhao Ziyang's blueprints for political reform, it is clear that his thinking did not originate from notions of universal values, inalienable rights, or normative theories, but from the need for Chinese socialism to combine economic growth with justice, acceptance and transparency. He trusted that economic development under one-party rule enabled certain achievements, especially in the economy, infrastructure, education, and welfare, but development under extractive political institutions was feeble and unstable because it encouraged infighting from rival factions within the CCP wishing to take control of the state and the extraction it generated. He looked for ways to install checks and balances to control vested interests and contain deals behind closed doors. He viewed political institutions as instrumental rather than as normative, designed to serve the more fundamental goals of raising living standards and enabling fair distribution. He was convinced that it was necessary to constantly modify and redefine political institutions, even in socialism, as new problems and risks to these goals emerged.[36]

Equally important are Zhao's political actions. That he opted for a dialogue with the protesting students on Tiananmen Square proved his belief in political accountability. And above all Zhao refused to succumb to the tradition of purged leaders bowing to Party criticism and writing self-criticisms. During the entire time from 1989 until his death he resolutely protested the Party's decision that he had done wrong and he never ceased to try to have it overturned.[37] Unlike a long line of earlier CCP leaders from Peng Dehuai to Liu Shaoqi, Deng Xiaoping, and Hu Yaobang, who gave in to the Party's demand to admit mistakes even though history showed that their positions had been correct, he never bowed to this dark tradition within the CCP that he should accept blame. Just like the founder of the CCP, Chen Duxiu, Zhao Ziyang refused to give in to Party pressure and he stood up for his fundamental beliefs. And like Chen Duxiu, Zhao was sidelined for the rest of his life: both stand as examples of paths not taken, or rather abandoned.

Despite China's breathtaking economic success over recent decades, which to no small degree is based on Zhao's achievements, political institutions in China remain brittle. Hence the CCP's survival inevitably hinges on political reform and liberalization.[38] When and how China will embrace a more participatory and legitimate system, and whether the Party will survive that process, are the main questions that need to be asked about China's political future. One conclusion can be safely drawn from the history of reform since 1978: without more accountability, pluralism, and a greater degree of popular participation in political life, a more sustainable and stable development seems difficult to imagine, and future political crises seem likely. Given the increasing repressive climate in China today, it seems more urgent than ever to revisit the reform proposals laid out by Zhao Ziyang in the late 1980s. Yet there are no signs that the CCP under Xi Jinping is willing to draw on its own legacy of political reform.

Chapter 8 – 1990s

The 1980s saw a period of daring reform in the Party, begun by Deng Xiaoping's leadership and taken up by a new generation of top leaders, Hu Yaobang and Zhao Ziyang, Deng's immediate successors. Yet conservative forces within the Party resisted and the decade saw a back-and-forth between audacious reform (the end of the communes, the beginnings of market reform, village elections) and repressive reaction (the dismissal of Hu Yaobang the reformist General Secretary and the Anti-Spiritual Pollution campaign of the mid-1980s). These tensions came to a head in 1989, when the Communist leadership ordered the violent suppression of popular demonstrations in Tiananmen, the main square in Beijing south of the Forbidden City, and in many other major Chinese cities to which the protests had spread. The result was a resounding crushing of political reform and intellectual dissent.

The 1990s began with retrenchment but Deng Xiaoping restarted economic reform – minus political reform – with his 1992 Southern Tour. What soon emerged has defined China ever since: authoritarian rule buttressed by market economics. This is the world in which Wang Yuanhua, the protagonist of this scene from the life of the Party, made sense of his world and contemplated the future of the Party and of China. Wang was a leading Party intellectual, but he was not a happy man. In fact, he was worried, worried for China, for the revolution he had served, and for China's intellectuals and their elite civilization. His critique of the faults of Maoism and Party rule are biting, but they are not based on Western liberal theory. Rather, Wang's is an internal critique of a Party intellectual, drawing from Chinese history and culture as well as from a fresh reading of Marxist ideology and nineteenth-century European and Russian literature. Everything in this scene contrasts with our last Party intellectual, Wang Shiwei, whom we met in Yan'an in the 1940s in Chapter 3. We find Wang Yuanhua in his apartment in Shanghai, not in the political center of Beijing. His venues of activity are not Party committees. And he does not engage with Party leaders, as was the case for Wang Shiwei in the 1940s. Rather, it is private spaces, including a cabin by Rattan Lake in the far south of China, limited public spaces such as newspapers and blogs, and elite *intellectual debates that defined Wang Yuanhua's life in the 1990s. Post-Mao intellectuals were paying the price of autonomy: loss of political influence. Wang Yuanhua was no dissident, but he represents the disenchantment of Party intellectuals by the century's end.*

The author of this chapter, Xu Jilin, is one of the two PRC-based Chinese historians in this volume (along with Zhang Jishun in Chapter 4). His voice is important to the mosaic we present, but readers may find his tone and style surprising. He addresses the Party indirectly for reasons that should be obvious; he and his subject often speak in the metaphors of history and historical figures. But their message is clear: tolerance, not ideological conformity, is what Party intellectuals require of their leaders in the new century.

THE 1990s
8 Wang Yuanhua: A Party Intellectual Reflects
XU JILIN*

Summer, 1993. Shanghai is unbearably hot, muggy, over-
cast, oppressive. In a high-rise on Wuxing Road in the old French
Concession area an old man of seventy-three sits before his desk,
writing. The red line of the thermometer has already passed thirty-
five degrees. The electric fan blows only hot air. The old man simply
throws off his singlet, torso bare, and goes on writing quickly.

This is Wang Yuanhua, one of the initiators of the intellectual liberation and New Enlightenment movements of the 1980s, a
celebrated spiritual leader of intellectuals.

The sound of the telephone rings out; Wang answers,
"Young Xu? I'm just reading that essay by Du Yachuan you sent
over. That Du Yachuan really is something! So many of the
questions I am pondering now he already thought through seventy years ago. I can't stop on my essay, the more I write the
longer it gets!"

The essay Wang is writing is the foreword for *Selected
Works of Du Yachuan*. Du was the famous editor of *The Orient*
(*Dongfang zazhi*) early in the previous century during the May
Fourth Movement. He has always been considered a cultural con-
servative opposed to the New Culture Movement.[1]

A month later Wang's essay appears in the *Literary Gazette*
(*Wenhui bao*) running over two full pages of the newspaper. The
title: "Du Yachuan and the debate on Eastern and Western culture."
The article on a debate from some seventy years ago is a bombshell
in Chinese intellectual circles. In no time north and south of the
Yangzi and across the country contrary opinions fly: "Wang

Yuanhua defending conservatism? Has the leader of the New Enlightenment movement 'crossed the aisle'"?[2]

The term "crossed the aisle" (*zhuanxiang*) came into Chinese from Japanese and it is derogatory. It means to turn traitor to your original political position. Hearing this chatter, Wang Yuanhua demurs. "I'm not 'crossing any aisle'; I am reflecting."

Reflection. This has been the heart and soul of Wang Yuanhua all his life. There are two different kinds of intellectuals. One sort, when they have determined their values and politics, never change for the rest of their lives. Another sort responds to changing times, challenges their own standpoint, and overcomes their original self. This has been Wang Yuanhua's path. Wang has had two periods in his life of serious reflection and reconsideration. The one that began in 1993 was by far the more significant. It sprang from the political environment of the early 1990s in China.

The 1980s were China's most lively period of reform and opening. However, the 1989 Tiananmen Incident was an immense tragedy. It pierced the heart of every Chinese intellectual. After June Fourth, many intellectuals privately pondered, how in the end did this tragedy come to pass? Why did this become an antagonistic life-and-death struggle between the Party and the student demonstrators? What were the deeper causes? Why was revolutionary radicalism the mainstream of twentieth-century China and not moderate liberalism?

Wang Yuanhua was one of the first intellectuals in the early 1990s to reflect on this question. He was more sensitive to this than most because in his career the young Wang had been a sincere Marxist revolutionary.

Wang Yuanhua was born in 1920 to a Christian household. His maternal grandfather, Gui Meipeng, was an Anglican vicar in the central Chinese city of Shashi, Hubei (on the Yangzi River). He and his wife were both devout Christians. Although Wang Yuanhua himself was not a Christian, the influence of this worldview in his family prevented him from ever blindly worshiping any particular person. Without believing in God, he was always alert to the dark side of human nature. In 1953 Wang saw Mao Zedong for the first time, at the opening ceremony for the Second National Conference of Literature and Arts Workers. Mao Zedong led a delegation of senior leaders on the rostrum. Wang Yuanhua was below the stage, surrounded by people with tears in their eyes excitedly shouting, "Long live Chairman Mao! Long live Chairman Mao!" But Wang wasn't excited. He felt anxious; he suspected that he lacked appropriate feelings for the leader. Only in his old age did Wang realize that it was the Christian gene that prevented him from losing his sense of proportion.

Wang's father, Wang Fangquan, studied in Japan and America, and mastered English. After returning to China, he became a professor of English literature at Tsinghua University in Peiping (as Beijing was called in those days). Wang Yuanhua had three elder sisters and one younger sister; he was the only son. And so, of course, he was prized by his father and doted on by the family. Growing up in this sort of scholarly family and living in the beauty and elegance of the Tsinghua campus, Wang Yuanhua's character naturally tended to an intellectual disposition. Even though he would later join the Revolution, he was unlike some other "hardened" Communists, being bookish and aloof.

He set great store by his Tsinghua University origins. In later life he gave his home the memorial name Tsing Garden. Originally Tsinghua University had been a preparatory school for students aiming to study in America. It was the most American in spirit of Chinese universities. This duality was inscribed on Wang – both the free and independent spirit of the West and the Chinese sense of dignity and pride in their own civilization. These Chinese and Western elements constituted the two conflicting sides of Wang Yuanhua's personality which he tried to harmonize.

But for the Japanese invasion of China in the 1930s, Wang Yuanhua would most likely have gone overseas to study in preparation for a splendid and comfortable career like many other sons of prosperous families in this period. However, when he was fifteen years old, the December 9th Movement against Japanese imperialism erupted in Peiping. Wang, who was then studying in a church middle school, was inspired by this spirit of nationalism. He threw himself into the anti-Japanese movement and joined the National Liberation Vanguard, a Communist front organization. Prior to this, scions of wealthy families rarely joined the Revolution, but nationalism succeeded in mobilizing these heretofore privileged youth, and they headed straight for the Communist Party.

After the outbreak of war, Wang Yuanhua went to Shanghai, where he secretly joined the underground Party. Before 1949 the Communist Party basically comprised intellectuals and peasants. There were two great periods of recruiting intellectuals into the Party. The first was the beginning of the 1920s with the establishment of the Party. Those founding leaders of the Party, each and every one of them, were ordinary intellectuals, with a few notable exceptions, such as the early leaders, Chen Duxiu and Li Dazhao. The second great intake was in the December 9th Movement in the mid-1930s. Caught up in the fervor to save the nation, a much greater range of intellectual youth threw themselves into the Revolution. Wang was assigned to the CCP Jiangsu Province Cultural Committee, an extraordinary intellectual community in Shanghai. For Wang, who had not attended college, the Jiangsu Cultural Committee undoubtedly was his university and it formed his character for life.

Wang Yuanhua was certainly a Communist, but in his own eyes he was first of all an intellectual, a Communist of intellectual disposition. In his later years in a private letter to Li Rui, a famous reformist Party intellectual, he lamented,

> It's been half a century since I joined the Party. I'm ashamed that I have yet to fulfill the mission and responsibility of an intellectual. In this time of social instability, I haven't exerted myself to encourage others, and when I awake at night I can't get back to sleep.[3]

Like Li Rui, Wang Yuanhua joined the revolution determined to save the nation. They were "old-school" Communists, meaning that they were part of a generation of idealists who joined the Party to realize their ideals of liberty, democracy, and independence. This can be contrasted with those "new-style" Communists who might be seen to join the Party to seek power and money. Having passed through the tribulations of the Cultural Revolution, intellectuals such as Li and Wang became the first to reconsider their history in the 1980s and became pioneers in advocating reform and opening for the Party.

The young Wang Yuanhua had a hero complex. The heroes he admired were not the twentieth-century heroes of Soviet communism but rather the German Nietzsche, the French Romain

Rolland, and China's modern writer Lu Xun. He was convinced that this filthy world could only be saved by the extraordinary will of individual heroes. In those years, Lu Xun was the one he worshiped the most. When Wang was forced to flee occupied Peiping, all he took was a drawing of Lu Xun that he had made himself, hidden in his clothes. If it had been discovered by Japanese soldiers, it could have cost him his life.

The young Wang Yuanhua was a fine writer and had something of a reputation within the Party. In 1949, when the Party had taken power, this thirty-year-old who had just come to prominence was appointed head of the Shanghai Literature and Arts Press – a proper section chief. Enjoying success at such a young age, he was full of pride. His coworkers said Wang Yuanhua had an insulting arrogance and a fierce temper.[4]

However, the strict discipline of the Communist Party did not tolerate this sort of young man. In the mid-1950s, a group of left-wing writers with views incompatible with the mainstream ideology of the day were condemned as the "Hu Feng Counterrevolutionary Clique" because they had offended Mao Zedong. Wang Yuanhua was not part of Hu Feng's circle, but because he appreciated Hu Feng's work and had published some of his books, one dark night Wang was arrested, locked up in isolation and placed under investigation.

In prison Wang had to write endless confessions each week, reporting his relations with the Hu Feng Counterrevolutionary Clique. In the end, the investigation couldn't turn up any incriminating evidence. The interrogator said to him, "You only need to acknowledge that Hu Feng is counterrevolutionary, then you'll be fine." Wang Yuanhua replied, "If you want me to acknowledge that Hu Feng committed political errors, I admit it. But, if you want me to say that Hu Feng is counterrevolutionary, I can't see that, so I can't agree to it." The interrogator exploded, "Wang Yuanhua! Here we run into all sorts – Kuomintang spies, reactionary military officers, Trotskyites – but not a one as obstinate as you!"[5]

Because of his refusal to conform, Wang was thrown out of the Party. He was sent down to the Literature Research Institute of the Shanghai Writers' Association as an ordinary researcher. Two years of isolation and investigation with nothing but cold looks and harsh rebukes, he later recalled, "were a huge shock. The things that

I had long believed to be beautiful and sacred were destroyed in an instant." During his isolation and interrogation he read a great deal, mainly works of philosophy from Mao Zedong and Lenin to Marx and Hegel. The vicissitudes of life and the wisdom of these philosophers made him introspective, and changed him from a radical literary youth into a reflective thinker.

The book he read most carefully while in prison was Hegel's *Science of Logic*. Wang discovered in Hegel's thinking the origins of leftist dogmatism in Chinese communism – Hegel's epistemology. According to Hegel, in the process from perceptual knowledge to rational knowledge there is also a stage of intellectual knowledge which abstracts from material things, which generalizes. Once the intellect is made absolute, however, replacing the dialectical process of rational knowledge, one can fall into rigid dogmatism – for example, by only recognizing the class nature of people and denying human nature and the rich variety of individuals, or by only talking about the universal nature of things and ignoring their respective differences. This was Wang Yuanhua's first ideological reassessment. In those days such reflections based on these classics of German philosophy were undoubtedly utterly heretical. Only in the movement to liberate thought in the early 1980s was it possible to share these ideas in public.

In 1982, Zhou Yang represented the Party center as its literary authority to give a report at a meeting to commemorate the hundredth anniversary of Marx's death. His topic was "An exploration of a few theoretical questions in Marxism." He invited a few open-minded thinkers among the reformist group including Wang Yuanhua to join him in drawing up this report. Wang Yuanhua took on the section on the origin of dogmatic thought in the substitution of intellect for rational knowledge, and he edited the final draft. Of course, a report full of the values of liberated thought such as this was immediately criticized by conservatives within the Party. This contributed to the "Anti-Spiritual Pollution" campaign during which Wang Yuanhua, who had just been reinstated as the head of the Shanghai Propaganda Department, was forced to step down before he even started his job.[6]

In the liberation of thought and New Enlightenment movements of the 1980s, Wang Yuanhua was the most influential thought leader in the south. He gave talks, penned essays, and ran a magazine, *New Enlightenment*, inviting a group of notable new-thinking writers to contribute. However, after publishing just two issues the magazine caught the attention of Party officials and it was banned.

After the Tiananmen Incident of 1989, intellectual circles were silenced. Wang Yuanhua's home fell silent. Friends no longer dared to visit. For a while Wang moved far to the south to Guangdong, to a cottage by Rattan Lake in Zhuhai. He described his mood there in a letter to a friend:

> Here I am cut off from the outside. Beyond the mundane world. I enjoyed this tranquility as a child. Before my lodgings is a small garden, replete with a lawn with flowers and trees. In warm and sunny weather, I sit on the grass and gaze up at the changing forms of the clouds. Agitation slips away and tranquility returns.[7]

Later, he confessed,

> When I was young, I just started writing, but only in the 90s could you say I reached the level of thought ... The 1990s was my era of reflection. Only in the 90s was I able to make a relatively thorough self-criticism of the ideological concepts I had accumulated over the years.[8]

In his later writings, Wang Yuanhua favored two words: "thinking" and "rethinking" (thought and reflection). Some people are reluctant to reflect or rethink, believing that they have always been correct. Wang Yuanhua holds that such reflection and reconsideration are an expression of the worrying mind-set of intellectuals (*youhuan yishi*), worrying about China. It is the natural instinct of his life. For him, rethinking is not simply one way to ponder; it is a way of life. And it is a painful path because its object is not someone else, but your own opinionated self. Solitary reflection by the banks of Rattan Lake made Wang alert to the tragedies of twentieth-century Chinese Revolution and radicalism and set him on a trail to discover the historical origins of these ideas.

We began this story with mention of an article about Du Yachuan. It was a prelude to Wang Yuanhua's second period of reflection and rethinking. Wang discovered the answers to his search for the origins of the political disasters he had lived through in the experiences of this "conservative" from early in the century. Wang found that the earliest ideological origins of twentieth-century revolutionary radicalism, the radicalism that caused the political disasters in his life, trace back to anarchism during the last years of the Qing Dynasty and the early years of the Republic of China in the first two decades of the twentieth century. By the time of the famous May Fourth Movement in 1919, this radicalism lay hidden within the enlightenment thought of the day. Wang found this intolerant radicalism in the debate over Western and Eastern culture during the 1920s in the person of Du Yachuan's adversary, Chen Duxiu – the first General Secretary of the Chinese Communist Party, whom Mao Zedong called "the commander-in-chief of the May Fourth Movement." Chen had an "only-I-am-correct" dictatorial disposition. He believed he was absolutely right, so revolutionaries could disregard ordinary life and sacrifice all without regret for the lofty goals of the revolutionary ideal.

By 1993 the May Fourth idealism that Wang had learnt to love and support from his own youth now appeared to him to be infected with basic assumptions that not only did not support intellectual enlightenment but instead contributed to the radical excesses of his Party across the century. Wang categorized those negative ideas into four types: first, vulgar evolutionary theory, believing that all that is new will vanquish the old; second, radicalism, exhibiting extreme attitudes, fanatical thought, a tendency toward extremes, and a fondness for violence; third, utilitarianism, an attitude toward knowledge where the goal is not learning but rather achieving various political strategies; and fourth, an ethic of ultimate ends (in Weber's sense), in which questions of truth are treated without a spirit of seeking truth from facts, where a political standpoint takes precedence, being forever for something and against something.[9]

A child of the May Fourth Movement and deeply influenced by Hegel's thinking, Wang Yuanhua had always firmly believed in the omniscience of human reason. With the guidance of this reason, people should be able to smash the old world and create an ideal new world. However, the tragedies of the twentieth century had testified to the many crimes committed in the name of an extreme form of reason. Wang wrote,

The spirit of reason and human effort brought humanity out of the darkness of the Middle Ages. However, once that reason was deified and claimed to itself mastery of ultimate truth, in the name of that truth it denounced any who opposed it or disagreed with it as heretics. It did not seek to reform such heretics but to destroy them.[10]

Wang Yuanhua himself once was just such a committed Hegelian, but by the 1990s part of his reflections and rethinking was precisely to come to terms with the poisons of absolutism and dogmatic theory in Hegel and in Marxist ideology.

The now seventy-five-year old Wang Yuanhua spent a great deal of time and effort rereading Rousseau's *Social Contract* and reflecting on the links between his General Will and totalitarian thought. In his letter to Li Rui, Wang wrote,

The General Will must be embodied; it needs authority, and requires a charismatic figure with unblemished political morality. The unfortunate fact is that this sort of General Will, one that understands the needs of the people better than the people themselves, is but an apparition, an illusion. It is nothing more than an abstract universality that strips away all individuality and particularity. The state apparatus built in the name of this magnificent General Will recklessly expands its range of powers, interfering in every aspect of people's lives. In short order it kills off any individuality, replacing flesh-and-blood society with abstractions, and forces everyone to pay with their freedom.[11]

This is no empty theorizing; Wang here offers a profound philosophical reflection based on his own painful history.

Just as Wang Yuanhua was rethinking the lessons of China's twentieth-century revolutions, China in the 1990s was undergoing unimaginable changes. During his Southern Tour in 1992 Deng Xiaoping determined to revive the political legitimacy of the Party by opening the door to economic reform. This road to wealth and power began in 1993 as China's economy took off. Along with the new model of a socialist market economy on the one hand there emerged the polarization of the rich and poor of "capitalism," while on the other hand there continued the dictatorship of "socialism." Back in the 1980s, enlightenment intellectuals generally agreed on China's current state and future prospects: dump the socialist planned economy and, with the West as the model, build a democratic market economy. But from the mid-1990s what emerged was a distorted, state-controlled market economy. And so intellectuals now split over what to make of these developments and where China was heading: liberals and New Left. The liberals reckoned that China's problems were the fault of "socialism"; the government was too strong and was interfering with the autonomous development of the market and of society. The New Left intellectuals held that China had already become "capitalist" and the only way to solve China's problems and overcome inequality was to return to the "socialist" tradition.[12]

The intellectual divisions of the 1990s included not just the liberal and New Left camps, but also divisions between the "enlightenment school" and the "national-studies school." The enlightenment school carried on the antitraditionalism of the 1980s. They wanted to replace the traditional culture of China with the universal values of the West. The national-studies school, on the other hand, represented a new trend of thought in the 1990s. They held that China could not possibly emulate the West completely, that China's tradition had positive value, and that it was necessary to return to China's ancient Confucian classics, to interpret them afresh and to give new life to China's tradition. The enlightenment school and the national-studies school, like the liberals and the New Left, appeared as different as fire and ice, and they constantly argued.

Where did Wang Yuanhua, as a Party intellectual, stand in this great intellectual division?

Through painful reflection, Wang had already come to realize that truth is not dictatorial; it is never all on one side but rather exists somewhere between opposing sides, in some "golden mean." The intellectuals of the enlightenment camp in the 1980s cherished shared ideals and faced common enemies and they tolerated differences amongst their colleagues. But in the 1990s intellectual factions sprung up that denounced their intellectual opponents. This was heartbreaking to Wang. He pondered, why can't intellectuals have reasonable, normal relations? Invoking Isaiah Berlin's metaphor, if they are not porcupines ignoring each other, they are jackals and wolves out to kill each other. He was disgusted by their forming factions, raising flags, and making personal cliques, and even more by their exclusion of and attacks on dissidents, forever calling people this -ism or that faction, passing off private profit as public interest.

Among Party intellectuals of the 1990s Wang was in the liberal and enlightenment camp, but he was not alone. At the time, intellectuals spoke of "Southern Wang and Northern Li." "Northern Li" referred to Li Shenzhi (1923–2003) in Beijing. He had been the vice president of the Chinese Academy of Social Sciences and a famous specialist on America who had traveled to the US with Deng Xiaoping in 1979. In the 1990s, Li was China's most famous spiritual leader of liberalism. He regularly wrote courageous and pointed articles, reflecting on China's revolution, criticizing contemporary politics, fighting against tradition, and continuing the enlightenment project by pursuing universal values with the West as the exemplar.[13] "Southern Wang" was Wang Yuanhua. Even though he was not as politically courageous as Li Shenzhi, Wang's thorough investigation into the principles of liberal theory earned him the universal regard of his peers. This is why they evoked the "Southern Chen and Northern Li" of the May Fourth era (referring to the famous left-wing intellectuals Chen Duxiu and Li Dazhao) to honor Wang and Li.

Li Shenzhi openly identified as a member of the enlightenment group and as a liberal. But Wang Yuanhua, seeing the profound divisions among intellectuals, did not want to make any simple identification with a single camp. Although clearly a liberal, he tried to transcend factional positions, to rise above the ideological battles. This advocacy of a "middle path" and his reflections often stirred up debate. Because he criticized the radicalism of Chen Duxiu in the May Fourth era while sympathizing with the moderate Du Yachuan, Wang was misunderstood as "crossing the aisle" and even as a conservative belonging to the national-studies school. When he heard this, Wang would become furious and firmly declare, "Nowadays intellectuals are forming cliques and organizing factions, but I won't join the mutual-aid team nor the co-operative; I'll be a private farmer to the end."[14]

Painfully aware of the divisions among intellectuals, Wang Yuanhua especially stressed the importance of tolerance. The spiritual leader of liberalism in the Republican period, Hu Shi

(1891–1962), had a dictum in his old age: "Tolerance is more important than freedom." He meant that even though Chinese intellectuals seek freedom, they do not tolerate their opponents but rather are arbitrary and dogmatic. Wang firmly agreed and increasingly came to believe that tolerance is more important than freedom. Tolerance is not the hypocrisy of "I'm OK, you're OK, we're all OK," nor is it abandoning your position to accommodate someone else's opinion. Rather, it is to listen carefully to your opponent and to seek mutual understanding.

Wang Yuanhua's approach to friendship bore this out, even with those with whom he disagreed. Wang criticized the thesis of the Chinese-American scholar Lin Yusheng on the radical iconoclasm of Chinese intellectuals in the twentieth century. Lin Yusheng published a rebuttal. According to Chinese practice, this polemic should have resulted in hard feelings on both sides. Yet, two years later at a conference in Hawaii, Wang met Lin Yusheng and talked it through, and they became close friends able to talk about anything with confidence in each other. Reflecting on this, Wang said, "To be able to do this, first of all both sides must be dedicated to seeking truth and must value academic democracy and the freedom of discussion. Only in that way can one find the good, and treat people as equals, rather than putting on airs and seeking victory alone."[15] In this, Wang Yuanhua was different from most Chinese intellectuals. He was not concerned with different positions or opinions, but only sought kindred spirits.

When Wang Yuanhua was alive, his living room was always full of interesting and notable people from all walks of life, with all sorts of opinions. No matter the voice, as long as it was reasoned and had grounds, Wang would listen attentively. Yet beneath his gentle persona was another, fearsome side. He would often say, "I'm from Hubei, so I have some of the wild man of Chu in my nature."[16] There was a furnace in Wang's heart. When he encountered fundamental questions of right and wrong, he was capable of explosive emotions. Friends who did not know him well would frequently take fright. This was something one would never guess from his published writings.

Why this contrast between his writings and his character? Wang explained to one of his students, "Never write an essay when your emotions are stirred. If you write that way, whatever you write will certainly see anger triumph over reason. Wait until you have calmed down and use your intelligence, then you can make a sound argument." Wang Yuanhua's heart was ardent, but his essays are moderate and reserved. Yet behind those reasonable words you can sense volatile feelings.

The many guests who visited Wang Yuanhua's "Tsing Garden" parlor, whether students, friends, or admirers, all experienced the same thing. When someone was banging on in ostentatious tones, Wang's expression would convey a lively but dignified awareness of the foolishness of such talk and the truth behind surface appearances. As a revolutionary, Wang had always been concerned with politics, but in his later years he seemed to have seen beyond the mundane world and seen through political pretenses. With intensive reading of ancient books added to the ups and downs of a seventy-year career, this old man, full of history and knowledge of human nature, was no longer interested in the politics of the day. In his view, heroes come and go on the historical stage, but the important things in history do not change. This often left him anxious about the future. He felt that even if you could establish a democratic system, if it lacked a humane spirit and public ethics even democracy would degenerate.

The elder Wang Yuanhua worried about the decline of humanity's ancient civilizations, especially the diminution of the spirit of the humanities. In 1995, as the market economy swept across China and the search for wealth and material benefits became universal, intellectual circles held a great debate on the humanistic spirit in the Chinese tradition. Even though Wang did not participate in this debate, he shared the fear that mass culture would overwhelm elite culture accumulated over millennia of human history. He often said, "Art cannot be judged by ancient or modern, Chinese or foreign, new or old. It can only be distinguished as sublime or paltry, exquisite or vulgar, meaningful or moronic."[17] There are good things in mass culture, but when it is the dominant culture it erases the standards for art itself. It blindly pursues popularity and fashion and substitutes market taste for art itself. Wang was most against playing to the gallery. Over and over he would say, "A social culture that puts fashion first has no truly profound life of the spirit to speak of."

Wang's commitment to an independent intellectual spirit, the lesson of his life of revolution, embraced both Chinese wisdom and cosmopolitan conversation. In 2002, through the recommendation of Lin Yusheng, Wang read the last essay written by Harvard University's Benjamin Schwartz, "China and contemporary millenarianism: something new under the sun."[18] This essay gave Wang a great shock. In the spirit of the ancient prophets, the dying Professor Schwartz warned the world of the dangers lurking in human civilization: technological progress and various new sciences have given humanity consumerism and materialism, which has become a sort of "materialist apocalypticism" in which the humanistic spirit that the axial-age civilizations have bequeathed us is declining. Wang felt a strong resonance with Schwartz's argument. He realized that the decline of the human spirit is not just a problem which China is facing but also a common menace that confronts all human civilization. He wrote specifically on this, pointing out his worry: "China today has no reason to be excited by universal ideas from the West that are full of consumerism and materialism."[19]

In the years that followed, Wang Yuanhua's anxieties only increased. Like so many intellectuals of his generation, Wang was not only a nationalist but also a cosmopolitan. Wang Yuanhua's generation continued the tradition of *Tianxia* (All under Heaven) in Chinese culture, in which they approached problems not from the standpoint of nation and state, but from the perspective of all humanity. In his letter to Lin Yusheng, Wang wrote with a heavy heart,

> Isaiah Berlin said that the twentieth century was a terrible century, but in light of current trends the twenty-first century will see the collapse of civilization . . . Every time I think of this I am overcome by grief. I am already in my final years, I don't need anything. But when I think of our descendants, when I think of our long-standing cultural traditions, to imagine that they could be lost in a moment is a disaster that I cannot bear.[20]

The twentieth century is unbearable to recall; the twenty-first century is just a dim prospect. So Wang Yuanhua, in his final years, began to feel a certain nostalgia for that not-so-distant time, the nineteenth century. In 2001 in an important interview, "Dialogue on the humanistic spirit and the twenty-first century," he openly declared, "I have more feeling for the nineteenth century than for the twentieth century. Even today Western literature from the nineteenth century is my favorite reading ... In spirit I am a child of the nineteenth century; I grew up drinking the milk of writers of the nineteenth century."[21]

Why was Wang Yuanhua so stuck on the nineteenth century? What does it signify? For Wang the nineteenth century first of all represented breadth. It was a "vast field" of culture. The spirit of that age was open, an ocean receiving the waters of a hundred rivers, combining East and West. Wang Yuanhua was once a child of May Fourth, devoting himself to the grand project of enlightenment and defending the May Fourth spirit. In the 1990s, his reflections on May Fourth led him to see that, as the spirit of the twentieth century, the May Fourth Movement was narrow-minded. Looking back at the enlightenment scholars of the nineteenth and early twentieth centuries, he saw people like the publicist Liang Qichao, the translator Yan Fu, and the scholar Wang Guowei who saw no gulf between East and West and who worked to understand both civilizations. This reflected cultural self-confidence, the bearing of a civilized great nation, neither humble nor overbearing. These men were his models for China's future.

There was another reason for Wang's fondness for the nineteenth century. In his reading, the enlightenment thinking of the nineteenth century exemplified the humanistic spirit. In 1937 after he fled to Shanghai, nineteenth-century European literature became his only spiritual nourishment. From the English Dickens and the Brontë sisters, to the French Balzac and Romain Rolland, to the Russian Chekhov and Dostoyevsky, these writers formed Wang's inner being throughout his life. He said, "I love that nineteenth-century literature goes so deeply into people's emotions, takes such concern over their fates, lays such importance on their spiritual life, and affirms the most beautiful of sentiments."[22]

The core of the humanistic spirit is to take man as the goal, to value the individuality and dignity of each person. Wang Yuanhua considered that word "dignity" to be of the utmost importance. Having lived through the Cultural Revolution, Wang was especially sensitive to issues of dignity or honor. He said, "You cannot insult a person's dignity ... Thought is a strange thing. You cannot force thought upon another, nor can the force of another destroy your thought." Human dignity comes from our spirit, because man is a thinking being. In a letter to his students, Wang wrote, "Throughout my life – especially during the Cultural Revolution and similar political campaigns – I have experienced too much ruthlessness, callousness, and brutality. And so I hope that your generation will not have such insults to your honor, that you will be able to preserve your human dignity."[23] Human dignity suffered humiliation at the hands of power in the political campaigns of the past, and today, Wang feared, it would be lost to the vulgarity of the market. This broke Wang's heart. Over and over he would repeat the intellectual's credo: "Independent spirit, free thinking," to inspire this generation and to encourage his colleagues.[24] This independence and freedom are directed not just against imperious authority but also to resist commercialization and wealth.

Although in his old age he had accounts to settle with Hegel, still Wang kept as his lifelong motto Hegel's saying on the importance of human thought and the power of the spirit: "the power of the spirit cannot be underestimated or slighted." Wang Yuanhua wrote,

> I am a man who works with the pen. My greatest desire has been to fulfill the responsibility of a Chinese intellectual. Without toadying, without selling out, to offer something of value for people. And in whatever circumstance never to lower my aspirations or disgrace myself, never to chase fame or run away from danger.[25]

On May 9, 2008, Wang Yuanhua departed this life with dignity.

Chapter 9 – 2000s

After the suppression of the 1989 Tiananmen movement, Party leaders had shied away from political reforms, focusing on economic growth at all costs instead. By the year 2000 this had begun to lift China out of poverty and catapulted it into the ranks of the global economic superpowers. The political system remained unchanged, but during the 1990s and early 2000s the CCP and its new leader, Jiang Zemin, watched over the fastest-growing economy in the world (and probably in history). Chinese enterprises were integrated into the global market and the effects of globalization were visible everywhere.

A profound and unprecedented social change took place. Now there was an urban real-estate market and job mobility. The open economy provided a solid foundation for an increasingly mobile society and enabled the creation of a wealthy middle class and different types of civil-society organizations that asked for more political participation. The advent of the Internet in China allowed Chinese citizens to participate in political discussions and organize effective protests against perceived injustices. Market forces also fundamentally changed cultural practices. New technologies and the expansion of the market economy transformed the formerly uniform and relatively homogeneous public culture into a diverse and pluralistic culture that reflects the diversity of individual experiences in the reform era. At the same time, China's economic miracle had to contend with widening income inequalities, corruption, ethnic conflicts, and social fragmentation. In parallel with the growth in prosperity, the need for resources and raw materials also grew, which has come at great expense to the environment.

The rise of China also had an impact on global conditions beyond national borders. The country began to seek its economic influence with the confidence and the intentions of a future global superpower in search of raw materials, in Africa and beyond. China's growing economic power coincided with an increasingly assertive foreign policy. China built aircraft carriers, nuclear submarines, and stealth aircraft.

In the 2000s, as the Party faced a deeply transformed country, marked by prosperity for many though by no means for *all, by national pride, and by new forms of diversity, it was becoming a victim of its own success. There was increasing unease and unrest. Lively, concerned, and critical debates questioned the direction of Chinese society in the midst of extensive and rapid change. There were also concerns about the sustainability of Chinese development and questions about the widening gap between economic liberalization and the political monopoly of the Party. The far-reaching and rapid changes for society, politics, and culture in China thus tested the limits of the Party's capacity and resilience. After years of restless change, the question arose as to how long this development of unbridled growth could continue and to what extent the Party would be able to maintain its control over China. General Secretary Jiang Zemin officially stepped down in 2002, but in fact he was the looming presence overseeing this decade.*

9 THE 2000s
Jiang Zemin and the Naughty Aughties
JEREMY GOLDKORN

On October 1, 2009, the Chinese Communist Party celebrated the sixtieth anniversary of the founding of the People's Republic with an enormous military parade in Beijing. There were tanks, helicopters, planes, armored cars, amphibious vehicles, and thousands of soldiers from every major division of the People's Liberation Army. State media proudly enumerated the numbers: 10,000 troops, fifty-two weapons systems, 151 warplane flyovers, and twelve intercontinental-range missiles. The parade also gave the world a glimpse of what was said to be the world's first anti-ship ballistic missile (ASBM), the Dongfeng 21-C, nicknamed "aircraft carrier killer."

The parade included what the *New York Times* called "improbably, a female militia unit toting submachine guns and attired in red miniskirts and white jackboots, and a fleet of floats with representations of a giant fish and Mount Everest."[1] Among the floats were four carrying outsized portraits of each of China's post-revolutionary leaders, each decorated with two of the pictured leader's trademark slogans:

MAO ZEDONG
Long live Mao Zedong Thought
The Chinese people have stood up

DENG XIAOPING
Persevere with Deng Xiaoping Theory
Push forward with reform and opening up and the modernization of socialism

JIANG ZEMIN

Adhere to the important thoughts of the "Three Represents"

Comprehensively build a moderately prosperous society

HU JINTAO

Implement the scientific outlook on development

Unswervingly follow the path of socialism with Chinese characteristics

Two of the men depicted on the floats were still alive, and watching the parade: former president and General Secretary of the Communist Party Jiang Zemin, who stood behind the incumbent, Hu Jintao.

The last time Jiang had reviewed a military parade in Beijing – in 1999 for the fiftieth anniversary of the founding of the People's Republic – Deng had been dead for two years, Jiang was leader of the Party, and no one was breathing over *his* shoulder. But for the next decade, Jiang would breathe over the shoulder of Hu Jintao, a president and Party General Secretary who never really succeeded in marking out his own political turf. This meant that the first decade of the twenty-first century, the naughty aughties, when China went from third-page news to front-page story in the *Wall Street Journal*, was really the time of Jiang's Communist Party.

What were the aims of the Communist Party from 2000 to 2010, under Hu, who was under Jiang? Was the Party at that time a reformist organization? Was Jiang a leader who could or did change the Party? Fundamentally, was the Party he left behind different from the Party of Deng? What did China's increasingly globalized society make of this reformed Party?

Answers are difficult. China was a Wild West boomtown in the Naughties, an era of pregnant possibilities, with much craziness and vibrancy. The ghost of Jiang Zemin floated above it all. He continued to shape events through his proxies, the so-called Shanghai Gang or Shanghai Clique,[2] a group of Jiang loyalists who had worked with the former leader when he ran the city of Shanghai as mayor and Party secretary from 1985 to 1989. Developments that he had set in train, or pushed along, or agreed to in the 1990s, such as China's entry into the WTO, came to fruition in this decade.

I was living in Beijing at the time, working as an entrepreneur. My business was publishing a website (the now defunct *Danwei.org*) that covered Chinese media and politics critically. The Beijing city commercial authorities granted me a business license for technology consulting, which gave me legal cover to run a company that was producing uncensored media. Nobody ever checked up on what I was doing with my company. It felt like China was on the brink of a new era: I actually believed that I would be able to run an independent media company in Beijing, and the Communist Party would let me do it. The Party seemed open to new ideas: the Ministry of Culture even commissioned my company to arrange a forum attended by various foreign specialists in media and cultural fields to advise the ministry on how to engage with foreigners. Those were heady days. (My website was blocked in 2009, as the last of Jiang's powers were waning.)

The era is too close to our own to allow for a steady bearing, but seen from today, in the first decade of the twenty-first century, the Party seems to have been making an uncertain but genuine attempt to withdraw its tentacles from society.

Ruling from behind the Screen

Jiang had served as General Secretary of the Communist Party of China from 1989 to 2002, chairman of the Party's Central Military Commission from 1989 to 2004, and president from 1993 to 2003. But for most of that time, Deng Xiaoping had remained "paramount leader." When Deng died in 1997, his *People's Daily* obituary called him "One of the major leaders of the People's Republic,"[3] while the *New York Times* said that while he "formally retired from his last important post, chairman of China's central military commission, in 1989 ... he continued to wield immeasurable influence, reserving final say in all important political matters for several years afterward, and finally relinquishing power only as he grew frail and disoriented."[4]

Despite his frailty, Jiang's hold over the Party remained questionable for the last few years of Deng's life. "Veiled attacks on Jiang's theories of governance" in Party magazines would "continue through 1997," writes political scientist Bruce Gilley[5] – a sign that powerful forces inside the Party were opposed to Jiang's leadership. But by the end of 1997, Deng was truly gone, and Jiang was in charge. That year was "a landmark for Jiang Zemin," according to Willy Wo-Lap Lam:[6]

> He presided over the historic July 1 Hong Kong handover. The Chinese economy grew by 8.8 percent while inflation dipped to two percent. The president shoved aside two long-standing enemies, Qiao Shi and Liu Huaqing at the 15th Chinese Communist Party Congress in September. A month later [he] achieved the long sought-after stature of world statesman by holding a historic summit with US President Bill Clinton at the White House.

But by that point, Jiang had only five years to go as official leader. The system of leadership transition set up by Deng that led to Jiang's rule meant he was supposed to retire after two "terms," or roughly a decade. Jiang stepped down as General Secretary of the Party in November 2002 to make way for Hu Jintao. But the elder leader waited until September 2004 to relinquish his post as chairman of the Party's Central Military Commission, and another six months to resign from his chairmanship of the state's Central Military Commission. In other words, Jiang had formal power over the barrel of the gun until more than two years into Hu's first term as leader. An equivalent would be an American president retaining the title of commander in chief of the armed forces more than two years after he had left the White House.

Jiang's influence remained powerful even without a formal title: Six of nine new Politburo Standing Committee members appointed at the 16th Party Congress of 2002 were members of the "Shanghai Gang."[7] Three of Jiang's men stayed on the Standing Committee after the 17th Party Congress in 2007.

So although Hu Jintao assumed all the trappings of China's top leadership position when he took over as General Secretary in 2002, he seemed chosen almost for his weakness and lack of revolutionary credentials. He was an uninspiring speaker, sometimes caricatured as a robot. He was the first leader of the People's Republic without any direct ties to the Revolution. Although Jiang did not fight in the Civil War, he had been an underground student organizer in Shanghai, whereas Hu not only came from a merchant (capitalist!) family, he was just seven years old in 1949, and only joined the Party in 1964. He had never studied in the Soviet Union (or anywhere else outside China).

Hu Jintao and the "Most Democratic Body in the World"

Hu's relative weakness was often said to demonstrate a strength of the Party's method of collective leadership, by both Western commentators and Party leaders themselves. One of the Wikileaks Cablegate documents (dated July 2009) is illuminating:[8]

HU JINTAO AS CHAIRMAN OF THE BOARD?

Chinese Communist Party Politburo decision-making is similar to executive decision-making in a large company, two well-connected contacts say. Chen Jieren, nephew of Politburo Standing Committee (PBSC) Member He Guoqiang and editor of a Communist Youth League website, told PolOff [US Embassy political officer] May 13 that Party General Secretary Hu Jintao could be compared to the Chairman of the Board or CEO of a big corporation.

Wu Jiaxiang, who served under now-Premier Wen Jiabao on the Central Committee General Office staff in the late 1980s, used the same analogy in a May 18 meeting with PolOffs. Wu said that PBSC decision making was akin to a corporation in which the greater the stock ownership the greater the voice in decisions. "Hu Jintao holds the most stock, so his views carry the greatest weight," and so on down the hierarchy, but the PBSC did not formally vote, according to Wu. "It is a consensus system," he maintained, "in which members can exercise veto power."

Chen had told PolOff previously that he knew "on very good authority" that "major policies," such as the country's core policy on Taiwan or North Korea, had to be decided by the full 25-member Politburo. Other more specific matters, he said, were decided by the nine-member PBSC alone. Some issues were put to a formal vote, while others were merely discussed until a consensus was reached. Either way, Chen stated sarcastically, the Politburo was the "most democratic body in the world," the only place in China where true democracy existed.

What Chen did not say is that outside observers had no way of knowing what was driving the decision making. If more than half of the Politburo members were under the influence of Jiang Zemin, the process was perhaps a little less democratic than Chen would have his interlocutor believe.

The Golden Age of Chinese Liberalism under Hu Jintao, and Jiang Zemin

Democratic or not, the first decade of the twenty-first century was a time of rapid change and economic opening up for Chinese society, which was accompanied by an influx of foreign technologies and ideas. At the same time, the government continued to remove itself from its citizens' private and cultural lives. Civil society grew as activist lawyers, NGOs, university professors, and journalists pushed the boundaries of the politically possible.

The major events that defined China's new reality in the 2000s happened under Jiang Zemin's leadership, before Hu Jintao became General Secretary and president. First, in July of 2001, the International Olympic Committee selected Beijing as the venue for the summer games of 2008. Second, China became a member of the World Trade Organization (WTO) in December 2001. This was negotiated by Jiang's government, or, to be more specific, by his premier, Zhu Rongji, who was much beloved by his Western counterparts and was one of the people who did most to convince Western business elites that China was in safe hands.

Jiang had laid the ideological groundwork for Communist China to join the WTO in the 1990s, with his "Three Represents" contribution to Party theory. This theory states that the Communist Party of China "should be representative of advanced social productive forces, advanced culture, and the interests of the overwhelming majority." This was a welcome to "entrepreneurs" (what the ideologically unenlightened might call capitalists) as representatives of "advanced social productive forces" to join the Party, a reassurance to China's educated elite (as "forces of advanced culture") that the Party respected and valued their knowledge, and a promise to Chinese society that the Party would take a backseat. Making money and having fun was OK as long as one did not challenge the Party's right to rule.[9]

While it is often mocked for its ridiculous-sounding name, the theory was actually translated into practice – essentially, that the Party should welcome businesspeople into its fold, and be more responsive to citizens who are not Party members, including respect for China's educated elites. The policy led to important changes: Almost every significant Chinese entrepreneur is now co-opted into the Chinese government as an adviser to the Chinese People's Political Consultative Conference (CPPCC), and Chinese tycoons sometimes join the entourage of presidential visits, as their Western counterparts do. This was a remarkable change for a party that still called itself Communist: the country's biggest capitalists were (and continue to be) not only welcomed but celebrated by state media and propaganda organizations. Likewise, a fair number of China's intellectuals found work and rewards working in the Party, for the Party's goals, or by aligning their public voices to avoid open contradiction with Party rule. While dissidents remained, China's establishment intellectuals, now pocketing a nice salary (or two), found ways to couch their political criticism as advice to the Party. At universities and a growing number of think tanks, intellectuals found productive, prestigious, and well-paid work as teachers in classrooms and as researchers.

Fears that China would turn its back on economic reform after the death of Deng Xiaoping in 1997 were thoroughly dispelled by the reformed Party under Jiang's leadership. In fact, Jiang oversaw a period of extraordinary growth, an economic boom of a scale the world had never seen.

With WTO membership, China's status changed, very suddenly. No longer was the country a poor developing nation that Wall Street bankers and international political leaders could afford to ignore. Now it was a market of nearly 1.3 billion people that made every multinational-company executive salivate, and go on to lose a mint. Now it was preparing to host the most ambitious Olympic Games ever, a "coming-out party" on the world stage.[10]

In the first decade of the twenty-first century, China became the world's second-largest economy and the world's largest goods exporter. The country experienced the fastest growth in GDP per capita of any major economy in human history – in 2001 China's GDP was US$1.3 trillion. By 2010, it was $6.1 trillion. Average GDP growth was around 10 percent for a whole decade. Foreign direct investment (FDI) in China leapt from under $1 billion in the year 2000 to more than $100 billion in 2010. Companies and entrepreneurs from all over the globe arrived in China, seduced by the promise of a gargantuan market and a government that seemed to encourage any kind of business activity, as long as it helped grow China's economy. Even Google – which at the time still promoted its old corporate slogan "Don't do evil" – set up shop in China in 2006, promising to expand the range of information available to Chinese Internet users (it beat a hasty retreat in 2010).[11]

Although foreign companies tended to get more anglophone press, Chinese companies, both private and state-owned, were perhaps even greater beneficiaries of China's entry into the WTO and the positive buzz that the coming Olympic Games generated. Nowhere was this more obvious than in the Internet industry. Companies like Alibaba, Baidu, Sina, and Tencent began life as clones of Western tech services in the late 1990s, but by 2010 they had established themselves as major global players with user numbers matching and exceeding their American peers like Google and Facebook. The framework that the Party gave these companies under Jiang Zemin's leadership provided some, but not all, of the conditions for this growth. China blocked outside Internet companies effectively with what scholars Geremie Barmé and Sang Ye dub "The Great Firewall of China."[12] Thus, the Chinese companies did not have to compete for the China market with Facebook and later Twitter and Google. Outside of tech, Chinese companies also began competing globally: from shipbuilding to real estate, chain restaurants to fashion brands – China stepped up its capitalist game at an awesome speed under the rule of Hu Jintao, and the man standing behind him at the military parade in 2009, Jiang Zemin.

With the flows of money came people: a population census conducted in 2010 found more than a million foreign citizens residing legally in China, including citizens of Hong Kong, Macao, and Taiwan, but not including short-term visitors and businesspeople living in China without a long-term work visa.[13] In the previous census of the year 2000, foreign citizens were not even counted. The foreigners brought capital, and intellectual property, but they also brought ideas. Deng Xiaoping is supposed to have said, "If you open the window for fresh air, you have to expect some flies to blow in," meaning that opening China's market to the world meant a certain acceptance of values and ideologies that were anathema to the Party. The flies swarmed in.

During the 2000s, foreign and domestic money poured into the Internet, opening up channels of direct communication between citizens and enabling small provincial newspapers to get nationwide exposure for reporting. This had consequences for the Party, especially in local governance. For example, in 2003, the *Southern Metropolis Daily*, a Guangzhou-based newspaper, published an investigative report about a migrant named Sun Zhigang. Sun was arrested in Guangzhou for not having a "residence permit" and was beaten to death while in police custody in Guangzhou. The article went viral among China's then 80-million-strong population of Internet users. By June of that year, the government abolished the "custody and repatriation" policy established in 1982 that had led to Sun's detention.[14] The power of China's "intranet" netizens would only grow, as we shall see in Chapter 10 in the Guo Meimei case.

That same year, a young journalist with the online name "Mu Zimei" (木子美) started a blog in which she recorded her sexual experiences. After publishing a rather negative "review" of her experiences with a well-known rock musician, her diary became an overnight Internet hit, read by millions of Chinese youngsters. Blogging became a household word as millions of ordinary citizens – and professional journalists – discovered the joy of publishing without an editor or censor.[15] In December of that year, *Menbox*, China's first openly gay glossy magazine, began distributing to newsstands in Beijing, Shanghai, and other large cities. The magazine was produced in partnership with the prestigious Chinese Academy of Social Sciences.

In 2004, the advertising operations of the state-owned *Beijing Youth Daily* Newspaper Group were listed on Hong Kong's stock market – the first such listing of a mainland media company. As government departments ceased subsidies to local and some national newspapers, these publications were forced to go to the market for money, and the market rewarded interesting news over propaganda. For the first time in the history of the People's Republic, there was a powerful commercial force encouraging journalists and editors to take risks.

Some of these challenging social developments came through entertainment. In 2005, Hunan television station's reality talent show *Super Girls* (*Chaoji Nüsheng*) broadcast the final, knockout competition. The finalists were far from conventionally feminine, nor did they fit any model of youth or womanhood that the Party would endorse. But the show was a nationwide hit, drawing advertisers away from the stodgier programs on China Central TV (CCTV) and giving viewers a tiny taste of democracy: winners were decided by vote via mobile phone text message.[16] Some 8 million people "voted" on the final night of the show. In 2006, the Rolling Stones played a concert in Shanghai. Also that year, the Uyghur economist Ilham Tohti founded a website called *Uyghur Online*, which published critical commentary in Chinese and Uyghur on social issues. (In 2014, Tohti was found guilty of "separatism" and sentenced to life imprisonment.) The Party had given an inch in the "Three Represents," but society tried to take a mile.

In fact, as the 2008 Olympic Games approached, the Party advertised its openness to the world and allowed an unprecedented amount of unsupervised intellectual and cultural activity. In retrospect, some commenters called it the "golden age of Chinese liberalism under Hu Jintao and Wen Jiabao." But perhaps it should be the "golden age of Chinese liberalism under Jiang Zemin," because the elder leader's presence was undeniable, both physically and ideologically.

Jiang appeared in public on multiple occasions during every single year of Hu Jintao's tenure, often accompanied by senior leaders still in office. Jiang loyalists and relatives remained in key positions in the Party bureaucracy. They also commanded power in the growing economy of state assets under private or semiprivate control. But more importantly, Jiang's Three Represents – which was included in amendments to the Party and state constitutions at the 16th Party Congress in 2002 – set the tone for the next decade.

By contrast, Hu Jintao's contribution to Party theory, the "Scientific Outlook on Development," was a veritable nonevent. Party propagandists struggled to define this as anything more than reheated leftovers of "socialism with Chinese characteristics" (Deng's policy from the 1980s).

It got worse. The other slogan associated with Hu Jintao is the schoolmarmish "Eight Honors, Eight Shames," which he began promoting in 2006 as a moral code for all Chinese, but especially Communist Party cadres:[17]

- Honor to those who love the motherland, and shame on those who harm the motherland.
- Honor to those who serve the people, and shame on those who betray the people.
- Honor to those who quest for science, and shame on those who refuse to be educated.
- Honor to those who are hardworking, and shame on those who indulge in comfort and hate work.
- Honor to those who help each other, and shame on those who seek gain at the expense of others.
- Honor to those who are trustworthy, and shame on those who trade integrity for profits.
- Honor to those who abide by law and discipline, and shame on those who break laws and discipline.
- Honor to those who uphold plain living and hard struggle, and shame on those who wallow in extravagance and pleasures.

China has a history of moral codes for Communists: Liu Shaoqi's 1939 pamphlet *How to Be a Good Communist* guided Party members on self-cultivation and subordinating personal interest to the greater – that is, the Party's – good.[18] Lei Feng embodied selfless devotion to the collective and Mao Zedong Thought in the 1960s. But unlike Liu's text, Hu's moral code was not written for a revolutionary party: the context was a growing sense among the public – reflected in the Chinese media and Internet commentary – that China's rapid economic development had left the country in a spiritual vacuum: the old ideologies and Communist values had disappeared, replaced only with rampant materialism, corruption, and moral decadence. Lei Feng had been revived, but the Communist boy scout was laughed off as a meme for stupidity. The emptiness of the "Scientific Outlook on Development" did not succeed in rallying the Party and country around a set of values, but the Eight Honors, Eight Shames had even less impact. Even worse for Hu Jintao's legacy, by 2006 China's Internet population was heading for 200 million, and a number of those people were writing blogs that ruthlessly mocked Hu's campaign.

The Olympic Games and the Global Financial Crisis

Despite growing public cynicism about the Party's confused ideological messaging, for most citizens the extraordinary economic growth of the post-WTO years and its concomitant rise in living standards were more than enough to compensate. The Olympic Games became a promise and then an achievement of the Party that resonated with large numbers of Chinese people who were genuinely proud of the country's apparent arrival on the world stage. Not even riots in Tibet in March 2008, nor the Wenchuan earthquake in Sichuan in May of that year that killed around 70,000 people, dented public enthusiasm for the Olympics, and for China's new image as a major global player. In fact, together with the games, those two events helped solidify a sense in China that the country had finally stood up.

A new generation of Internet-savvy young Chinese people who understood English were horrified by the way their country was represented in Western media coverage of the protests and subsequent ethnic conflicts in Tibet, which tended to be sympathetic to the Tibetans. This trend was epitomized by the website *Anti-CNN.com*, founded by a student in Beijing named Rao Jin, dedicated to exposing the alleged hypocrisies of the Western press. (Disillusionment with Western ideas and Western media was not novel: the 1996 best-selling "China Can Say No" (*Zhongguo keyi shuo bu*) by former Americophiles Song Qiang and Zhang Zangzang expressed similar attitudes).[19] These were informed and independent critics, not just Party stooges. These young intellectuals "jumped the firewall" (accessing Western media by using VPN software). The Party may have become more irrelevant for many Chinese youth, but ardent patriotism (that tends to buttress Party legitimacy) had taken root and took issue with slanted Western portrayals of China. *Anti-CNN.com* was just the latest example of young Chinese people defending the PRC and its government without direct coercion from the Communist Party, something that continues to be underemphasized in media reports about young Chinese nationalists.

The Party even managed to turn the Wenchuan earthquake into a propaganda success. In the first few weeks after the quake, journalists and bloggers had exposed deadly local government malfeasance, such as schools built with substandard materials, so local officials could skim money off the top, which collapsed during the quake, killing thousands of students. But the government soon silenced such reporting and dispatched Premier Wen Jiabao to the epicenter of the quake to pose for photos and assure the people that the central government had their back. (A similar dynamic would play out in early 2020 as Beijing turned the narrative about the COVID-19 epidemic from one of government cover-ups and bungling to a story of disease-fighting success and global leadership.)

By the time the Olympic Games opening ceremony began at the auspicious date and time of 8 p.m. Beijing time, August 8, 2008, the Communist Party had succeeded in convincing much of the Chinese population into celebrating. The event comprised a mass concert of dance, music, and lighting involving thousands of performers at the Beijing National Stadium, also known as the Bird's Nest. The show was produced by film director Zhang Yimou, with fireworks by visual artist Cai Guoqiang. Both artists were once considered avant-garde in China (and beloved by the international art scene), but now the two men had found comfortable positions producing light shows for the party-state. Jiang's "Three Represents" at work.

And what a show it was. It wowed the audience in Beijing. Television viewers across the world were suddenly exposed to a China that looked rich, modern, and powerful. China's "Prosperous Age" was at hand. The rest of the games did not disappoint: China ran a smooth operation, the country looked good on global television, and China raked in the lion's share of gold medals, forty-eight compared to America's thirty-six and Russia's twenty-four.

Jiang Zemin and Hu Jintao both attended the opening ceremony of the games. They must have been very happy with that evening's performance, and with the rest of the games, which were incident-free and competently managed. They would soon have cause to be even happier.

The games ended on August 24. Less than a month later, on September 15, 2008, the investment bank Lehman Brothers collapsed, heralding the global financial crisis of 2008. Within a year, the economic contagion had put much of the globe into recession, but China was partly insulated because its economy was not completely interconnected with world financial markets. And the

Chinese government kept the country's economy steaming along with enormous stimulus packages. China came out on top.

This had consequences. The Olympic success, combined with the Western financial woes, convinced many that China's day had come. Deng Xiaoping had advised "hiding our strength and biding our time." No more. By 2010, the scholar David Shambaugh – not a China hawk by any means – was writing about Beijing "showing its claws,"[20] and many other observers began to observe a new swagger in the manner of senior Party officials. If Beijing was showing its claws abroad, at home it was also baring its fangs. Although the Chinese economy emerged from the financial crisis unscathed, the Party had plenty to worry about: perhaps most importantly, a deadly ethnic riot in Xinjiang in August of 2009 and fears about an increasingly critical – and exponentially growing – social media commentariat. Events abroad were worrying: Iran was experiencing its "Facebook revolution," cheered on by techno-utopians and much of the Western press.

In response to these threats, the Leninist machinery of the party-state began to reassert itself. Domestic Internet censorship intensified. Veteran dissident and literary critic Liu Xiaobo, who had headlined an effort by a number of Chinese intellectuals to push for democratic reforms in Charter '08 as an Internet open letter, was peremptorily arrested for the effrontery. He would be convicted and die still under incarceration in 2017. Preparations for the sixtieth anniversary military parade in Beijing attended by Jiang and Hu involved chasing further dissidents and other trouble-makers out of Beijing. By the end of 2009, all major foreign social media websites had been blocked. Rights activists, lawyers, journalists, and bloggers saw the end of the golden age of liberalism under Hu Jintao (and Jiang Zemin), and even in business the talk was less about the private sector and more about "the state advancing and the private sector retreating." The Party began to take back that "mile" from society.

The Ten Grave Problems of the Hu–Wen Era

In the closing years of the Hu Jintao administration, the Party had even more to worry about. There was a popular perception that corruption was out of control. Citizens and senior officials alike could hear the environmental destruction wrought by decades of breakneck economic growth in the coughs of their children. Extreme inequality was obvious in Chinese cities where Bentleys competed for road space with bicycle couriers earning a couple of hundred dollars a month. In 2011, a high-speed train crash near the city of Wenzhou that killed forty people prompted even the Communist Party mouthpiece, *People's Daily*, to wonder in an editorial whether China had not lost its way pursuing a "blood-soaked GDP."[21] Stories of corruption abounded. The Chinese Internet lit up in March 2012 after reports that the son of top Hu Jintao adviser Ling Jihua died in a car crash in Beijing – in a Ferrari, accompanied by two half-naked women.[22] Also in that year, the *New York Times* and *Bloomberg* published separate stories detailing the wealth accumulated by close family members and relatives of both incumbent premier Wen Jiabao and president-to-be Xi Jinping.[23]

By the end of the naughty aughties messaging in state media and scuttlebutt from diplomats reported in the media had already begun to make it clear that the Communist Party machinery was settling on a choice of successor for Hu Jintao. It was Xi Jinping, the son of one of the founding fathers of the Chinese Revolution, Xi Zhongxun. Xi did in fact assume leadership of the Party and the country. The era of Jiang Zemin, Hu Jintao and Wen Jiabao came to a formal end on November 15, 2012, when Xi Jinping was appointed General Secretary of the Communist Party and chairman of the CPC Central Military Commission by the 18th Central Committee of the Communist Party of China. His rise was not a sure thing: Bo Xilai, another son of a revolutionary leader, was widely seen as a powerful rival to Xi, but his career came to a dramatic end after his wife was found guilty of murdering a British businessman in 2012.[24] Bo himself ended up behind bars on corruption charges, leaving Xi untouchable.

Both Jiang and Hu attended the meeting when Xi's ascent was formalized. For them, it was not, perhaps, as happy an occasion as the sixtieth anniversary military parade three years earlier. This time they watched from the sidelines: there was a new man in charge. However, many observers, both inside and outside China, looked forward to Xi taking power as General Secretary and president. *New York Times* columnist Nicholas Kristof predicted that Xi would "spearhead a resurgence of economic reform, and probably some political easing as well."[25] Kristof bravely, or naively, went on to forecast that "Mao's body will be hauled out of Tiananmen Square on his watch, and Liu Xiaobo, the Nobel Peace Prize-winning writer, will be released from prison." (Needless to say, Liu Xiaobo died in prison in 2017 and Mao Zedong's corpse is still in the mausoleum at Tiananmen Square.)

Even commentators who did not see Xi as a reformer recognized that he had inherited a government that was struggling to cope with the result of its successes. In 2007, Wen Jiabao himself had warned of the "Four Uns" – that the Chinese economy had become "unbalanced, unstable, unco-ordinated, and unsustainable." In August 2012 – a few months before Xi was anointed top leader – Deng Yuwen, a senior editor at the Party School journal *Study Times*, published an editorial titled "Ten grave problems left behind by the Hu–Wen administration."[26] The ten problems were:

1 no breakthroughs in economic restructuring and constructing a consumer-driven economy;
2 failure to nurture and grow a middle class;
3 an increased rural–urban gap;
4 population policy lagging behind reality;
5 bureaucratization and profit-incentivization of educational and scientific research;
6 environmental pollution continuing to worsen;
7 government failure to establish a stable energy supply system;
8 moral lapses and the collapse of ideology;
9 "firefighting" and "stability-maintenance"-style diplomacy, lacking vision, strategic thinking, and specific measures;
10 insufficient efforts to push political reform and promote democracy.

Xi had his work cut out for him.

Toad Worship in Xi Jinping's New Era

Jiang's network of loyalists in the Party leadership were almost completely removed by the 18th Central Committee that selected Xi as General Secretary and president in 2012 and 2013, respectively. Within months, Xi began a crackdown on corruption (and his political enemies), civil society organizations, and the media. Xi strengthened governing techniques invented during Jiang's rule: the crackdown on Falun Gong since 1999 became a template for religious repression in Tibet and, under Xi, in Xinjiang. The Great Firewall was invented in the 1990s; Xi fortified it and promoted it as a positive feature of Internet sovereignty.

However, it would take a few years for Xi's autocratic tendencies to be widely acknowledged. In 2013, it was not yet obvious that Xi's China would be a much more repressive place. State media and official reports from Party meetings frequently quoted Xi on the need for reform, and observers read what they wanted into that word. Nicholas Kristof was only one of many believers in the liberal possibilities of Xi's rule.

That year, Dutch artist Florentijn Hofman inflated an enormous yellow duck and tethered it near the waterfront of Hong Kong island. The installation immediately inspired copies in cities across China, initially all yellow ducks, but later a whole menagerie of floating animals. By 2015, there was a giant inflatable toad floating on Kunming Lake at the Summer Palace in Beijing. Photographs of the toad circulated on the Internet and online wags soon began comparing the toad's expression to former president and General Secretary of the Communist Party Jiang Zemin – the resemblance lay in his thick black spectacles and pants pulled up way past his waist.

Despite the mockery inherent in comparing an elderly Party leader to an inflatable toad, an online fan culture dedicated to Jiang began to develop called "toad worship culture" (*hama wenhua*).[27] Adherents, who called themselves "toad fans," created online groups to share videos, photos, memes, and quotes by Jiang. By 2015, it was also apparent that Jiang's China had been a much more tolerant place than the country ruled by Xi Jinping. Part of the appeal of toad culture seemed to be nostalgia for a time when China's leader was more approachable, given to off-the-cuff remarks to journalists in several languages, and playing the erhu or piano in front of foreign dignitaries and television cameras. And nostalgia for a time when it seemed that Chinese civil society and freedom of expression were expanding.

Compared to Xi Jinping's grim efficiency, Jiang appeared in a whole new light to young Chinese Internet users, who might not even have been born when the Elder (*zhangzhe*) – as some toad fans called Jiang – was in office. Was he a more enlightened ruler than

Xi? How much responsibility does Jiang bear for the illiberal nature of the Chinese Communist Party under Xi Jinping?

In a caustic essay criticizing Xi for his handling of the COVID-19 outbreak, the legal scholar Xu Zhangrun – whose recent writings have earned him suspension from his teaching duties at Tsinghua University and house arrest – had this to say:

> The Three Represents and the ideas [and policy changes of the time] represented a relative apogee of possibility; since then there has been an evident downward curve which, in recent years, has indicated that the Communists are ever more obsessed with control over their Rivers and Mountains, in particular by means of big data totalitarianism.[28]

Toad culture is nostalgia for that "apogee of possibility," but is the toad himself worthy? Perhaps not. The Three Represents may have been a sincere attempt to democratize the Party, or at least give it a mechanism to hear public feedback and allow citizens to participate in the political process a little more than previously. But when he left office, Jiang left in place a caretaker administration that was never powerful enough to make any real changes. Hu and Wen, with Jiang watching from behind, just kicked the can down the road when it came to so many urgent problems facing China, from inequality to environmental degradation to deteriorating relations with ethnic minorities. Writing in 2015, Chinese journalist Shi Feike commented on toad culture with a judgment that may ring true when the Party eventually leaves the stage:

> The nostalgia wave for the "toad" is a natural outcome of the comparison with the "bun" [a derogatory nickname for Xi Jinping]. But actually, there is nothing to be nostalgic about.
>
> The trend in the past three decades has always been that each leader is less accomplished than his predecessor.

Chapter 10 – 2010s

From arid Party babble to the Internet fashion of "toad worship" for former General Secretary Jiang Zemin, the 2000s reflected the increasing alienation of the Party from daily life in China. A rising urban middle class was mesmerized by the new consumerism. Struggling rural families labored in the villages to make ends meet and sent husbands and adult children to the cities to work as "migrant laborers." Life no longer turned around Party events. Political study campaigns came and went without anyone – other than the more than 80 million Party members – taking much notice. The party-state was a fact of life, but it was the local state that dominated daily life, sometimes delivering the services of a somewhat intrusive nanny state and sometimes preying on citizens in the form of rent-seeking local officials.

The Party seemed to be retreating to some sort of predictable, authoritarian politics, something more akin to the later years of the Nationalist Party on Taiwan in the last decades of the twentieth century: freedom to make money and enjoy yourselves, so long as you keep out of politics. The Party delivered two notable achievements – entry into the WTO in 2001 and a boisterously successful Olympics in 2008. But the major achievement was a decade of tremendous economic growth. On top of that, China survived the global Great Recession of 2008–2009. Yet Party ideology became something of a farce. Jiang Zemin's revision of Maoism in the "Three Represents" mostly garnered mockery from intellectuals, while the "Scientific Socialism" of the next General Secretary, Hu Jintao, brought yawns from all concerned. While both the Party and the public took pride in China's rise and began to doubt the West as it stumbled financially, the reformed Party increasingly looked aloof and unconcerned about China's growing domestic problems: pollution and the plight of some 200 million underpaid and displaced migrant workers. But importantly the Party was unable to control rampant corruption.

Coming into the 2010s the Party faced the twin challenges of legitimacy: relevance to people's lives and the ability to curb corruption, pollution, and the woes of the working poor, as well as *the frustrations of the rising middle class. The Party had lost control of the national story. Into this maelstrom strode an audacious young woman, flaunting her newfound wealth: Guo Meimei was an Internet sensation and then a public pariah who set off a public firestorm over government corruption.*

THE 2010s

10 Guo Meimei: The Story of a Young Netizen Portends a Political Throwback

GUOBIN YANG

Due to the coronavirus disease outbreak, the entire city of Wuhan was locked down on January 23, 2020. The crisis induced by the epidemic has prompted much soul-searching among commentators and citizens alike. Some protest that the epidemic would not have spread so fast if the Wuhan police had not silenced whistle-blowers by accusing them of spreading rumors on the Internet. One key criticism is that it is the lack of an open and free-speech environment that kept the public ill-informed of the coronavirus disease in its critical early period. Such a political environment, however, did not appear overnight. Rather, it is the result of long-term CCP efforts to censor online speech, especially the policies and campaigns implemented since Xi Jinping became CCP General Secretary in November 2012.

The coronavirus epidemic exposed the flaws in the current Party regime. To understand the origins of these flaws, let us return to 2011, when the Chinese Internet was anything but quiescent. Instead, it was full of riotous and contentious activities. That was the Internet that the new Party leadership under Xi Jinping would set out to tame after 2012.

The year 2011 was also pregnant with political uncertainties and even dangers for the Party's dominance of the PRC state. It was the year of the Arab Spring revolutions. In January 2011, Tunisian President Zine El Abidine Ben Ali fled his country. On February 19, barely ten days after Egypt's Hosni Mubarak was forced from office by revolutionary insurgents, anonymous calls for a jasmine revolution in China appeared on overseas Chinese-language websites. They called on people to rally at designated times and places in thirteen Chinese cities. Party authorities acted pre-emptively by rounding up prominent dissidents and installing a heavy police presence. The strong pre-emptive measures taken against even the tiniest manifestations of a popular movement revealed the anxieties of Chinese Party leaders.

Their anxieties had multiple sources. After the scandal of the Sanlu melamine-tainted milk powder in 2008, the urban middle class had lived in fear of food safety. Many people saw the root cause of the food-safety problems as a failure in Party governance. They did not believe that Party leaders were doing their job supervising the dairy industry. Other social concerns included rising food prices, unstoppable housing prices, unemployment, and growing costs for medical care and education. A crisis of trust plagued public institutions. This loss of public trust constituted a challenge to those in charge, an implicit challenge to the claim of the Party to be leading China forward.

Party leaders were not blind to these problems. To gauge public sentiments, then Premier Wen Jiabao went online three times to interact with netizens, the most recent of which took place on February 27, 2011. This was unprecedented. New laws and policies were also introduced to tackle the issues. Barely a year after the melamine milk scandal, China passed its first food-safety law. And yet just as the new law came into effect, melamine-tainted milk powder resurfaced on the market in early 2010. Clearly, the problem was systemic and patching up potholes here and there was no longer an option. China's political system was gasping for breath.

It was against this background that Hu Jintao, then the General Secretary of the Chinese Communist Party, chaired a Politburo meeting on May 30, 2011, to address the question of strengthening and innovating social management. Soon afterwards, on July 5, the Party issued a policy document concerning the very same issue of social management.[1] The message was clear: the Party had trouble handling all the social problems and must innovate its methods of governance.

There were other anxieties. The top CCP leadership was slated to change in 2012. Fierce elite negotiations and power shuffles happened in 2011. On February 6, 2012, the elite power struggle spilled into public view, when Wang Lijun, deputy mayor and chief of police in the western Chinese city of Chongqing, shocked the world by entering the American Consulate in Chengdu to seek protection (but was turned back over to Chinese authorities by the American Consulate the following day). Wang Lijun was the right-hand man of Bo Xilai, the party secretary of Chongqing and Xi Jinping's rival for the top CCP leadership position. Soon afterwards, on March 15, 2012, Bo Xilai was removed from office; he was tried and sentenced to life in prison in 2013 for bribery, graft, and abuse of power. In November 2012, Xi Jinping became the new CCP General Secretary and China's top leader.

Guo Meimei and the "Red Cross Commercial Society"

In this roiling political season, the protagonist of our story was thrust into public view. Guo Meimei was barely twenty years old on June 21, 2011. Her name means Beauty Guo. If it were in 1966, she might have replaced the "beauty" in her name with a more militant and revolutionary-sounding word. She would have been a Red Guard making loyalty oaths to the Chinese Communist Party and Chairman Mao and chanting quotations from Mao's Little Red Book. She would have been most proudly dressed in secondhand army uniforms, the national youth fashion of the time.

But 2011 was not 1966. Forty years is a long time in modern Chinese history. None of the things above would mean anything to Guo Meimei now. Instead, like others of her age, she was a netizen, or *wangmin*, spending lots of time online. On Sina Weibo, China's leading social media platform in 2011, she had posted photographs of herself and her Maserati and Lamborghini automobiles, dozens of Hermes handbags, and expensive jewelry. Times have changed. Revolutionary virtue no longer has much currency in today's China. Wealth is the new virtue.

Nor is there exactly anything wrong about what Guo was doing on social media. In an age of selfies and in a country with 500 million Internet users as of 2011, displays of personal wealth and success on social media could not be more common. In China, as in the rest of the world, Internet culture feeds endless online reality shows by enticing users to update their online status and share their personal lives. In 2011, Guo Meimei was just one of millions who displayed their glamorous lives on Sina Weibo.

But the hapless Guo made the mistake of identifying herself as the general manager of a Red Cross Commercial Society on her Weibo account. On June 21, 2011, this job title became a headline on Tianya, one of China's most popular online communities: "New discovery on Weibo! A 20-year-old general manager of 'Red Cross Commercial Society,' all sorts of wealth shown off! Hurry up and go see!"[2] The posting linked Guo's wealth to the Red Cross Society of China (RCSC) and ended provocatively, "Whoever continues to donate money to the Red Cross must be a moron!"

To the infinitely curious minds of Chinese netizens, Guo's job title was an invitation to investigation. Many suspected that the Red Cross Commercial Society must be related to the Red Cross Society of China (RCSC). To them, Guo's story provided an opportunity to expose the RCSC. At a time of declining trust in China's official institutions, there was nothing more gratifying to them than to discredit a public agency like that.

The RCSC made a good target. A member of the International Federation of the Red Cross, the RCSC is a ministerial-level quasi-governmental agency qua charity organization. It is led by individuals boasting high-ranking Party leadership credentials. In 2011, the RCSC executive vice president and Party secretary was Zhao Baige, who was a former deputy director and vice Party secretary of the National Population and Family Planning Commission. As of February 2020, RCSC executive vice president and Party secretary was Liang Huiling, former head of the Commission for Discipline Inspection in Hebei Province. For netizens, a challenge to the RCSC was an indirect challenge to the legitimacy of the CCP. And as students of Chinese politics well know, in the protest culture of contemporary China, indirection is a safer strategy than direct confrontation.

An unorganized but concerted online hunt for Guo's connections to the Red Cross thus started. Overnight, Guo and the RCSC became the center of a national Internet storm.

Weiguan: Online protest culture

By 2011, an online protest culture had long taken shape, characterized by a playful style, crowd-sourced searches, massive participation, and inventive methods to dodge censorship. One item in this digital repertoire of contention has the ghastly name "human flesh search" (人肉搜索). In a human flesh search, large numbers of individual users mobilize their Internet search skills to hunt for information aimed to expose the identities and alleged misdemeanors of individuals ranging from Party officials suspected of corruption to animal abusers. Searches may also be conducted offline, but the information acquired offline is then shared online. Sometimes viewed as a form of Internet vigilantism, a human flesh search resembles a collective quest for truth or social justice. There is usually a mystery, and the goal of a human flesh search is to solve that mystery by uncovering information using whatever means are available. For example, in a case in 2007, a peasant in Shaanxi Province named Zhou Zhenglong posted photographs of what he claimed to be a China tiger which he claimed he had discovered in the mountains near his village. The mystery in this case was, were the photographs authentic, or did he forge them? A sustained period of online search, which included the widespread sharing of very technical analyses of the photographs, proved unequivocally that the photographs had been forged and that Zhou had made up his story at the behest of local forestry officials in their attempt to obtain more government funding. The exposure of these forged photographs led to the downfall of several local Party officials.

Another item in the repertoire of online protest is *weiguan* (围观), or spectating. *Weiguan* was once associated with the passivity and numbness of a citizenry unable to take action when seeing fellow citizens in trouble. It was an image of the Chinese nation which the famous writer Lu Xun created in his writing in the early twentieth century in the hapless character of Ah Q, who loved to watch troubles on the street. The playful crowd wisdom of Internet culture gives the term a new lease of life. It now refers to online participation by paying attention. Liking or retweeting a post is paying attention. When tens of thousands of people pay attention, it becomes a form of collective power, and the target of *weiguan* is turned into an object of public gaze. Thus, for some time, "*weiguan* is power" becomes an Internet meme. This transformation of the meaning of *weiguan* suits well the attention economy of the information age. Social media platforms like Sina Weibo depend on user attention. No users, no business. To encourage *weiguan* is to encourage user participation.

Weiguan-style participation can be serious or playful. With such a large Internet population in China, there is inevitably a fair amount of voyeurism and spectacle. To attract attention and interest, discussions about even serious social issues often adopt a humorous style. Jokes, cartoons, parody, and emojis abound. Yet in this process, netizens do bring some issues to public attention and often can create pressure on Party authorities to take action. In a case in 2009, a young man in a detention facility in Yunnan Province was pronounced dead. The reason given for his death was that he accidently hit his head on the wall when he was playing hide-and-seek with other detainees. How could a young man just accidently knock himself to death while playing hide-and-seek? An online outcry in the forms of *weiguan* and a human flesh search led to an investigation, which concluded that the detainee had not killed himself but was beaten to death by prison bullies. This led to the exposure of serious management problems at the detention facility.

The Guo Meimei incident was the result of the same style of online participation. Before the appearance of Sina Weibo and WeChat, Tianya was one of the most popular online communities in China. It was also one of the most liberal-oriented, where many online protests originated. It is not surprising that the Guo Meimei incident started there. But the news was quickly spread to Sina Weibo, where screenshots of photographs of Guo's luxury possessions were circulated. Many users left comments on Guo Meimei's Weibo account, such as, "What a complicated plot in this play!"[3] "How intriguing! I'm going to stay awake and continue to follow [the event]." There was palpable excitement, as if people were watching a mystery drama. Intentionally or unintentionally, they were all characters in the drama and were enacting it through their own participation.

Guo initially responded that the RCSC and the "Red Cross Commercial Society" were two different entities and she had nothing to do with the RCSC.[4] Shortly afterwards, she deleted this post and posted another message claiming that she had made up the name "Red Cross Commercial Society" and that in reality no such organization existed. She also stated that her verified identity on Weibo was originally "singer and actress," not "general manager of the Red Cross Commercial Society." On June 22, 2011, the Chinese Red Cross issued a statement on its website which summarily dismissed the public accusations. Instead of dispelling public doubts, the responses of Guo Meimei and the RCSC provoked more intense online searching and questioning. Xi Jinping was fighting for Party leadership, but the "masses" were busy trying to expose unaccountable Party-led institutions.

The "masses" included many regular Internet users, who made up the tens of thousands who participated by reading, retweeting, or querying and commenting on postings. They also included the so-called "Big-Vs," referring to people with verified Weibo accounts with often huge followings. Big-Vs were China's de facto Internet opinion leaders, because of the large numbers of followers they could reach. Often using highly provocative language, their postings were designed to dramatize. For example, the popular scholar–blogger Yu Jianrong, with close to 2 million followers on Sina Weibo, stated that unless the RCSC reformed itself and built a transparent system, he would boycott it. In a posting on June 24, 2011, another celebrity blogger directly addressed her several million followers to complain about censorship: "How frustrating! In only a matter of ten minutes, the long thread on Tianya was gone [deleted]. People had just dug up information about who Guo Meimei's mother was. That was such critical information."

This post alone was retweeted over 5,000 times and received over 3,000 comments. That Tianya deleted discussions about Guo Meimei was taken by netizens as new evidence that powerful hidden forces must be behind Guo Meimei and should be exposed.

Popular bloggers' postings propelled the drama by enticing run-of-the-mill netizens to participate. The well-known sports commentator Huang Jianxiang posted the following message on June 27, 2014: "The state of things has come to such that I personally think that Guo Meimei is a really great person! She is more fucking awesome than Yu Zecheng!"

The hero in a popular spy television drama series, Yu Zecheng was a Communist mole in the Nationalists' powerful spy agency in the 1940s who always managed to outmaneuver his opponents. Comparing Guo Meimei to Yu Zecheng is a playful way of saying that Guo Meimei is a mole planted within the RCSC to bring it down. This analogy fed netizens' imagination with a narrative of suspense.

Finally, participants included those who became known in the middle of the incident through their active participation. They were the organic opinion leaders and the most interesting type. Up to that point, they were China's unknown keyboard warriors. Some media channels dubbed them "unofficial detectives," because they acted as detectives to unearth and analyze information. They included, among others, a wheelchair-bound man in a small town in Sichuan, a student at Peking University, a female government employee in Sichuan, a noodle shop owner, and a middle-aged man with a passion for charity. The wheelchair-bound man was a forty-year-old blogger called Mr. Zhou, who named his Weibo account "@truth-digging machine" to stress his self-designated role as a truth warrior. Spending much of his daily routine browsing the Web from home, Mr. Zhou happened upon postings about Guo Meimei. He told journalists that these made him very angry. He believed that the Red Cross must have been involved. Mr. Zhou used to be a vocational-school teacher. After a traffic accident disabled him in 2007, he spent much of his time in bed, using a wireless mouse to browse the Web with the monitor of his computer hung above his bed. In search of clues, he read all of Guo Meimei's postings on her Weibo timeline as well as the postings of Guo's followers.[5] He built a large following on Weibo with his frequent posts about Guo and the RCSC.

Another minor celebrity during the Guo Meimei incident was a blogger called Jiang Pengyong. In media interviews, Jiang claimed he had met Guo Meimei once at a party and knew some insider stories. Thus, when he saw his friends forwarding Guo Meimei's tweets, he began to follow the event. His active participation earned him the name of an Internet anticorruption warrior. Jiang enjoyed his online celebrity status, saying, "I've already been pushed to the front. What can I do? I cannot retreat. I cannot stand hearing people say that I'm retreating ... I'm now a vanguard. Soon I will become a martyr ... I'm a spiritual leader, the kind whose portrait is hung on the wall."[6]

The experiences of these two bloggers reveal the complex motivations for participating in online protest events. Some are genuinely outraged about corruption and social injustices. Others go online to seek a sense of human connection and belonging in a world they find cold and indifferent.

Furthermore, online participation is encouraged by Internet firms because it is completely in line with the commercial logic of social media. By this logic, one's social media status, measured by the number of followers, is a measure of one's actual social and professional status, and therefore it is imperative to be actively engaged on social media. But of course, the success of social media platforms as a business also depends on user engagement. Personal status and business success are interdependent. One consequence of this social media logic is the tendency toward sensationalism and entertainment, because sensationalizing and entertaining postings tend to attract more attention. As a result, participation may become a form of spectatorship. There is a public relish, sometimes bordering on the vicious, in the scandalizing of private lives and the debunking of a public institution. The Guo Meimei case abounds with such sensationalizing and entertaining elements. Party control of "the message" was notably absent from the whole drama.

Guo Meimei's Fall as a Lack of Public Trust

The Chinese Red Cross held a news conference on June 28, 2011, to respond to the ongoing crisis. Its spokesperson denied all the accusations and announced that police authorities had started investigating the case. On July 7, 2011, the municipal public security department in Beijing announced that police investigations had found no direct connections between Guo Meimei and the RCSC. But the Internet uproar had done the damage. Between June and August 2011, charity donations nationwide fell by 80 percent. When a major earthquake struck Lushan county in Sichuan Province on April 20, 2013, the RCSC raised a paltry $23,000 of disaster relief funds in the first twenty-four hours after the quake, while the private One Foundation raised $3 million. In the words of RCSC executive vice president Zhao Baige, "It took only three days for an unverified Internet incident to completely destroy us. Three days destroyed one hundred years [of the Red Cross]."[7]

Beginning in July 2011, several other social crises happened which diverted public attention from Guo Meimei and the Red Cross. On July 23, a high-speed train crashed near the city of Wenzhou, causing forty deaths. The Ministry of Railways came under public attack because of the way it handled, or rather mishandled, the disaster. On September 21, 2011, villagers of Wukan in Guangdong Province began several months of organized protest against village cadres who had been accused of selling village land for personal profit. In the middle of the protest, a villager who was detained by the police died during detention, leading to the intervention of the provincial government. The protest ended with villagers electing their own head. This event turned out to be one of the biggest social protests in recent decades. On October 13, 2011, in a small town in Guangdong Province, a two-year-old girl called Yueyue was run over by two trucks one after the other near her home. Eighteen pedestrians walked past Yueyue; none of them gave any help to the poor child. It was the nineteenth person who walked by, a middle-aged woman, who picked her up and took her to the roadside, when Yueyue's mother finally appeared. Yueyue died in hospital the following day, and the incident triggered a national debate about the awful moral conditions of Chinese society.

These incidents revealed similar social problems as the Guo Meimei story, especially the crisis of trust in public institutions and their officials. Thus, although Guo Meimei and the Red Cross temporarily receded from public view, the social issues and public protest persisted, albeit in different forms. On December 20, 2011, an independent investigation team charged to investigate Guo Meimei's connections with the Red Cross concluded that Guo Meimei's wealth had nothing to do with the RCSC and public donations and that her alleged position as the general manager of the Red Cross Commercial Society never existed. However, the investigation report confirmed several pieces of critical information that had been exposed online. It found that the RCSC did have an affiliated organization known as the Commercial Red Cross Society which had commercial transactions with a private firm. The CEO of the firm was at some point simultaneously the vice president of the Commercial Red Cross. The report castigates the RCSC for failing to provide adequate and responsible supervision over the operations of its affiliated organization, the Commercial Red Cross, and recommends a series of changes, including establishing a more transparent information system to boost its social credibility.[8]

At this point, one might think that the curtain had fallen on this melodrama. Not quite. Guo Meimei did not get off the hook easily. Three years later, on July 10, 2014, she was arrested in Beijing on charges of gambling. On September 10, 2015, she was put on a televised trial, convicted of operating gambling facilities, and sentenced to five years in prison. Pleading not guilty, Guo insisted that she might have committed the crime of gambling, but not of operating a gambling business. Gambling carries a sentence of up to three years in prison while the crime of running a gambling business carries five years in prison. Guo served the full length of five years in a prison in her hometown in Hunan and was released on July 13, 2019.

From the time when she was arrested in 2014 to her release in 2019, Sina Weibo had undergone significant change as well. Indeed, the entire Chinese Internet ecology and social and political landscape had changed profoundly. In so many ways, the rise and fall of Guo Meimei's personal fortunes and her Weibo status are symptomatic of these changes. As of this writing, Guo's Sina Weibo account is still accessible. Her Weibo timeline is completely clean and empty, with all postings removed. Yet she still has 1.3 million followers, a reminder of a once feisty social media past. In its stead, Xi Jinping's "positive propaganda" has increasingly filled the Internet.

The Heyday of Online Public Opinion

When Guo Meimei was thrust into unwanted public limelight in 2011, the Internet in China was at the zenith of its public engagement. For at least a decade prior to 2011, Chinese netizens had filled the Internet with their vociferous voices, despite China's highly controlled Internet environment. Frequent online protest events turned the Internet into a weathervane of public sentiment about Party policies and the behavior of Party leaders.

Because people could turn to the Internet to air grievances, tracking, monitoring, and analyzing online communication became an important way of gauging public opinion. This led to the appearance of an online public-opinion industry. In 2009, the Media Opinion Monitoring Office of *People's Daily Online* took the lead as the first official institution to publish regular survey reports on the so-called "Internet mass incidents," a euphemism for mass protests. The reports were sold to Party and business subscribers at a handsome price. Short-term courses for training public-opinion analysts offered by *People's Daily Online* and the Ministry of Industry and

Information Technology cost up to 10,000 yuan for just a few days. While *People's Daily Online* led the pack of this online public-opinion industry, many research institutions, commercial and academic, joined the fray. Using social surveys and public-opinion polls for social control and governance has a history dating back to the Republican era.[9] Mining big data of online sentiments for commercial and surveillance purposes, however, has been a recent fad.[10]

These online public opinion survey reports serve at least two purposes for the Party and for businesses. First, they track hot-button incidents on social media, including online protests, and provide metrics showing whether a specific incident has generated positive or negative energy and whether the online sentiments associated with it are positive or negative. The reports may then be used to guide the Party in managing online expression, or as training manuals to help government officials or business managers better understand and control Internet incidents and crisis situations. Second, they create and help to popularize a new vocabulary of Internet governance that is being adopted in both official and public media discourse. A distinct feature of these survey reports is the use of indicators to attribute degrees of emotionality, rationality, hopefulness, apathy, and pessimism to Internet incidents. This provides a convenient and seemingly scientific approach to measuring the degree of positive or negative energy in online speech, which can then be deployed by Party bureaucrats for more effective "social management." The measures of emotionality and rationality ultimately serve to delegitimate online speech that is critical of the CCP, because they advocate a vision of online speech that sees critical emotions in online expressions as political threats and social pollution.

For example, in 2011, the Public Opinion Monitoring Office of People's Net found in its survey report on Internet public opinion for that year that the intensity of Internet public opinion in China was unparalleled in the world. Earmarked by the two major events involving Guo Meimei and the high-speed train crash, 2011 was an extraordinarily dynamic and vociferous year in contemporary Chinese history. In these contentious activities, Sina Weibo and other social media platforms played a critical role.

Ironically, the ending of the Guo Meimei drama also coincided with a national crackdown on the Internet and the unfolding of a new approach to Internet control. Party leaders had had enough. On December 16, 2011, Sina Weibo introduced its real-name registration requirement, clearly a response to the raucous drama of Guo Meimei seemingly spiraling out of control on Weibo. The real-name registration rule makes users think twice before they post anything lest their posting is censored. But it was only a prelude to what was to come. The summer of 2013, in the first year of Xi Jinping's leadership, saw the launching of a national crackdown on China's social media influencers known as Big-Vs. On August 23, 2013, one such Big-V, Internet celebrity qua venture capitalist Xue Manzi, was detained in Beijing on charges of soliciting prostitution. A naturalized American citizen, Xue was an active commentator on current affairs on Sina Weibo. It was widely believed that his detention was related to his influential voice on Weibo. Making an example of him was a warning to other Internet celebrities to restrain their voices. And he was made an example of about three weeks after his detention, when he was shown on China's television news channels repenting his misdemeanor. He confessed on camera that as a popular blogger with 12 million followers on Weibo, he sometimes felt like an emperor and relished that feeling. He apologized for posting unverified information and misguiding his followers. It became clear that Xue Manzi was a selected target in what turned out to be a series of national campaigns to sanitize Internet expression.

Wenming: Disciplining the Online Public

In Chinese political culture, both negative and positive examples are commonly used for mass education, mobilization, social control, and human development. While public shaming uses negative examples to teach moral lessons to the public, positive exemplars are also common in the Party's efforts to innovate social management.[11] One method is the honoring of model civilized websites and civilized netizens. For example, in August 2015, the Cyberspace Administration of China (CAC), in collaboration with the propaganda department of Jiangxi Province, launched a national competition of essays and creative works to recognize "2015 China Good Netizens" (中国好网民). Similar projects of selecting model websites and netizens are carried out at the local level. For example, an announcement posted on August 31, 2015, on the website of the government of Yixing City in Jiangsu Province details a citywide competition to select "civilized websites." Its published criteria for evaluating websites have twenty-three items, each with a score, totaling 100 points.

One might wonder what the Party hopes to achieve through selecting model websites and model netizens. Of course, winning a "civilized" website award brings positive publicity. But perhaps more importantly, the real purpose of these competitions is not so much to recognize individuals and organizations as to create public opinion and a social atmosphere inhospitable to "uncivil" online behavior that might bleed over into criticism of the government or the Party. As the news release launching the 2015 China Good Netizens award makes clear, the goal of the activity is "to create a strong social atmosphere ... for building a clear and bright Internet space."[12]

There are other disciplinary methods in the Party's repertoire. Major Internet firms are mobilized to make self-regulation pledges. In November 2014, Lu Wei, then head of the CAC, following an old Party strategy of building united fronts, went out of his way to make friends with Internet celebrities. Instead of using a united front to join with a competing political party as Sneevliet had forced the young CCP to do in the 1920s, here the Party was in charge and invited Internet celebrities to dinner to build personal relations with them. Along with this networking, the Party adopts a systematically designed and implemented propagation of discourse on *wenming* (文明), which may be translated as "civility" or "civilization." The discourse of *wenming* has been integral to Chinese modernity since the late nineteenth century. To be civilized has long been viewed as a sign of modernity. Under Xi Jinping, the discourse of *wenming* is elevated to new ideological heights.[13] To promote this ideology of *wenming*, the Party's Propaganda Department runs an active website called wenming.cn. Among other things, it features news about Party meetings, information about important policies, and "models" (典型) of moral behavior and good persons (好人). An entire section is devoted to quotations of Xi Jinping's remarks on or related to *wenming*. As of February 22, 2020, the section features 284 Xi quotations from what is now called Xi Jinping Thought. The first of these is from a speech Xi made on December 29, 2012, about the China dream of "achieving the great rejuvenation of the Chinese nation." A more recent quotation is from a speech Xi made on January 29, 2020, about fighting the coronavirus. A quotation from Xi's speech at the study session of the Politburo on January 25, 2019, goes,

> No matter what type of media, whether they are online or offline, whether they have big screens or small screens, there are no places above the law, no special enclaves for public opinion. Supervisory agencies must perform well their duties of supervision and strengthen the management of emerging media according to the law, in order to make our cyberspace clearer and brighter.[14]

Many forms of Internet control are undertaken in the name of promoting this civility. Thus Internet commentators can serve as online civility monitors; national competitions are held to select model websites and model Internet users for their civil use of the Web; online protests can be shut down for being uncivil. An Internet uproar such as the one surrounding Guo Meimei could thus be censored in the name of civility. Civility serves the Party.

Methods designed to discipline online expression are buttressed by new laws designed to punish infractions. On September 8, 2013, the Chinese Supreme People's Court and Supreme People's Procuratorate issued a judicial interpretation, stating that people who post false information on the Internet may face up to three years in prison if the posting is viewed more than 5,000 times or retweeted 500 times. This new rule was applied on September 20, 2013, when a sixteen-year-old boy in a small town in remote Gansu Province was detained for posting a message on Weibo which had indeed been retweeted more than 500 times. He was charged with posting false information that led to a street demonstration and disrupted social order. Although the hapless lad was later released under public pressure, no doubt was left about the aggressiveness of the new campaign against Internet expression.

Meanwhile, institutions of Internet governance have been centralized to consolidate control under the Party. The Cyberspace Administration of China was established in 2014 as the agency in charge of Internet regulation and oversight. The CAC is placed under the supervision of a Party small leading group headed by none other than Xi Jinping himself. Also, in 2014, the National Security

Commission was established. It was also headed by Xi Jinping. Subsequently, a National Security Law and a Cybersecurity Law were introduced in 2015 and passed in 2017. As the names of these laws suggest, the Party increasingly uses language that elevates cyberspace security to the level of national security to legitimate Internet censorship and surveillance. In the same speech made on January 25, 2019, quoted above, Xi also said, "The construction of Internet content should be strengthened from the height of maintaining national political security, cultural security, and ideological security."[15]

It was in the middle of these political changes that the Guo Meimei drama was brought to an end in 2015. As in the 2013 case of Xue Manzi, television was enlisted as a medium of public shaming and condemnation. The one who errs on the Internet is forced to confess on television. Thus, according to the Party, is moral order restored. And to borrow Xi's own words, the Chinese cyberspace is made "clearer and brighter."[16]

The Internet was censored in China from the very beginning, when it became publicly available in the mid-1990s. Yet censorship efforts largely failed to contain it, as it became increasingly unruly with online protest. Since 2013, however, although Internet protests continue to appear, they are not as frequent as before. The Party has caught up with the technology, at least for now. Surveys by Chinese Internet research and monitoring institutions, including *People's Daily Online*, show that the overall number of online incidents declined after 2013 while the number of online events with "positive" public sentiments —that is, sentiments supportive of government agendas – has increased. Unsurprisingly, in 2015, Xi Jinping called upon all media to "tell China's story well." Thus, to some extent, the combined methods of rewards, discipline, and punishment under Xi Jinping have tamed China's boisterous cyberspace.

The Managed Worlds of WeChat Circles

As is so often the case, other ironic twists of plot were happening right at the moment of this transformation of China's cyberspace. Particularly notable was the rapid growth of new social media platforms and practices. When the Guo Meimei incident happened in 2011, Sina Weibo was at the height of its popularity. But just as Sina Weibo was enjoying its glory, its soon-to-be business rival WeChat (*Weixin* 微信 in Chinese) was quietly released in January 2011. By 2014, partly as a result of the crackdown since the summer of 2013, Sina Weibo was widely reported to be losing users, while WeChat, Tencent's mobile instant messaging app for the new smartphones, was quickly rising as China's super-app. By integrating multiple easy-to-use services such as messaging, WeChat pay, group chats, public accounts, and a variety of applications, WeChat has become a social media platform popular with all age groups, but also heavily commercialized. WeChat public accounts are often used for moneymaking purposes. Numerous individuals and firms post sensationalizing information to gain clicks, attention, and profit.

And then there was the simultaneous rise of livestreaming and short-video industries. The video-sharing portals Youku and Tudou merged in 2012.[17] Livestreaming social media apps such as Miaopai, Meipai, YY and Douyu were launched or became popular around 2013 and 2014.[18] In 2016, the Chinese version of TikTok, Douyin, came on the scene and quickly became a key player. By 2018, there were 425 million livestreaming users in China,[19] and the short-video and livestreaming industries had eclipsed China's domestic box office, with an estimated worth of about US$18 billion and as many as 21 million content creators.[20]

The monetary value of these new social media platforms attests to their high degree of commercialization, but commercialization does not necessarily conflict with the logic of Party control. In fact, in its efforts to civilize and "occupy" the Web, the CCP often incorporates elements of the market logic to enhance its appeal. To grow followers and gain user attention on WeChat and livestreaming platforms, accounts run by government agencies post clickbait headlines in the style typical of commercial accounts. Some of the most influential public accounts on social media platforms are now operated by official entities. A study by a Chinese communication scholar at Tsinghua University shows, for example, that the most popular short videos on Douyin for the period May 1 to November 30, 2018, were almost all released by state-owned media agencies, including *Global Times*, Xinhua News Agency, China Central Television (CCTV), and *People's Daily*.[21] A glance at a few titles of these viral videos shows that they are no different from commercial accounts in their attention-grabbing strategies.

Whether Guo Meimei has personal accounts on these new social media platforms no longer matters. She has already made history and paid a high price for that. I did search for information about her on WeChat, and found the same news about her release from prison which I found on Sina Weibo. Eight years after Guo Meimei caught national attention and five years after she was jailed, Guo Meimei's story feels as recent as if it were yesterday. No one can say that rowdy online incidents like the Guo Meimei case will no longer happen in China's curtailed cyberspace. Other cases have indeed happened, albeit less frequently. But Guo Meimei will live on in public memory as a symbol of the times and the awkward position of the Party regime, a symbol mingling money, power, wealth, consumerism, spectatorship, online vigilantism, and digital citizenship, all on full display in China's vast digital spaces.

AFTERWORD
The Party and the World
PHILIP BOWRING

Looking back over 100 years shows how the history of the Chinese Communist Party and hence of China intersects with so many of the key global events of the century. That may surprise because it is often seen more as the product of uniquely Chinese circumstances than may actually be the case. So we need to look back at the Party's international links and roles to see its relevance to the present, and the future.

Looking ahead, we must ask whether the Party's power monopoly will end under pressure for some form of democratization and power sharing. There are precedents from elsewhere, such as Mexico, where the Institutional Revolutionary Party was in power for seventy-one years of patronage-based rule, its ideology shifting to suit the opinions and interests of the incumbent leader. It eventually succumbed to its inability to accommodate enough interest groups as society became more complex and economically advanced.

A second possibility is that the Party will remain in power for many more decades but will lose all pretense at ideology while also curbing any ambitions to throw its weight around at home and in the world. With Western influence in further decline and no obvious threats from its neighbors, and no longer dependent on imported technology and energy, it may focus on domestic challenges brought about by climate change, demography, and its ever-fractious western provinces.

A third alternative is that the creed, however interpreted, of Marxism–Leninism continues to have a global life with China as its standard-bearer. In this world, Beijing will be the new Rome or Baghdad, just as those cities, not Medina or Jerusalem, became the imperial hearts of Christianity and Islam. Just as America's

Jeffersonian democracy has found admirers around the world, will China's example become a template and Beijing its ideological center? This would not be the revolutionary agenda of Mao's Little Red Book but a practical primer on how to harness the power of a Marxist–Leninist party to deliver prosperity and a degree of personal freedom while keeping a nation stable and united. The state which taught others about the revolutionary potential of the peasantry can now teach the further stages in the never-ending road to socialism.

Even in the 1960s and 1970s when China was largely cut off from the world, it still played an international role of significance. As in the Soviet Union, there has also been an inherent conflict between national interest and ideological purity. The issue of the internationalization of an ideology takes us back to the beginning of the CCP and the role of an idealistic Dutchman, Henricus Sneevliet, whom we met in Chapter 1. Expelled from the Dutch East Indies (now Indonesia), where in 1914 he founded the party which became the Indonesian Communist Party, he served as its representative at the Second World Congress of the Communist International (Comintern) in 1920, at the high point of hopes for revolution across Europe and beyond. It was as a true believer in the importance of the need for the internationalization of revolution that he was sent to China.

Such idealism was not to last, inspiring the first big split in the Soviet leadership after Lenin's death in 1924. Stalin advocated Socialism in One Country and split with Leon Trotsky, whom Lenin had preferred to Stalin, and maintained that the latter's views were contrary to Marxist theory. "Trotskyism" was to become a term of abuse – Wang Shiwei, the independent Communist critic in Yan'an we met in Chapter 3, would be purged as a "Trotskyite" in the 1940s – but it remains an idea which still survives. The split was thus typical of how differences of opinion and personal rivalries came together and were then further fueled by the importance of correct theory in Marxism–Leninism and the necessity of revolutionary bloodshed. Stalin set a particularly gruesome example, but Mao's China was not far behind. Centralization of party power in an individual, the logic of secular ideology, and the paranoia bred by secretive elite politics have elsewhere made the killing of rivals the default option, though China itself now prefers imprisonment.

The history of the Party and then the state is bound up with the relationship with its original mentor, Moscow. Socialism in One Country did not, of course, mean Stalin's abandonment of the Comintern. Quite the opposite. It was now to be focused on the policy interests of the Soviet Union. In the Chinese context this saw the replacement of Sneevliet with a Russian, Mikhail Borodin, aiming to keep the Chinese Party closer to Moscow and to the Soviets even as Russia flexed its imperial muscles in 1929, seizing back the Chinese Eastern Railway. Its influence continued through the 1930s and 1940s and right up to the Sino-Soviet break following Khrushchev's 1956 denunciation of Stalin's purges and personal dictatorship and his pursuit of coexistence, not revolution. In response, Mao denounced Soviet "revisionist traitors." Almost necessarily, this led to a border conflict between the Soviet Union and China in the late 1960s which had its roots in the clash between nineteenth-century Russian imperialism and the Qing empire.

The importance of Russia to the Chinese Party took a different tack with the 1991 collapse of the Soviet Union, which came not long after the June 1989 Tiananmen killings. The protests the previous month coincided with the Beijing visit of the Soviet tribune of glasnost and perestroika, Mikhail Gorbachev. Beijing, not least Xi Jinping, has become obsessed with the need to avoid a similar fate, the end of empire as well as of party rule. Soviet economic failures of the 1970s and 1980s were a lesson in the need for the Chinese Party to deliver prosperity by opening its economy to foreign trade and capital and replacing bureaucratic planning with market mechanisms. Gorbachev's failure to handle the challenges of political reform is Xi Jinping's excuse for maintaining the Party's dictatorship. The Soviet specter still haunts the Party.

In recent years, Xi Jinping and Russia's Putin have found common cause in opposing the US. For one, the main issue is the South China Sea, for the other, Ukraine, and both react against America's assumptions of moral superiority. China's need for Russian energy resources has seen rapid trade growth and earlier post-Soviet worries about Chinese migration overwhelming Russia's thinly populated Far East have faded, for now. Another piece of history now on hold concerns the so-called unequal treaties. Parts of the Russian Far East and Kazakhstan were ceded by the Qing in the nineteenth century at the same time as now recovered parts of China such as Hong Kong. The issue is dormant but not beyond reawakening if other circumstances make it a useful nationalist tool.

The two countries also share concern over Muslim identity in Central Asia. The Soviet collapse and the independence of Kazakhstan and Kyrgyzstan took Russian troops away from China's western border and hence any ability to stir up Xinjiang. But they also increased the sense of Turkic and religious separateness in the province and the desire not to be a small minority in a large, culturally different, empire. Events in Xinjiang over the past few years suggest that Communist China may face the same challenges in holding the Qing empire together as the Soviets had in maintaining the Czarist one. It is often forgotten that China is an empire now as it was in the nineteenth century when Westerners made a distinction between "China" and "Chinese Empire." Xi's 2019 draconian crackdown on Islam and Turkic sentiment will probably work for the time being. But given the attention it has attracted, it has damaged Beijing's global image, particularly among Muslim Turkic peoples who dominate so much of the overland of Xi's cherished Belt and Road project. The future probably favors the indigenous due to their fertility rate and the diminishing attraction of Xinjiang and Tibet for Han migration. Likewise, European Russia in the 1980s had an aging population, with a low birth rate there but higher in the Asian and Caucasus republics. China now has an even more rapidly aging population, with gender imbalance adding to a low fertility rate. China's nineteenth-century population growth spurred the Han colonization of Manchuria and Mongolia and the establishment of communities in many countries; that demographic advantage is passing.

Population pressure also propelled Japan's imperialism. Without Japanese aggression in the 1930s Mao would have been a footnote and Chiang Kai-shek might have presided over the rapid modernization of a China which, like Japan, retained its cultural roots while learning Western technology. That might well have been a better outcome for Chinese people before and after 1949 but would probably not have led China to have the remarkable global impact that Mao and his legacy provided.

Zhou Enlai, representing the new China, was a major figure at the 1955 Bandung Conference which spawned the Non-Aligned Movement, confirming China's status as outside the Soviet camp. Nine years on, this writer was present at Khartoum airport in

January 1964 to witness the arrival of Zhou Enlai on what was China's first concerted effort to engage Africa, visiting ten countries. The visit led to China building the 1,800-kilometer Tanzania–Zambia railway, a huge revolutionary investment in the defeat of white-ruled southern Africa. That commitment carried on through China's own upheavals, inspiring and providing training and material support to African liberation movements, not least that of Zimbabwe's Robert Mugabe.

That history provided fertile ground for China when its companies looked to investment in Africa to feed demand for raw materials and in their wake came tens of thousands of Chinese setting up small businesses across the continent and stimulating economic activity. Most recently, Africa has become the location for major Belt and Road projects such as the Mombasa–Nairobi and Djibouti–Addis Ababa railways. However, the goodwill that China has built up now faces obstacles. Chinese state enterprises have to face the same real difficulties in operating as exist throughout Africa and in finding profits hard to generate. They are perceived as no less mercenary than their Western counterparts. Resentment against the use of Chinese workers in China-funded projects is common and Chinese small businessmen may be no more popular than the Indian ones who arrived with Western colonialism. China will remain an important trading partner for the continent but its need for many raw materials may have already peaked as its economy becomes more technology- and service-oriented. It will be a long time before China can develop the social and linguistic links that most African countries still have with their former colonizers, the devil that they know. Nonetheless, the Party makes a difference. China's political system, with an ideology and a disciplined party, will find appeal in Africa as an alternative to messy attempts at democracy or the "Big Man" rule of tyrants and kleptocrats.

If the Maoist influence in Africa was somewhat positive, the same could not be said elsewhere. Land reform or decolonization were not enough. Fervent devotees wanted to follow the Great Leap Forward and the Cultural Revolution, remaking society from the bottom up according to both a fixed theory and their power interest. The Khmer Rouge in Cambodia, led by a tiny French-educated clique, succeeded in making Mao's massacres seem modest. As we have seen in Chapter 6, in Peru Abimael Guzmán was similarly committed to violence by his Shining Path movement, which would remake society. In the West, Maoism found many, mainly young, people who would admire it from a safe distance. A few killed, bombed, and kidnapped in its name. Yet for all Maoism's violence and failures, the image of Mao and his Little Red Book became more firmly implanted in the global mind, far ahead of Lenin, Stalin, and Trotsky – equal, perhaps, to Marx and his little book, the *Communist Manifesto*. Although China today is so different, foreign and especially Western fears owe much to the Communist Party's ability to mobilize the obedience of 1.4 billion people. Xi's partial return to a command society dominated by a party led by an individual is for many foreigners as troubling as China's military buildup.

Neighbors are particularly aware of that buildup but also find themselves at the intersection of ideology with national interests and ethnicity. In Vietnam, Ho Chi Minh learned from Mao the need to mobilize the peasantry as well as the importance of party dominance. During the war against the French he received massive Chinese support and followed Chinese land reform policies. But Ho preferred a slower road to socialism and his ideas also reflected a Confucian-based commitment to frugality and personal ethics. Vietnamese distrust of an overbearing China never went away and flared into the 1979 border war to "smack the child" (in Deng's words) for its intervention in Cambodia. China's military setback in that war against a small country which had learned conventional as well as guerrilla tactics spurred Deng Xiaoping's quest for modernization.

The exodus of Vietnamese-Chinese after 1974 was a setback for the Vietnamese economy but should be another reminder to Beijing of the vulnerability of its erstwhile compatriot communities in Southeast Asia. Beijing today may feel it needs to be a protector of ethnic Chinese everywhere. It clearly has economic clout in its Southeast Asian neighborhood. But the links can be counterproductive and enrage the majority. Indonesian Chinese suffered particularly, though far from exclusively, in the anti-Communist and intercommunal killings which followed the failed 1966 coup in that country. At the time official Chinese policy distanced itself from overseas Chinese, unless they were of Maoist disposition.

The difficulty of separating party from ethnicity has long been a problem for the CCP. Chinese in Malaya and Singapore resisted the Japanese but few Malays did. The postwar Communist uprising in Malaya led by Chin Peng was largely a Chinese affair. Few non-Chinese saw it as a war of liberation. Mao's official policy was to support socialism generally without regard to ethnicity. He denounced "Han chauvinism" but in practice Chinese were identified as leftists and, in the case of Lee Kuan Yew's Singapore, leftists were bracketed with "Han chauvinists."

Socialism's appeal to overseas Chinese fell as they prospered and China stagnated under Mao. Economic policies for long followed a Soviet pattern, but less successfully. Stalin's 1930s collectivization of agriculture and the forced extraction of rural surpluses to develop heavy industry, albeit at a high cost in lives, helped the Soviets to fight Germany. Mao's version in the 1950s, the Great Leap Forward, failed on all counts, with famine but little industry to compensate.

Post-Mao China was lucky in two ways. The first was that it already had nearby examples, Japan and Korea, of what could be achieved by a combination of good, scientifically focused education, market forces, and openness to foreign trade and hence the ideas and investment they could bring. With open policies even small agriculture-based states like Thailand could urbanize and industrialize.

Second, the three decades from 1980 saw the global fall of many barriers to trade, bringing specialization and new cross-border supply chains. Capital flows increased massively and stock exchanges sprouted around Asia. But the biggest plus for China specifically was the US–Soviet rivalry. The US was happy to see China develop as a counterweight to Moscow, even after the collapse of the USSR. At the same time, the US had a dream that by encouraging China to open up by offering trade access and capital it would remake Communist China into a liberal democracy. All roads led to the easy entry of China into the WTO and nearly two more decades of rapid growth. The stories in this book show how that American dream was a fantasy.

In its own neighborhood, however, China's economic success of the past three decades has done five things to resurrect the specter of ethnic friction that is now cast in terms of communism and the Party by Western states and commentators:

Trade and investment opportunities offered by China may be seen as mainly benefiting the ethnic Chinese prominent in big business.

The pride that Chinese may feel at the PRC's remarkable successes sharpens ethnic difference.

Han chauvinism is reappearing in China, as instanced by policies in non-Han regions.

There are attempts by Beijing to draw political support from ethnic Chinese citizens of other countries. The "once-a-Chinese-always-a-Chinese" approach not only causes frictions with distant countries such as Sweden but is noticed in a neighborhood where there is a history of sometimes violent anti-Chinese sentiment.

China is making efforts to establish hegemony over the South China Sea, though most of its shores are those of neighbors with significant Chinese minorities.

The era of China's "peaceful rise" has gradually come to an end during the Xi era. The South China Sea claims were not new but have been pursued with particular disregard for the other littoral states, and for the many countries who fear the seas becoming a "Chinese lake." These regional claims, as well as the increasing ethnic frictions, are widely seen as driven by the Party, which, after all, claims to represent the Chinese nation.

Chinese money remains very welcome and can buy political favors as well as build roads and fill tourist hotels. It has been particularly welcome in countries starved both of capital and of the resources to undertake major construction works. Yet the euphoria over Xi Jinping's signature policy, the Belt and Road Initiative, has died away. For sure it offers some useful infrastructure, sometimes on generous terms. But there are resentments about the lack of local involvement in construction and the import of Chinese workers. There are worries about the debt burdens it can impose on small countries, and fears, particularly among neighboring countries, that items such as Indian ocean ports and a railway through Laos are driven by China's strategic interests, not commerce. The Belt and Road is also an expense which the Chinese people may come to resent. Already it is a small burden now that the nation no longer runs a large foreign-exchange surplus.

China's corporate interests will continue to expand, acquiring foreign assets which they hope will offset much slower domestic growth, and state-backed money will continue to flow into overseas infrastructure projects. China's investment in manufacturing in the developing world will increase but from a small base compared to Japan and others. The Party claims credit for these successes, or at least for making them possible. These same claims worry actors around the world – wondering if all Chinese companies are compliant tools of the one-party state.

For all its success, China faces daunting problems of a declining workforce, environmental degradation, continuing wide income gaps, and so on. Some advanced industries, such as the telecommunications firm Huawei, are already the best in the world and the Party is throwing huge sums into research, notably into artificial intelligence and other IT-related projects. China has the scale to do these things without starving the broader economy of capital. In the CCP it has the power to make them happen. But return on capital has been falling and focus on state enterprise can only make it worse.

Under Xi Jinping, the needs of the nation are conflated with those of the Party to a greater extent than since Mao. Years of making some space between Party and state under Deng, Jiang Zemin, and Hu Jintao have now been reversed. The leadership of the Party in all areas, not least big business, is an invitation both to bureaucracy and to the supremacy of political over commercial priorities. Xi's goal to make China independent in a range of key technologies is ultimately a quest for autarky, a return to times – most of its history – when foreign trade was marginal. This Party autarky is driven by the Leninist concern to maintain power by maintaining access to resources and information.

Since the Revolution the Party's economic choice, as in the Soviet Union, was autarky, a form of defense against a mostly hostile capitalist world. For a while, it worked and by the 1960s the Soviets were looking to catch up economically with the West. They had education, resources, and expertise. But it foundered on a party dedicated to that autarky being closed and rigid, suppressing initiative and controlling information. Deng Xiaoping's policy was a rejection of both Mao and the Soviets and put China in a position where it is a global power and aspires to fill the space long occupied by the West.

China has done so well out of opening up that gradual closing might seem improbable. But with politics in command and a revived Party organization, China could yet fall back on more of Mao's prescriptions, Party control and correct ideology. The result need not be a return to Cultural Revolution upheavals but a Chinese replay of the grind of the stultifying, authoritarian, and uninspiring Brezhnev–Andropov–Chernenko years in the Soviet Union.

So far, Xi Jinping has been lucky in the decline of his adversaries. Trump's America has probably done more damage to the interests of its allies, ranging from Japan to Mexico, Canada, and the EU, than to China. His withdrawal from the Trans-Pacific Partnership (PPT) was an open goal for China. Trump's personality and erratic behavior have drawn attention away from Xi's repressive domestic policies and memories of the Bo Xilai affair, and cast Xi, by contrast, as a more predictable and reliable leader. But whoever or whenever his successor, Trump will leave behind the sense, not just in the US, that China under the Communist Party is ambitious and potentially dangerous.

Yet the Party under Xi can show that in addition to military advances, China's external financial position has strengthened, its macroeconomic policies are pragmatic, and its technological development is impressive. Its claims to favor open trade have partial credibility at a time when the US is uncertain of its global role and is hobbled with Trump's tariffs and trade wars. The US anyway is overdue for a recession and has massive foreign debt. The 2020 coronavirus shock may even show that the disciplined authoritarianism of the Chinese Party machine is better equipped to handle such challenges (including climate change) than liberalism beset by democratic indecision and legal obstacles.

Xi Jinping has concluded that only the Party can save China, and only he can save the Party. However, from Henricus Sneevliet in the 1920s to Wang Ming in the 1930s and Mao since the 1940s, not to mention Deng Xiaoping and Jiang Zemin after Mao, confident leaders have shaped the Chinese Communist Party to their will, just as Xi Jinping is doing today, only to discover that it, or the constellation of actors who make up the Party and the society in which it operates, would not comply. Party intellectuals like Wang Shiwei in the 1940s and Wang Yuanhua in the 1990s, leading figures like Wang Guangmei in the 1960s and reformist General Secretaries like Zhao Ziyang in the 1980s, all interpreted or adapted the visions of the supreme leaders to produce something else again. All failed – leaders and led alike – to achieve their personal goals, but all succeeded in constructing a powerful and resilient political body that lives today. We cannot predict the future life of the Party, but it is unlikely to stray far from the range of examples we have met in these ten moments in the life of the Party.

APPENDIX
Selected Further Readings

Historical Context: Useful General Histories

Spence, Jonathan, *In Search of Modern China*, 2nd edition (New York: W. W. Norton, 1999)

Mühlhahn, Klaus, *Making China Modern: From the Great Qing to Xi Jinping* (Cambridge, MA: Harvard University Press, 2019)

van de Ven, Hans, *China at War: Triumph and Tragedy in the Emergence of the New China* (Cambridge, MA: Harvard University Press, 2018)

Cheek, Timothy, *The Intellectual in Modern Chinese History* (Cambridge: Cambridge University Press, 2015)

Party Writings in Translation

Selected Works of Mao Tse-tung and other official Mao texts/images available at the Mao Zedong Internet Archive: www.marxists .org/reference/archive/mao/index.htm

Mao's Road to Power, 1912–1949, ed. Stuart R. Schram (New York: M. E. Sharpe, 1992–; London: Routledge, 2015–) (the standard scholarly edition with commentary in ten planned volumes, up through 1945 published by 2015)

Cheek, Timothy, *Mao Zedong and China's Revolutions: A Brief History with Documents* (Boston, MA: Bedford Books, 2002) (selected texts with historical background)

Saich, Tony, *The Rise to Power of the Chinese Communist Party: Documents and Analysis* (Armonk, NY: M. E. Sharpe, 1996; London: Routledge, 2016) (one thousand pages of reliable documents and helpful commentary)

Studies by Topic and Period
(per Chapters of This Book)

1920s

Ishikawa, Yoshihiro, *The Formation of the Chinese Communist Party*, trans. Joshua A. Fogel (New York: Columbia University Press, 2013) (new research by a senior Japanese scholar on the international origins of the CCP)

Landsberger, Stephan, *Chinese Propaganda Posters*, www.iisg.nl/~landsberger (an excellent website including posters and commentary on Party policies, etc.)

Saich, Tony, *Finding Allies and Making Revolution: The Early Years of the Chinese Communist Party* (Leiden: E.J. Brill, 2020) (a vivid retelling of the origins of the Party drawing from Comintern archives)

1930s

Averill, Stephen J., *Revolution in the Highlands: China's Jinggangshan Base Area* (Lanham, MD: Rowman & Littlefield, 2006) (explains the shift from city to rural revolution in rich ethnographic context)

Sun Shuyun, *The Long March* (London: Harper Perennial, 2007) (a contemporary journalist retraces the Long March and talks to survivors)

1940s

Apter, David and Tony Saich, *Revolutionary Discourse in Mao's Republic* (Cambridge, MA: Harvard University Press, 1994) (an analysis of why many believed in the Yan'an rectification movement)

Gao, Hua, *How the Red Sun Rose: The Origins and Development of the Yan'an Rectification Movement, 1930–1945*, trans. Stacy Mosher and Guo Jian (Hong Kong: The Chinese University Press, 2018) (seminal and critical study of Mao and the Party by a Chinese historian writing in China)

Pepper, Suzanne, *Civil War in China: The Political Struggle* (Lanham, MD: Rowman & Littlefield, 1999) (a classic study of the Communist–Nationalist struggle for minds and territory)

1950s

Altehenger, Jennifer, *Legal Lessons: Popularizing Laws in the People's Republic of China, 1949–1989* (Cambridge, MA: Harvard University Press, 2018) (shows the Party's efforts to rule their new nation with a focus on the 1950s)

Brown, Jeremy and Paul G. Pickowicz, eds., *The Dilemmas of Victory: The Early Years of the People's Republic of China* (Cambridge, MA: Harvard University Press, 2010) (a well-edited collection that gives the social history of the Party's national victory)

Chen, Jian, *Mao's China and the Cold War* (Chapel Hill: University of North Carolina Press, 2000) (uses newly released materials to create a fresh interpretation of Mao's role in the Korean War and the Cold War more broadly)

Dikötter, Frank, *Mao's Great Famine: The History of China's Most Devastating Catastrophe* (London: Bloomsbury, 2010) (detailed and critical history of the Party's Great Leap Forward and its disastrous outcomes)

1960s

Brown, Jeremy and Matthew D. Johnson, eds., *Maoism at the Grassroots: Everyday Life in China's Era of High Socialism* (Cambridge, MA: Harvard University Press, 2015) (shows life under Party rule during Mao's ascendency, mid-1950s to mid-1970s)

MacFarquhar, Roderick and Michael Schoenhals, *Mao's Last Revolution* (Cambridge, MA: Belknap Press of Harvard University Press, 2008) (the best narrative history of the Cultural Revolution decade, 1966–1976)

Morning Sun (Boston: Longbow Group, 2002) (an excellent two-hour documentary focusing on the Cultural Revolution and Mao,

available on DVD and supported by an intelligent website, www
.morningsun.org)

1970s

Butterfield, Fox, *Alive in the Bitter Sea*, enlarged edition (New York:
Times Books, 1990) (award-winning journalist's account of life in
the early reform period after 1978)

Lovell, Julia, *Maoism: A Global History* (New York: Knopf, 2019)
(a vivid narrative of the impact of Maoism around the world,
1960s to today)

1980s

Baum, Richard, *Burying Mao: Chinese Politics in the Age of Deng
Xiaoping* (Princeton, NJ: Princeton University Press, 1994) (still
one of the best accounts of the clash of ideas and values between
the old generation of revolutionaries of the Maoist era and their
younger, more pragmatic successors in the 1980s)

Vogel, Ezra F., *Deng Xiaoping and the Transformation of China*
(Cambridge, MA: Belknap Press of Harvard University Press,
2013) (magisterial biography that focuses on Deng's reform of
the Party from the late 1970s)

Zhao Ziyang, *Prisoner of the State: The Secret Journal of Premier
Zhao Ziyang* (New York: Simon & Schuster, 2009) (Zhao's
posthumous autobiography, which he secretly recorded on a tape
recorder while under house arrest)

1990s

Fewsmith, Joseph, *China since Tiananmen: From Deng Xiaoping to
Hu Jintao*, 2nd ed. (New York: Cambridge University Press,
2008) (readable and reliable account of Party reform in the
1990s, updated to the mid-2000s)

Wang, Chaohua, *One China, Many Paths* (London: Verso, 2003)
(Chinese voices from the 1990s on the Party, reform, and new
challenges)

2000s

Fewsmith, Joseph, *The Logic and Limits of Political Reform in China* (New York: Cambridge University Press, 2013) (engaging case studies of why Party rural administrations resist reform)

Shambaugh, David, *China's Communist Party: Atrophy and Adaptation* (Berkeley: University of California Press, 2008) (a clear and comprehensive political-science assessment of the Party in the 2000s)

2010s

Brown, Kerry, *China's Dream: The Culture of Chinese Communism and the Secret of Its Power* (Cambridge: Polity Press, 2018) (a serious assessment of what Party leaders under Xi Jinping believe and why)

deLisle, Jacques, Avery Goldstein, and Guobin Yang, *The Internet, Social Media, and a Changing China* (Philadelphia: University of Pennsylvania Press, 2016) (studies of Internet populism, stressing citizen resistance to Party abuses)

Tang, Wenfang, *Populist Authoritarianism: Chinese Political Culture and Regime Sustainability* (Oxford: Oxford University Press, 2016) (a challenging analysis of why so many Chinese support the Party's authoritarian regime)

NOTES

Chapter 1

1 The long history of failed Western efforts to make China "more like use"
is vividly chronicled in Jonathan Spence, *To Change China: Western
Advisers in China* (New York: Penguin, 1980).

2 Henricus Sneevliet, "Zhi gongchan guoji yuandong shujichu de xin"
(Letter to the Far East Secretariat of the Comintern), trans. Li Yuzhen, in
"Gongchan guoji daibiao Malin guanyu Zhongguo gongchanzhuyi
yundong ji Zhonggong chuangjian de wufen wenxian" (Five documents
from Comintern Representative Maring [Sneevliet] about the Chinese
Communist Movement and the establishment of the CCP), *Dang de
wenxian* (Party Documents), no. 4 (2011), pp. 5–9, 11.

3 Sneevliet, "Bericht des Genossen H. Maring fur die Executive" (Report of
Comrade H. Maring to the Executive), July 1922, Archive of the
Amsterdam District Court, 797/33.

4 Sneevliet, "Letter to Zinoviev, Bukharin, Radek, and Safarov," June
1923, International Institute for Social History, Amsterdam, Sneevliet
Archive, Number 231. Hereafter Sneevliet Archive.

5 Sneevliet, "Met en Bij Soen Yat Sen, Eenige Persoonlijke Herinneringen"
(Together with Sun Yat-sen: personal recollections), *Klassenstrijd* (Class
Struggle), 1:3 (1926), pp. 65–69.

6 Harold Isaacs, "Documents on the Comintern and the Chinese
Revolution," *China Quarterly*, 45 (January 1971), p. 104.

7 Sneevliet, "Uit Het Verre Oosten" (From the Far East), *De Tribune*, May
6, 1922.

8 Ibid.

9 Chen Duxiu, "Chen Duxiu zhi Wu Tingkang de xin" (Letter from Chen
Duxiu to Voitinsky), April 6, 1922, in *"Erda" he "sanda": Zhongguo
gongchandang di 2, 3 ci daibiao dahui ziliao xuanbian* (The Second and
Third Party Congresses: Selected Materials) (Beijing: Zhongguo shehui
kexue chubanshe, 1985), p. 36.

10 Chen Duxiu, "Chen Duxiu zhi Wu Tingkang de xin" (Letter from Chen Duxiu to Voitinsky), June 30, 1922, in *"Erda" he "sanda"*, p. 55.
11 Sneevliet, *Bericht des Genossen Maring*.
12 Sneevliet, "Die revolutionäre nationalistiche Bewegung in Südchina" (The revolutionary nationalist movement in south China), *Die Kommunistische Internationale*, September 13, 1922.
13 Ibid.
14 Sneevliet, "Letter to Zinoviev, Bukharin, and Radek," June 20, 1923, Sneevliet Archive, Number 231.
15 Chen Duxiu, "A letter to all comrades," translated in *Chinese Studies in History*, 3:3 (Spring 1970), p. 227; Chang Kuo-t'ao, *The Rise of the Chinese Communist Party: The Autobiography of Chang Kuo-t'ao* (Lawrence: University Press of Kansas, 1971), vol. 1, p. 254.
16 "Notes of Sneevliet's about co-operation with the KMT," end of November–early December 1922, Sneevliet Archive, Number 270.
17 Sneevliet and Grigory Voitinsky, "Concerning our work in colonial and semi-colonial countries in general and in China in particular," Sneevliet Archive, Number 294.
18 Sneevliet, "Letter to van Ravesteyn," February 26, 1923, International Institute of Social History, Amsterdam, van Ravesteyn Archive, Number 18.
19 "Resolution passed by the ECCI of the Comintern on the relations of the Communist Party of China to the 'Kuomintang Party,'" January 12, 1923, Sneevliet Archive, Number 272, original emphasis.
20 Karl Radek, "The tasks of the Chinese Communist Party," Sneevliet Archive, Number 282.
21 Grigory Voitinsky, letters to Safarov, head of the Eastern Department of the ECCI, March 8 and March 24, 1923, and telegram to Safarov, March 1923, in RKP(B), *Komintern und die national-revolutionäre Bewegung in China, Dokumente* (The Comintern and the national-revolutionary movement in China, Documents) (Paderborn: F. Schöningh, 1996), vol. 1, 1920–1925, documents 65, 68, 70. Hereafter *The Comintern*.
22 Karl Radek and Grigory Voitinsky, "Entwurf der Direktive der Ostabteilung des EKKI für den Vertreter der Ostabteilung des EKKI auf dem 3. Parteitag der KPCh" (Draft for a directive by the Eastern Department of the ECCI for its representative to the Third Party Congress of the Chinese Communist Party), May 23, 1923, in *The Comintern*, document 74.
23 "May 1923 directive of the ECCI to the Third Congress of the Chinese Communist Party," Sneevliet Archive, Number 274.
24 Sneevliet, "Telegram to Davtian," June 5, 1923, and "Letter to Davtian and Joffe," July 20, 1923, Sneevliet Archive, Numbers 230, 232.

25 Sneevliet, "Letter to Zinoviev, Bukharin, Radek, and Safarov," June 20, 1923, Sneevliet Archive, Number 231.

26 Ibid.

27 Sneevliet, "Notes of delegates' comments at the Third Party Congress on the question of co-operation with the Kuomintang," June 1923, Sneevliet Archive, Numbers 275, 276.

28 Sneevliet, "Speech to the Congress," Sneevliet Archive, Number 277.

29 "Report by H. Sneevliet on the period June 23–July 15, 1923," Sneevliet Archive, Number 301.

Chapter 2

1 John Bell, *The Bulgarian Communist Party from Blagoev to Zhivkov* (Stanford: Hoover Institution Press, 1985), p. 47.

2 China National Library, ed., *Chinese Fighters in the Spanish Anti-Fascist War* 中国勇士血洒西班牙 (Beijing: Forbidden City Publishing House, 2008).

3 "Notes on the Chinese question: From Dimitrov's diary, November 11, 1937," www.marxists.org/reference/archive/dimitrov/works/1937/china2.htm.

4 "The history of Wang Ming's defiance of Mao Zedong after his return from Moscow" 1937 年王明回国后与毛泽东分厅抗礼, http://cul.sohu.com/20080229/n255441318_1.shtml.

5 "The CCP's ten main guidelines for resisting Japan and saving the nation," in Central Committee Archives, *A Selection of CCP Central Committee Documents* 中共中央文件选集, XI, p. 328. Hereafter ZZWX.

6 "Central Committee resolution on the current situation and the party's tasks," ZZWX, XI, p. 326.

7 "Record of Wang Ming's report to the Politburo of the Central Committee of the Chinese Communist Party," December 9, 1937, quoted in Jin Chongji, *Biography of Mao Zedong* 毛泽东传 (Beijing: CCP Central Committee Documentation Center, 1996), p. 506.

8 Jin Chongji, *Biography of Mao Zedong*, p. 507.

9 Ibid.

10 Guo Dehong, *Chronological Biography of Wang Ming* 王明年谱 (Anqing: Anhui People's Press, 1991), p. 94.

11 "Impressions of Hankow," *Manchester Guardian*, December 21, 1937.

12 Chiang Kai-shek, *Diary Entries on Striving in Adversity* 困勉集 (Taipei: Guoshiguan, 2011), II, p. 592.

13 Jin Chongji, *Biography of Zhou Enlai* 周恩来传 (Beijing: CCP Central Committee Documentation Center, 1989), pp. 393–394.

14 Chiang Kai-shek, *Striving in Adversity*, II, p. 591.

15 Liu Jixian, *Chronological Biography of Ye Jianying* 叶剑英年谱 (Beijing: CCP Central Committee Documentation Center, 2007), I, pp. 213–214.

16 Guo Dehong, *Chronological Biography of Wang Ming*, pp. 99–100; Liu Jixian, *Chronological Biography of Ye Jianying*, I, p. 221.

17 Chen Shaoyu (Wang Ming), "Summary of the March Politburo meeting," ZZWX, XI, p. 447.

18 CCP Central Committee Documentation Center, *Chronological Biography of Zhou Enlai* 周恩来年谱 (Beijing: CCP Central Committee Documentation Center, 1998). pp. 403–404.

19 "CCP Central Committee telegram to the KMT emergency national congress," ZZWX, XI, p. 481.

20 "Central Secretariat message about strategy toward the KMT emergency national congress to Chen Shaoyu, Zhou Enlai, Bo Gu and Kai Feng," ZZWX, XI, p. 509.

21 CCP Central Committee Documentation Center, *Chronological Biography of Zhou Enlai*, p. 395.

22 Ibid., pp. 400–404.

23 W. H. Auden and C. Isherwood, *Journey to a War*, pp. 39–40, quoted in Stephen MacKinnon, *Wuhan, 1938: War, Refugees, and the Making of Modern China* (Berkeley: University of California Press, 2008), p. 97.

24 This section is heavily indebted to MacKinnon, *Wuhan, 1938*.

25 Chen Kewen, *Diary of Chen Kewen* 陈克文日记, ed. Chen Fangzheng (Taipei: Modern History Institute of the Academia Sinica), I, p. 147.

26 Quote from Hans van de Ven, *China at War: Triumph and Tragedy in the Emergence of the New China* (Cambridge, MA: Harvard University Press, 2018), p. 111.

27 "Chinese refugees: a Hankow picture," *Manchester Guardian*, April 25, 1938.

28 Quoted in Van de Ven, *China at War*, pp. 99–100.

29 Ibid., p. 99.

30 Ibid., p. 102.

31 Quoted in CCP Central Committee Documentation Center, *Chronological Biography of Zhou Enlai*, p. 406.

32 "600,000 take part in Hankow propaganda week parades," *China Press*, April 14, 1938.

33 Wu Yan, "A discussion on the CCP–KMT co-operation during the War of Resistance"' 抗战期间国共合作述论, in *Southern Discussion* 南方论刊, 2016:5, pp. 51–53; Owen Lattimore, "From GSI to GOC HK" (July 7, 1937), UK National Archives, HW 106/5731.

34 This and the next paragraph are based on Liu Jixian, *Chronological Biography of Ye Jianying*, pp. 218–235.

35 "Unity against Japan pledged by Chinese," *New York Times*, July 17, 1938.

36 "Chinese casualties over million in year," *New York Times*, July 9, 1938.

37 Tillman Durdin, "Japanese planes near Hankow; 500 victims found," *New York Times*, July 13, 1938.

38 "We wish the National Political Consultative Conference enormous success," in Marxism–Leninism Institute of Sichuan University, *Sources for the National Political Consultative Conference* 国民参政会资料 (Chengdu: Sichuan People's Press, 1984), p. 251.

39 *Liberation* 解放, 45 (1938), pp. 6–17.

40 *News Digest* 新闻摘旬刊, I:5 (1938), pp. 4–5.

41 *The Critic* 时论丛刊, V (1939), pp. 28–33.

42 Georgi Dimitrov, *Notes on the Chinese Question: From Dimitrov's Diary* (November 11, 1937), www.marxists.org/reference/archive/ dimitrov/works/1937/china2.htm.

43 Chen Shaoyu, Zhou Enlai, and Qin Bogu, "Our thoughts on the defense of Wuhan and the third period in the War of Resistance," ZZWX, XI, p. 856.

44 "Trading space for time: China's new plan," *Manchester Guardian*, July 22, 1938.

45 Ibid.

46 Agnes Smedley, "The last days of Hankow," *Manchester Guardian*, October 28, 1938.

47 "Sending civilians from Hankow," *Manchester Guardian*, July 7, 1938.

48 "15,000 refugees in Hankow," *The Times* (London), October 8, 1938.

49 "The Chinese exodus," *Manchester Guardian*, June 17, 1937.

50 "Hankow hears the guns," *The Times* (London), October 25, 1938.

51 "In ruined Hankow," *The Times* (London), October 27, 1938.

52 Van de Ven, *China at War*, p. 108.

53 Jin Chongji, *Biography of Mao Zedong*, p. 515.

54 Wang Jiaxiang, "My recollection of the struggle between Comrade Mao Zedong and Wang Ming's opportunism" 回忆毛泽东同志与王明机会主义的斗争, *People's Daily* 人民日报, December 27, 1979.

55 On the instruction, see Gao Hua, *How the Red Sun Rose: The Origins and Development of the Yan'an Rectification Movement* (Hong Kong: Chinese University of Hong Kong Press, 2018), pp. 179–182.

56 Mao Zedong, "On the new stage," ZZWX, XI, p. 595.

57 Van de Ven, *China at War*, p. 141.

58 "Instruction regarding the defense of Wuhan," ZZWX, XI, p. 538.

59 Quoted in Jin Chongji, *Biography of Mao Zedong*, p. 520.

60 Gao Hua, *Red Sun*, pp. 284–285.

61 Ibid., p. 309.

62 Ibid., p. 311.

63 Ibid., p. 320.

64 "Wang Ming relates Mao's quest for one-man rule," Moscow, TASS, September 12, 1975, *FBIS Daily Reports*, FBIS-Sov-75-187.

65 Cao Min 曹敏, "The truth about the 'Wang Ming poisoning incident,'" *One Hundred Year Tide* 百年潮, V (2013); Guo Dehong, "The reality behind the two Wang Ming poisoning incidents," *General Review of the History of the Communist Party of China* 党史博览, IX (2010).

66 Peter Vladimirov, *The Vladimirov Diaries: Yenan, China: 1942–45* (London: Robert Hale, 1975), p. 185.

67 Mao Zedong, "To Comrade Dimitrov," included in *The Diary of Georgi Dimitrov, 1933–1944*, tr. Jane Hedges, Timothy Sergay, and Irina Faion (New Haven: Yale University Press, 2003), p. 295.

68 Mao Zedong, "On the new stage," ZZWX, XI, p. 658.

69 Wang Ming, *Fifty Years of the CCP* 中共五十年 (Beijing: Society for Modern History Sources, 1980), pp. 64–69.

70 "Wang Ming relates Mao's quest for one-man rule," Moscow, TASS, September 24, 1975, *FBIS Daily Reports*, FBIS-SOV-75-187.

71 "Armistice day," *The Times* (London), November 12, 1937.

Chapter 3

1 Wang Shiwei, "Ying gutou, ruan gutou" (Strong bones, soft bones), originally published in the Yan'an wall newspaper *Arrow and Target* (*Shi yu di*) in spring 1942, reprinted in Huang Changyong, *Wang Shiwei zhuan* (Biography of Wang Shiwei) (Zhengzhou: Henan renmin chubanshe, 2000), pp. 173–174. Another translation appears in Dai Qing, *Wang Shiwei and "Wild Lilies": Rectification and Purges in the Chinese Communist Party, 1942–1944* (Armonk, NY: M. E. Sharpe, 1994), p. 96 (with minor edits).

2 Edgar Snow and Baron von Richtofen, quoted in Mark Selden, *China in Revolution: The Yenan Way Revisited*, 2nd ed. (1995; reprinted London: Routledge, 2016), pp. 3–4.

3 Selden, *China in Revolution*, pp. 144–145; and Gao Hua, *How the Red Sun Rose, 1935–1945: The Origins and Development of the Yan'an Rectification Movement* (Hong Kong: Chinese University of Hong Kong Press, 2018), pp. 343–347.

4 The most recent biography of Wang is Wei Shiyu, *Wang Shiwei: wenyi zhengfeng yu sixiang gaizao* (Wang Shiwei: Literary Rectification and

Ideological Remolding) (Hong Kong: Xianggang chengshi daxue chubanshe, 2016).

5 Wang Shiwei, *Xiuxi* (Rest) (Shanghai: Zhonghua shuju, 1930), pp. 2, 85. Although an unspectacular piece, it was reprinted four times: 1930, 1931, 1934, and 1940.

6 See, for example, reminiscences in Dai Qing, *Wang Shiwei*, pp. 157–191; and the moving documentary produced by RTHK (Radio Television Hong Kong) in 2017, *Wang Shiwei: The Buried Writer*, introduced with a link to the video at MCLC Resource Center (Ohio State University), https://u.osu.edu/mclc/2017/01/20/wang-shiwei-documentary/ (accessed December 15, 2019).

7 Mao Zedong, "Zhong xuan bu xuanchuan daodian," translated in Stuart R. Schram and Timothy Cheek, eds., *Mao's Road to Power: From Rectification to Coalition Government, 1942–July 1945*, Vol. VIII (London: Routledge, 2015), pp. 9–10.

8 Mao Zedong, "Zhengdun xuefeng, dangfeng, wenfeng" (Rectify our study style, Party style and writing style), translated in Schram and Cheek, *Mao's Road to Power*, vol. VIII, p. 18.

9 Translated in Tony Saich, *The Rise to Power of the Chinese Communist Party: Documents and Analysis* (Armonk, NY: M. E. Sharpe, 1996), p. 1228; also Schram and Cheek, *Mao's Road to Power*, vol. VIII, p. 819 (with slightly different phrasing).

10 Ding Ling, "Women xuyao zawen" (We need *zawen*), *Jiefang ribao*, October 23, 1941, p. 4.

11 Wang's words come from Chen Boda's later critique, "Guanyu Wang Shiwei" (Concerning Wang Shiwei), published in *Jiefang ribao*, June 15, 1942, p. 4.

12 Wang Shiwei, "Zhengzhijia, yishujia" (Politicians, Artists), reprinted in Huang Changyong, *Wang Shiwei zhuan*, pp. 274–277, and translated in Dai Qing, *Wang Shiwei and "Wild Lilies"*, pp. 90–93.

13 Qi Su, "Du 'Ye baihehua' yougan" (Thoughts on Reading "Wild Lilies"), *Jiefang ribao*, April 7, 1942, p. 4.

14 Wang Shiwei, "Ye baihua" (Wild Lilies), *Jiefang ribao*, March 13 and 23, 1942, p. 4. Quote from March 13, p. 4. A slightly different translation appears in Dai Qing, *Wang Shiwei*, p. 7.

15 Wang Shiwei, "Ye baihua" (Wild Lilies), quote from March 23, p. 4 – drawing from Simon Leys's spirited translation in *Chinese Shadows* (New York: Viking Press, 1977), pp. 123–127.

16 Mao Zedong, "Oral political report at the Seventh National Congress of the Chinese Communist Party" (April 24, 1945), translated in Schram and Cheek, *Mao's Road to Power*, vol. VIII, pp. 852–853. Mao also

mentions wall newspapers of the time in his comments on the Party's historical resolution – ibid., p. 742.

17 "Mao Zedong tongzhi haozhao zhengdun sanfeng yao liyong baozhi" (Comrade Mao Zedong calls for the use of newspapers in the rectification of the Three Work Styles), *Jiefang ribao*, April 2, 1942, p. 1.

18 Mao Zedong's "Talks at the Yan'an Conference on Literature and Art," translated by Bonnie S. McDougall and incorporated into Schram and Cheek, *Mao's Road to Power*, vol. VIII, p. 106.

19 Ibid.

20 Ibid., pp. 106, 121.

21 Wen Jize, "Douzheng riji" (Diary of struggle), *Jiefang ribao*, June 28 and 29, 1942, p. 4. The following excerpts come from the translation in Saich, *The Rise to Power of the Chinese Communist Party*, pp. 1113–1122.

22 Ding Ling, cited in Dai Qing, *Wang Shiwei*, p. 50.

23 Cyril Birch, "Fiction of the Yenan Period," *China Quarterly*, 4 (1960), p. 11. On *Yangge*, see David Holm, *Art and Ideology in Revolutionary China* (Oxford: Clarendon Press, 1991).

24 Zhang Ruxin, "Zhongyang yanjiuyuan zhengfeng yilai sixiang gaizao zongjie – zai zhongyang yanjiuyuan zongjie dangfeng shide baogao" (General summary of ideological remolding in the Central Research Institute since the start of rectification: report on Party rectification in the Central Research Institute), *Jiefang ribao*, October 31 and November 1, 1942, translated in Dai Qing, *Wang Shiwei*, pp. 115–134, quote from p. 115.

25 Yang Shangkun, "Tuopai Wang Shiwei de huodong yu dang nei ziyou zhuyi," *Dang de shenghuo* (Party Life), October 31, 1942, translated in Dai Qing, *Wang Shiwei*, pp. 135–145. See also *Yang Shangkun nianpu, 1907–1998* (Chronological Biography of Yang Shangkun, 1907–1998), I (Beijing: Zhonggong dangshi chubanshe, 2007), p. 504.

26 Yang gives the formal name for Wang's "gang": *fandang wuren jituan* 反黨五人集團, made up of Wang, Pan Fang 潘芳, Zong Zheng 宗錚, Cheng Quan 成全, and Wang Li 王里. Dai Qing, *Wang Shiwei*, pp. 58–63, gives more details about their relationships.

27 Kang Sheng, "Kang Sheng zai xunlian ban de baogao (zhailu)" (Abstract of Kang Sheng's report to a training class), August 1943, trans. in Dai Qing, *Wang Shiwei*, pp. 146–155. Kang's "internal text" is quoted at length in Huang Changyong, *Wang Shiwei zhuan*, pp. 221–226.

28 Dai Qing, *Wang Shiwei*, p. 150; Huang Changyong, *Wang Shiwei zhuan*, p. 221.

29 See Peter Seybolt, "Terror and conformity: counterespionage campaigns, rectification, and mass movements, 1942–1943," *Modern China*, 12,

no. 1 (1986), pp. 39–74; David Apter and Tony Saich, *Revolutionary Discourse in Mao's Republic* (Cambridge, MA: Harvard University Press, 1994); and especially Gao Hua, *How the Red Sun Rose*, chapters 12, 13, and 14.

30 Zhao Chaogou, *Yan'an yi yue* (One Month in Yan'an) (Shanghai: Xinmin baoshe, 1947), pp. 147–148.

31 Vividly covered in Dai Qing, *Wang Shiwei*, pp. 3, 66–68.

32 Mao Zedong, "On democratic centralism," translated in Stuart Schram, *Mao Tse-tung Unrehearsed* (Harmondsworth: Penguin, 1974), pp. 185–186.

33 Gao Hua, *How the Red Sun Rose*, pp. 590 ff.

34 See Wen Jize, *Wang Shiwei yuan'an pingfan jishi* (Record of the Rehabilitation of Wang Shiwei's Unjust Case) (Beijing: Qunzhong chubanshe, 1993).

35 Hu Yaobang, General Secretary of the CCP, quoted in Dai Qing, *Wang Shiwei*, p. 159.

36 "Wang Shiwei yu 'Ye baihehua'" (Wang Shiwei and "Wild Lilies"), in Dai Qing, *Liang Shuming, Wang Shiwei, Chu Anping* (Nanjing: Jiangsu wenyi chubanshe, June 1989), pp. 41–110, is translated in full in Dai Qing, *Wang Shiwei*.

Chapter 4

* Translated by Melanie Faber and Lu Tian. The author would like to thank Liu Wennan, Jiang Jin, and Jeremy Brown for their help with the revision process.

1 Mao Zedong, "Zai Yan'an wenyi zuotanhui shang de jianghua," 在延安文艺座谈会上的讲话 (Speech at the Forum of Literature and Art in Yan'an), May 1942, in Editorial Board of Central Documents of the CCP, *Mao Zedong xuanji*, vol. 3, Beijing: Renmin chubanshe, 1991.

2 Chen Danyan, *Shanghai de hongyan yishi* 上海的红颜遗事 (Anecdotes of Shanghai Female Celebrities), Shanghai: Shanghai wenyi chubanshe, 2015, pp. 8–9.

3 Office for Intellectual Issues of the Municipal CCP in Shanghai (print), "Shanghai dianying zhipianchang dangwei shuji Lin Lin fayangao" 上海电影制片厂党委书记林琳发言稿 (Speech by Lin Lin, secretary of the Party committee of Shanghai Film Studio), February 24, 1956, Shanghai Municipal Archives (SMA), A22-1-275.

4 Deng Deng, *Daiyu yunmai yiban shan: ji wode fuqin Cheng Shuyao* 带雨云埋一半山－－记我的父亲程述尧 (Half Buried with Rain Clouds:

About My Father Cheng Shuyao), Shanghai: Shanghai renmin chubanshe, 2017, pp. 107–115.

5 Office for Intellectual Issues of the Municipal CCP in Shanghai, "Shanghai dianying zhipianchang dangwei shuji Lin Lin fayangao."

6 Interview with Wei Ran (Deng Deng), April 9, 2019, in Shanghai.

7 Office for Intellectual Issues of the Municipal CCP in Shanghai (ed.), "Shanghai dianying zhipianchang zhishifenzi qingkuang diaocha baogao" 上海电影制片厂知识分子情况调查报告 (Investigative Report on Intellectuals in Shanghai Film Studio), December 1955, SMA. A22-1-282.

8 Ibid.

9 Office for Intellectual Issues of the Municipal CCP in Shanghai, "Shanghai dianying zhipianchang dangwei shuji Lin Lin fayangao."

10 Ibid.

11 Ibid.

12 Office for Intellectual Issues of the Municipal CCP in Shanghai, "Shanghai shi gaoji zhishifenzi mingdan" 上海市高级知识分子名单 (List of High-Level Intellectuals in Shanghai); "Gaoji zhishifenzi biaozhun shuoming" 高级知识分子标准说明 (Notes on the Criteria for High-Level Intellectuals), February 1956, SMA, A22-1-285.

13 Pang Xianzhi and Feng Hui (eds. in chief), *Mao Zedong nianpu* 毛泽东年谱 (Chronicle of Mao Zedong), *1949–1976*, Beijing: Zhongyang wenxian chubanshe, 2013, p. 102.

14 Paul G. Pickowicz, *China on Film: A Century of Exploration, Confrontation, and Controversy*, Lanham, MD: Rowman & Littlefield Publishers, Inc., 2013, pp. 183–185.

15 Ge Kunyuan (comp.), *Shen Ji koushu shi* 沈寂口述史 (Oral History of Shen Ji), Shanghai: Shanghai shudian chubanshe, 2015, pp. 185–187.

16 SMA, A22-2-554.

17 Wang Danfeng, "Re'ai shenghuo, zhongyu yishu" 热爱生活，忠于艺术 (Love Life and Stay True to Art), *Film Art* (Beijing), 12 (1982), p. 38.

18 Interview with Wei Ran, "Yidai hongyan Shangguan Yunzhu" 一代红颜上官云珠, Beijing TV Station, Science and Education Channel, January 2012.

19 Zheng Keqing and Chang Zhi, "Cong jianguo yilai Mao Zedong wengao kan Mao Zedong dui Jiang Qing taidu de yanbian" 从《建国以来毛泽东文稿》看毛泽东对江青态度的演变 (The evolution of Mao's attitude toward Jiang Qing as seen in the *Manuscripts of Mao Zedong since the Founding of the People's Republic of China*), *Dangshi Bocai* 党史博采 (Shijiazhuang), 1 (2005), pp. 17–18.

20 Yan Changgui, *Yan Changgui tan Jiang Qing* 闫长贵谈江青 (Yan Changgui on Jiang Qing), Hongkong: Zhongguo wenge lishi chubanshe, 2017, pp. 34–35.

21 Qin Yi, "Yi Shangguan Yunzhu" 忆上官云珠 (Recollection of Shangguan Yunzhu), *Dazhong Dianying* 大众电影 (Beijing), 3 (1979), p. 9.

22 Pang Xianzhi and Feng Hui, *Mao Zedong nianpu, 1949–1976*, pp. 194–195.

Chapter 5

1 William Hinton, *Hundred Day War: The Cultural Revolution at Tsinghua University* (New York: Monthly Review Press, 1972), pp. 103–105.

2 Huang Zheng (黄峥), *Wang Guangmei fangtan lu* 王光美访谈录 (Transcript of Interviews with Wang Guangmei) (Beijing: Central Documents Press, 2006), p. 353.

3 Ibid., p. 353.

4 Zhang Jiang (张绛), *Wo suo zhidaode Wang Guangmei* 我所知道的王光美 (The Wang Guangmei I Know) (Beijing: Central Documents Press, 2012), pp. 113–114.

5 Ibid., p. 127.

6 Mao Zedong (毛泽东), "Guanyu siqing yundong de yici jianghua" 关于四清运动的一次讲话 (A talk on the Four Cleans movement) (January 3, 1965), in *Mao Zedong sixiang wansui* 马泽东思想万岁 [Long Live Mao Zedong Thought] (1968).

7 Zhang Jiang, *Wo suo zhidaode Wang Guangmei*, p. 157. Another translation of this text is available at Marxists.org: www.marxists.org/reference/archive/mao/selected-works/volume-9/mswv9_38.htm.

Chapter 6

1 Zhisui Li, *The Private Life of Chairman Mao: The Memoirs of Mao's Personal Physician*, trans. Tai Hung-chao (London: Arrow Books, 1996), p. 14. Other details of Mao's demise from ibid.

2 Geremie R. Barmé, *Shades of Mao: The Posthumous Cult of the Great Leader* (New York: M. E. Sharpe, 1996), p. 5.

3 Alexander C. Cook, ed., *Mao's Little Red Book: A Global History* (Cambridge: Cambridge University Press, 2014), p. xiii.

4 Barmé, *Shades of Mao*, pp. 6–11.

5 Private communication.

6 Private communication.

7 Abimael Guzmán Reinoso and Elena Iparraguirre, *Memorias desde Némesis 1993–2000* (2014), p. 404, at www.verdadyreconciliacionperu.com/admin/files/libros/801_digitalizacion.pdf (accessed March 19, 2020).

8 Ibid., pp. 405–408.

9 Ibid., p. 404.

10 Ibid., pp. 408–409.

11 Abimael Guzmán Reinoso and Elena Iparraguirre, interview with the Commission for Truth and Reconciliation, October 29, 2002 (Cassette BN 29/X/02 – AGR –EI), at http://grancomboclub.com/wp-content/uploads/2012/07/ABIMAEL-GUZMAN-REYNOSO-y-ELENA-IPARRAGUIRRE.pdf (accessed January 15, 2018).

12 Ton de Wit and Vera Gianotten, "The Center's Multiple Failures," in David Scott Palmer, ed., *The Shining Path of Peru* (London: Hurst, 1992), p. 45.

13 Matthew D. Rothwell, *Transpacific Revolutionaries: The Chinese Revolution in Latin America* (New York: Routledge, 2013), p. 45.

14 Ibid., p. 53; Ernesto Toledo Brückmann, . . . *Y llegó Mao: Síntesis histórica de la llegada del Pensamiento Mao TseTung al Perú (1928–1964)* (Lima: Grupo Editorial Arteidea, 2016), pp. 137–138.

15 Cynthia McClintock, "Peru's Sendero Luminoso Rebellion: Origins and Trajectory," in Susan Eckstein and Manuel Antonio Garretón Merino, eds., *Power and Popular Protest: Latin American Social Movements* (Berkeley: University of California Press, 2001), p. 66.

16 Carlos Iván Degregori, *El Surgimiento de Sendero Luminoso: Ayacucho 1969–1979* (Lima: Instituto de Estudios Peruanos, 2010), p. 36.

17 Santiago Roncagliolo, *La cuarta espada: La historia de Abimael Guzmán y Sendero Luminoso* (Barcelona: Random House Mondadori, 2007), p. 48.

18 Simon Strong, *Shining Path: The World's Deadliest Revolutionary Force* (London: Fontana, 1993), p. 31.

19 Carlos Iván Degregori, *How Difficult It Is to Be God: Shining Path's Politics of War in Peru, 1980–1999*, ed. Steve J. Stern, trans. Nancy Appelbaum (Madison: University of Wisconsin Press, 2012), pp. 104, 108, 106.

20 Rothwell, *Transpacific Revolutionaries*, p. 27.

21 Strong, *Shining Path*, p. 33.

22 See reminiscences in Guzmán Reinoso and Iparraguirre, *Memorias*, pp. 48–50.

23 Strong, *Shining Path*, p. 33.

24 Guzmán Reinoso and Iparraguirre, *Memorias*, p. 32.

25 Ibid., pp. 83, 82.

26 Ibid., pp. 84–85.

27 Abimael Guzman, "Interview with Chairman Gonzalo," interview by Luis Arce Borja and Janet Talavera, *A World to Win* 18 (1992), at

http://bannedthought.net/International/RIM/AWTW/1992-18/
GonzaloInterview-1988.pdf (accessed January 15, 2018), p. 79.

28 Toledo Brückmann, ... Y llegó Mao, p. 153.

29 Guzmán Reinoso and Iparraguirre, Memorias, pp. 258, 220, 209, 193,
90; Antonio Zapata, "Elena Yparraguirre: La Mirada de la Número
Tres," unpublished paper given at the Shining Path: Maoism and
Violence in Peru conference, Stanford University, February 2016,
p. 7.

30 Miguel La Serna and Orin Starn, The Shining Path: Love, Madness, and
Revolution in the Andes (New York: Norton, 2019). My thanks to the
authors for allowing me to access their manuscript prior to publication.

31 Guzmán Reinoso and Iparraguirre, Memorias, pp. 85, 98–99, 177,
169.

32 Ronald H. Berg, "Peasant Responses to Shining Path in Andahuaylas,"
in Palmer, The Shining Path, p. 98.

33 De Wit and Gianotten, "The Center's Multiple Failures," 46.

34 Gustavo Gorriti, The Shining Path: A History of the Millenarian War in
Peru, trans. Robin Kirk (Chapel Hill: University of North Carolina
Press, 1999), p. 91.

35 Ibid., pp. 17–18, 65.

36 Ibid., pp. 17–35.

37 Ibid., pp. 76, 98.

38 Ibid., pp. 104–105.

39 Ibid., p. 106.

40 Ibid., p. 110.

41 Ibid., p. 108.

42 Ibid., p. 69.

43 Strong, Shining Path, p. 104.

44 Robin Kirk, Grabado en piedra: Las mujeres de Sendero Luminoso
(Lima: Instituto de Estudios Peruanos, 1993), pp. 39–40.

45 Degregori, How Difficult, pp. 24–25.

46 State of Fear: The Truth about Terrorism (documentary), at www
.youtube.com/watch?v=WC1hAJOi6BE (accessed January 18, 2018).

47 For an account of these events, see Caretas, September 17, 1992.

48 Mohan Bikram Singh, interview, December 12, 2016, Kathmandu.

49 Ibid.; and Benoît Cailmail, "A History of Nepalese Maoism since Its
Foundation by Mohan Bikram Singh," European Bulletin of Himalayan
Research 33–34 (2008–2009), pp. 11–38.

50 Deepak Thapa with Bandita Sijapati, A Kingdom under Siege: Nepal's
Maoist Insurgency, 1996 to 2003 (London: Zed Books, 2004),
pp. 43–45.

51 Kiran, interview, December 13, 2016, Kathmandu.

Chapter 7

1 For an overview of the Tiananmen protests, including references to further reading, see Klaus Mühlhahn, *Making China Modern: From the Great Qing to Xi Jinping* (Cambridge, MA: Harvard University Press, 2019), pp. 518–526.

2 See Cheng Li, *Chinese Politics in the Xi Jinping Era: Reassessing Collective Leadership* (Washington, DC: The Brookings Institution Press, 2016).

3 Despite the fact that political reform and liberalization are widely regarded as crucial issues and are scattered in the publications on Deng Xiaoping and the period of reform and opening more generally, there are – with the exceptions cited below – virtually no systematic studies of Zhao Ziyang and Hu Yaobang in English.

4 David Shambaugh, *The Making of a Premier: Zhao Ziyang's Provincial Career* (Boulder, CO: Westview, 1984).

5 On land reform, see Mühlhahn, *Making China Modern*, pp. 402–404.

6 Zhao Ziyang, "Liangshi shengchan sudu keyi jiakuai" (Food production can be accelerated), *Renmin Ribao*, May 30, 1958, http://m.zlck.com/rmrb/news/HUXRM5OO.html.

7 *Nanfang Ribao*, October 8, 1959.

8 Zhao Ziyang, "Ren de sixiang geminghuade zhongda yiyi: zhongdu 'Guanyu zhengque chuli renmin neibu maodun de wenti'" (The great meaning of revolutionizing human thinking: rereading "On the correct handling of the contradictions among the people"), *Renmin Ribao*, April 4, 1964, http://m.zlck.com/rmrb/news/GBHFK6UD.html.

9 It is unclear which locality he was sent to. Shambaugh, *The Making of a Premier*, p. 65, assumes it was in Inner Mongolia.

10 Ibid., pp. 56–58.

11 Ibid., p. 59.

12 See www.cia.gov/library/readingroom/document/cia-rdp03t02547r000100910001-1.

13 Quotes are from from Anita Chan, Stanley Rosen, and Jonathan Unger, eds., *On Socialist Democracy and the Chinese Legal System: The Li Yizhe Debates* (Armonk, NY: M. E. Sharpe, 1985), p. 63; on Li Yizhe and its role, see Tim Cheek, *The Intellectual in Modern Chinese History* (Cambridge: Cambridge Unviersity Press, 2016), pp. 202–205; Roderick MacFarquhar and Michael Schoenhals, *Mao's Last Revolution* (Cambridge, MA: Belknap Press of Harvard University Press, 2006), pp. 352–354; Yan Jiaqi and Gao Gao, *Turbulent Decade: A History of the Cultural Revolution* (Honolulu: University of Hawai'i Press, 1996), pp. 451–452.

14 Shambaugh, *The Making of a Premier*, pp. 69–70.

15 His posthumous autobiography was published in 2009; it is called *Prisoner of the State: The Secret Journal of Premier Zhao Ziyang* (New York: Simon & Schuster, 2009). On Zhao's position on how to establish democratic centralism within the Central Committee, especially within the Politburo and its Standing Committee, see pp. 177–178.

16 Zong Fengming, *Zhao Ziyang ruanjin zhong de tanhua* (Zhao Ziyang: Captive Conversations) (Hong Kong: Open Press, 2007), p. 62.

17 Deng Xiaoping, "Emancipate the mind, seek truth from facts and unite as one in looking to the future," in *Selected Works of Deng Xiaoping (1975–1982)*, ed. Editorial Committee for Party Literature, Central Committee of the Communist Party of China (Beijing: Foreign Languages Press, 1984), 2: 151–165, here p. 165.

18 Mühlhahn, *Making China Modern*, p. 497.

19 Frederick C. Teiwes and Warren Sun, *Paradoxes of Post-Mao Rural Reform: Initial Steps toward a New Chinese Countryside, 1976–1981* (New York: Routledge, 2015), pp. 42–44.

20 Richard Baum, *Burying Mao: Chinese Politics in the Age of Deng Xiaoping* (Princeton, NJ: Princeton University Press, 1994), pp. 68–69.

21 Julian Gewirtz, *Unlikely Partners: Chinese Reformers, Western Economists, and the Making of Global China* (Cambridge, MA: Harvard University Press, 2017), pp. 39–63.

22 Julian Gewirtz, "The futurists of Beijing: Alvin Toffler, Zhao Ziyang, and China's 'new technological revolution,' 1979–1991," *Journal of Asian Studies* 78:1 (February 2019), pp. 115–140.

23 Zhao Ziyang, *Prisoner of the State*, pp. 125–126.

24 Mühlhahn, *Making China Modern*, p. 510.

25 White House Diaries, January 10, 1984, www.reaganfoundation.org/ronald-reagan/white-house-diaries/diary-entry-01101984.

26 Gewirtz, *Unlikely Partners*, p. 213.

27 Zhao Ziyang, *Prisoner of the State*, p. 113.

28 Chris Bramall, *Chinese Economic Development* (New York: Routledge, 2009), p. 351.

29 Zhao Ziyang, *Prisoner of the State*, pp. 91–94.

30 Bao Tong, "Remembering Zhao Ziyang," Radio Free Asia, February 2, 2005, www.rfa.org/english/news/politics/china_15th-20050201.html.

31 In his autobiography Zhao admitted, "[after 1978] I focused all of my attention for a time on reforming the economic system, ignoring the issue of political reform." Zhao Ziyang, *Prisoner of the State*, p. 256.

32 See several speeches and commentaries by Hu Yaobang in spring 1978; Hu Yaobang, "Yao jianchi shijian shi jiancha zhenli de weiyi biaozhun" (We need to assert that practice is the sole criterion of truth), *Hu*

Yaobang wenxuan (Selected Works of Hu Yaobang) (Beijing: Renmin chubanshe, 2015), pp. 89–94.

33 Hu Yaobang, "Zhengzhi tizhi gaige shi shehuizhuyi zhidu de ziwo wanshan" (Reform of the political system is the self-perfection of the socialist system), *Hu Yaobang wenxuan* (Selected Works of Hu Yaobang), pp. 652–654.

34 Richard Baum, "Zhao Ziyang and China's 'soft authoritarian' alternative," in *Zhao Ziyang and China's Political Future*, ed. Guoguang Wu and Helen Lansdowne (New York: Routledge, 2012), pp. 109–121.

35 In *Zhao Ziyang wenji* (Collected Works of Zhao Ziyang), Volume IV, 1987–1989 (Hong Kong: The Chinese University Press, 2016), pp. 207–216.

36 Andrew Nathan, "Zhao Ziyang's vision of Chinese democracy," *China Perspectives* 3 (2008), pp. 136–142.

37 See Zong Fengming, *Zhao Ziyang ruanjin zhong de tanhua*, pp. 6–21.

38 Baum, "Zhao Ziyang and China's 'soft authoritarian' alternative," p. 119.

Chapter 8

* Translated by Timothy Cheek. Xu Jilin's eulogy to Wang Yuanhua is translated by David Ownby, in Timothy Cheek, David Ownby, and Joshua A. Fogel, eds., *Voices from the Chinese Century: Public Intellectual Debate from Contemporary China* (New York: Columbia University Press, 2020), pp. 155–171.

1 Translator's note: the May Fourth Movement centered on the Chinese protests against the Versailles Treaty in 1919, and the New Culture Movement in the decade spanning that date promoted radical intellectual change. They are both considered by the CCP to be the origin of the national revolution led by the Party down to today.

2 Personal communication with the author.

3 Wang Yuanhua (王元化), *Qing yuan shujian* 清园书简 (Qing Garden Letters) (Wuhan: Hubei jiaoyu chubanshe, 2003), p. 153.

4 Li Ziyun (李子云), "Wo suo renshi de Wang Yuanhua" 我所认识的王元化 (The Wang Yuanhua I know), *Tianya* 天涯 (Ends of the World) 4(7) (2001), pp. 178–184.

5 Hu Xiaoming (胡晓明), *Wang Yuanhua hua zhuan* 王元化画传 (Pictorial Biography of Wang Yuanhua) (Beijing: Wenyi chubanshe, 2007), p. 93.

6 Translator's note: the Anti-Spiritual Pollution campaign was a formal rectification movement in the CCP that began in October 1983. It attacked Western ideas such as democracy and liberalism and saw the demotion and purges of liberal cadres.

7 Letter from Wang Yuanhua to Xu Jilin, in the author's collection.

8 Wang Yuanhua (王元化), *Jiushi niandai riji* 九十年代日记 (1990s Diary) (Hangzhou: Zhejiang renmin chubanshe, 2001), p. 528.

9 Wang Yuanhua (王元化), "Dui 'wusi' de sikao" 对"五四"的思考 (Reflections on 'May Fourth'), in Wang Yuanhua, *Jiushi niandai fansilu* 九十年代反思录 (Reflections on the Nineties) (Shanghai: Guji chubanshe, 2000), p. 127.

10 Wang Yuanhua (王元化), "Renwen jingshen yu ershiyi shiji de duihua" 人文精神与二十一世纪的对话 (Dialogue on the humanistic spirit and the twenty-first century), in Wang Yuanhua, *Qing yuan jinzuo ji* 清园近作集 (Recent Works from Qing Garden) (Shanghai: Wenhui chubanshe, 2004), p. 8.

11 Wang Yuanhua (王元化), "Yu youren lun Gongyi shu: zhi Li Rui" 与友人论公意书：致李锐 (Discussing the General Will with friends: letter to Li Rui), cited in Hu Xiaoming, *Wang Yuanhua hua zhuan*, pp. 173–175.

12 Translator's note: see Xu Jilin, "The fate of an enlightenment: twenty years in the Chinese intellectual sphere (1978–98)," translated by Geremie Barmé and Gloria Davies, in Edward Gu and Merle Goldman, eds., *Chinese Intellectuals between State and Market* (London: Routledge, 2004), pp. 183–203.

13 Translator's note: See *Select Writings of Li Shenzhi* (Dayton, OH: Kettering Foundation, 2010).

14 Wang Yuanhua, *Jiushi niandai riji*, p. 528.

15 Ibid., p. 85.

16 Translator's note: Wang is invoking Qu Yuan, the spirited minister, poet, and political critic of the King of Chu in the third century BCE. He was driven to death for his outspoken criticism of the king's errors.

17 Wang Yuanhua, *Jiushi niandai fansilu*, pp. 189–190.

18 Translator's note: published in *Philosophy East & West* 51/2 (April 2001), pp. 193–196.

19 Wang Yuanhua (王元化), "Guanyu 'Zhongguo yu dangjin qianxi'nianzhuyi' de jiju hua" 关于"中国与当今千禧年主义"的几句话 (A few words on "China and contemporary millenarianism"), in Wang Yuanhua, *Qing yuan jinzuo ji*, pp. 138–141.

20 "Wang Yuanhua zhi Lin Yusheng" 王元化致林毓生 (Wang Yuanhua to Lin Yusheng), *Caijing* 财经 (Finance & Economics), 143 (October 3, 2005).

21 Wang Yuanhua, "Renwen jingshen yu ershiyi shiji de duihua" (Dialogue on the humanistic spirit and the twenty-first century), in Wang Yuanhua, *Qing yuan jinzuo ji*, p. 2.

22 Wang Yuanhua, *Qing yuan jinzuo ji*, pp. 2–4.

23 "Wang Yuanhua zhi Wu Qixing" 王元化致吴琦幸 (Wang Yuanhua to Wu Qixing), in Wang Yuanhua, *Qing yuan shujian*, p. 117.

24 This credo comes from Chen Yinke's epitaph for Wang Guowei's tomb.

25 Wang Yuanhua (王元化), "Huojiang gan yan" 获奖感言 (Acceptance speech) at the Shanghai Philosophy and Social Science Awards Ceremony for Outstanding Achievement presenting him with a lifetime scholarly achievement award, *Wenhui bao* 文汇报 (Literary Gazette), December 17, 2006.

Chapter 9

1 "China celebrates 60 years of Communist rule," *New York Times*, October 2, 2009, www.nytimes.com/2009/10/02/world/asia/02china.html.

2 Willy Wo-Lap Lam, *The Era of Jiang Zemin* (New York: Prentice-Hall, 1999).

3 *People's Daily*, at http://news.sohu.com/20091012/n267279208.shtml.

4 "Deng Xiaoping is dead at 92; architect of modern China," *New York Times*, February 20, 1997, www.nytimes.com/1997/02/20/world/deng-xiaoping-is-dead-at-92-architect-of-modern-china.html.

5 Bruce Gilley, *Tiger on the Brink: Jiang Zemin and China's New Elite* (Berkeley: University of California Press, 1998), p. 285.

6 Lam, *The Era of Jiang Zemin*, p. 1

7 A popular joke told by the wags of Beijing's *hutongs* in the late 1990s focused on Li Peng, the one Politburo Standing Committee member not of the Shanghai Clique. The gag is that Li Peng comes back to his office after a meeting, visibly upset. His secretary asks him what the matter is, and if someone had done something hostile to Li. After asking several times without a response, Li screams at the secretary, "How the hell would I know if someone did something hostile, they were all talking Shanghainese!"

8 "Top Leadership Dynamics Driven by Consensus, Interests, Contacts Say," *Wikileaks*, https://wikileaks.org/plusd/cables/09BEIJING2112_a.html.

9 For an orthodox presentation, see "Three Represents," at *ChinaDaily.com* (July 10, 2007), www.chinadaily.com.cn/china/2007-07/10/content_6142053.htm.

10 Geremie Barmé, "China's Flat Earth: History and 8 August 2008," *China Quarterly* 197 (March 2009), pp. 64–86.

11 "Google and the China Pullout," *Sinica* podcast, https://supchina.com/podcast/google-china-pullout.

12 Geremie Barmé and Sang Ye, "The Great Firewall of China," *Wired* magazine (San Francisco), www.wired.com/1997/06/china-3.

13 *Wikipedia*, https://zh.wikipedia.org/wiki/%E4%B8%AD%E5%8D%8E%E4%BA%BA%E6%B0%91%E5%85%B1%E5%92%8C%E5%9B%BD%E7%AC%AC%E5%85%AD%E6%AC%A1%E5%85%A8%E5%9B%BD%E4%BA%BA%E5%8F%A3%E6%99%AE%E6%9F%A5.

14 "Why Is It Important to Remember Sun Zhigang?," *China Labour Bulletin* (Hong Kong), April 17, 2013, www.clb.org.hk/content/why-it-important-remember-sun-zhigang.

15 Jim Yardley, "Internet Sex Column Thrills, and Inflames, China," *New York Times*, November 30, 2003, www.nytimes.com/2003/11/30/world/internet-sex-column-thrills-and-inflames-china.html.

16 Susan Jakes, "Li Yuchun," *Time* magazine, October 3, 2005, http://content.time.com/time/world/article/0,8599,2054304,00.html.

17 David Bandurski, "Eight Honors and Eight Disgraces" 八荣八耻, *China Media Project* (Hong Kong), July 5, 2007, http://chinamediaproject.org/2007/07/05/eight-honors-and-eight-disgraces-%E5%85%AB%E8%8D%A3%E5%85%AB%E8%80%BB.

18 Liu Shaoqi, "How to Be a Good Communist," www.marxists.org/reference/archive/liu-shaoqi/1939/how-to-be/ch01.htm.

19 "Coming Out," *The Economist*, March 25, 2006, www.economist.com/special-report/2006/03/25/coming-out.

20 David Shambaugh: "The year China showed its claws," www.brookings.edu/opinions/the-year-china-showed-its-claws.

21 "Chinese newspapers defy ban to report on train tragedy," *The Guardian*, August 2, 2009, www.theguardian.com/media/greenslade/2011/aug/02/press-freedom-china.

22 "How son's death in a high-speed car crash led to powerful Chinese official's fall from grace," *South China Morning Post*, December 23, 2014, www.scmp.com/news/china/article/1668151/how-sons-death-high-speed-car-crash-led-powerful-chinese-officials-fall.

23 "The Wen family empire," *New York Times*, October 25, 2012, https://archive.nytimes.com/www.nytimes.com/interactive/2012/10/25/business/the-wen-family-empire.html; "Xi Jinping millionaire relations reveal fortunes of the elite,"*Bloomberg*, June 29, 2012, www.bloomberg.com/news/articles/2012-06-29/xi-jinping-millionaire-relations-reveal-fortunes-of-elite.

24 "Bo Xilai scandal: timeline," *BBC*, November 11, 2013, www.bbc.com/news/world-asia-china-17673505.

25 Nicholas Kristof, "Looking for a jump start in China," *New York Times*, January 6, 2013, www.nytimes.com/2013/01/06/opinion/sunday/kristof-looking-for-a-jump-start-in-china.html.

26 "Deng Yuwen," in *The China Story Yearbook 2013* (Canberra: Australian Centre on China and the World), www.thechinastory.org/yearbooks/yearbook-2013/chapter-7-fitting-words/deng-yuwen.

27 "为什么人们怀念长者？长者风靡网络背后的制度难题" (Why Are People Nostalgic for the Elder? The Difficult Questions Behind the Elder's Internet Popularity), *China Digital Times*, August 17, 2015,

http://chinadigitaltimes.net/chinese/2015/08/%E4%B8%8D%E7%9F
%A5-%E4%B8%BA%E4%BB%80%E4%B9%88%E4%BA%BA%
E4%BB%AC%E6%80%80%E5%BF%B5%E9%95%BF%E8%80%
85%EF%BC%9F%E9%95%BF%E8%80%85%E9%A3%8E%E9%
9D%A1%E7%BD%91%E7%BB%9C%E8%83%8C%E5%90%8E
%E7%9A%84.

28 "Viral alarm: when fury overcomes fear, by Xu Zhangrun, translated by Geremie R. Barmé," *ChinaFile*, February 10, 2020, www.chinafile.com/reporting-opinion/viewpoint/viral-alarm-when-fury-overcomes-fear.

Chapter 10

1 See Joseph Fewsmith, "'Social management' as a way of coping with heightened social tensions," *China Leadership Monitor*, 36 (January 6, 2012), www.hoover.org/sites/default/files/uploads/documents/CLM36JF.pdf.

2 Retrieved from www.tianya.cn/publicforum/content/funinfo/1/2691682.shtml, accessed February 23, 2020.

3 English translations of direct quotations of Web postings are my own. Original data are kept on file by author, but throughout this chapter, citation information is omitted to protect bloggers' anonymity.

4 Original quotations from Guo Meimei's Weibo messages are retrieved from http://vdisk.weibo.com/s/qo5X/1309155692.

5 Zhang Huan, Xu Zhen, and Wang Ning, "Zhuizong 'Guo Meimei' de minjian zhentan" (Unofficial detectives in search of "Guo Meimei"), *Vista (kan tian xia)*, July 11, 2011, www.dooland.com/magazine/article_147228.html, accessed April 24, 2012.

6 Ibid.

7 Fu Shan, "'Hong Shi Zi Hui' zaixuan yulun xuanwo, zhe liunian 'Hong Shi Zi' de naxie shi'er" (The "Red Cross", caught again in the middle of a storm – things that have happened to the "Red Cross" in the past six years), *The Paper*, July 21, 2014, www.thepaper.cn/newsDetail_forward_1257128, accessed February 23, 2020.

8 "Lianhe diaochazu guanyu shangye xitong Hong Shi Zi Hui xiangguan wenti de diaocha baogao" (Investigation report of the Joint Investigation Team on relevant problems in the "Commercial Red Cross Society"), December 20, 2011, http://news.ifeng.com/gundong/detail_2011_12/31/11702111_0.shtml. accessed February 23, 2020.

9 See, for example, Tong Lam, *A Passion for Facts: Social Surveys and the Construction of the Chinese Nation-State, 1900–1949*, Berkeley: University of California Press, 2011.

10 Rui Hou, "The commercialisation of internet-opinion management: how the market is engaged in state control in China," *New Media & Society*, November 27, 2019, https://doi.org/10.1177/1461444819889959.

11 Frank N. Pieke, "The Communist Party and social management in China," *China Information* 26/2 (2012), pp. 149-165.

12 Cyberspace Administration of China, "'2015 nian Zhongguo hao wangmin' wangluo zuopin zhengji pingxuan huodong zai Jiangxi qidong" (Selection of Internet writings by "2015 Good Chinese netizens" launched in Jiangxi), August 21, 2015, www.cac.gov.cn/2015-08/21/c_1116327355.htm, accessed February 22, 2020.

13 See Prasenjit Duara, "The discourse of civilization and pan-Asianism," *Journal of World History* 12/1 (2001), pp. 99-130, https://doi.org/10.1353/jwh.2001.0009; Ralph A. Litzinger, *Other Chinas: The Yao and the Politics of National Belonging*, Durham, NC: Duke University Press, 2000; Guobin Yang, "Demobilizing the emotions of online activism in China: a civilizing process," *International Journal of Communication* 11(2017), pp. 1945-1965.

14 Xi Jinping, Speech at the study session of the Politburo, January 25, 2019, www.wenming.cn/specials/zxdj/xzsjhwm_43255/201905/t20190524_5126562.shtml, accessed February 22, 2020.

15 Ibid. Xi's three securities are: 政治安全、文化安全、意识形态安全.

16 Ibid.

17 Ge Zhang and Larissa Hjorth, "Live-streaming, games and politics of gender performance: the case of Nüzhubo in China," *Convergence* 25/5-6 (December 1, 2019), pp. 807-825.

18 Junyi Lü and David Craig, "Firewalls and walled gardens: the interplatformization of China's Wanghong industry," in Guobin Yang and Wei Wang, eds., *Engaging Social Media in China: Platforms, Publics and Production*, East Lansing: Michigan State University Press, forthcoming, 2021.

19 China Internet Network Information Center (CNNIC), "Statistical report on Internet development in China," July 2018, http://cnnic.com.cn/IDR/ReportDownloads/201911/P020191112538212107066.pdf, accessed January 21, 2020.

20 Lü and Craig, "Firewalls and walled gardens."

21 Peng Lan, "短视频：视频生产里的'转机引'与栽培与再培育" (Short videos: The Transformation and Re-cultivation of Video Productivity), *Journalism and Mass Communication Monthly* (新闻界) 1 (2019), pp. 34-43.

INDEX